Lone Wolves

Florian Hartleb

Lone Wolves

The New Terrorism of Right-Wing Single Actors

Florian Hartleb
Hanse Advice
Tallinn, Estonia

ISBN 978-3-030-36152-5   ISBN 978-3-030-36153-2 (eBook)
https://doi.org/10.1007/978-3-030-36153-2

© Springer Nature Switzerland AG 2020
This work is subject to copyright. All rights are reserved by the Publisher, whether the whole or part of the material is concerned, specifically the rights of translation, reprinting, reuse of illustrations, recitation, broadcasting, reproduction on microfilms or in any other physical way, and transmission or information storage and retrieval, electronic adaptation, computer software, or by similar or dissimilar methodology now known or hereafter developed.
The use of general descriptive names, registered names, trademarks, service marks, etc. in this publication does not imply, even in the absence of a specific statement, that such names are exempt from the relevant protective laws and regulations and therefore free for general use.
The publisher, the authors and the editors are safe to assume that the advice and information in this book are believed to be true and accurate at the date of publication. Neither the publisher nor the authors or the editors give a warranty, expressed or implied, with respect to the material contained herein or for any errors or omissions that may have been made. The publisher remains neutral with regard to jurisdictional claims in published maps and institutional affiliations.

This Springer imprint is published by the registered company Springer Nature Switzerland AG
The registered company address is: Gewerbestrasse 11, 6330 Cham, Switzerland

Acknowledgements

The 21st century has now already become the century of individual, of so-called 'lone wolf' terrorism. The modern type of politically motivated brutality is "home-made" (*homegrown*) and cannot be attributed to Islamic fundamentalism as such. Individuals with far-right tendencies kill in order to establish a society according to their own standards, without requiring a great deal of organisation in the background, but autonomously and apparently unpredictably. The following book intends to take an in in-depth view of this phenomenon, a new dimension of virtual and international far right-terrorism, a recent dynamics including mutual inspiration.

I would like to extend my warm thanks to the publishers Springer Verlag, who put their trust in me and granted me the opportunity to write a non-fiction book at an academic level. The subject of "far-right extremist motivated lone wolves" has in the meantime adopted global relevance, attaining a new degree of networking and also of mutual inspiration. Accordingly, the author also hopes to reach an international audience. This is precisely the reason why I am very grateful that a leading think tank on security matters, the S. Rajaratnam School of International Studies in Singapore granted me financial assistance towards publication, by providing the funding costs for the translation. Mr. Charles Rose from Scotland realised this. He approached the project in a meticulous manner, which is the reason I am likewise very grateful to him. This topic has a certain dynamic. Originally, I had written a non-fiction book on lone wolf terrorism in German, published by the Hamburg-based trade publisher "Hoffmann und Campe". This was published in October 2018. New murderous assaults since then, for instance the attacks in Christchurch, New Zealand and in El Paso, New Mexico, gave me grounds to heavily update my book and, also to internationalise it.

The idea for the book had originated from what my work in the case of the murderous assault of 22 July 2016 uncovered—by no coincidence exactly five years to the day after the attacks by Anders Behring Breivik in Norway. Once I had been permitted to look over approximately 4000 pages of investigators' casework files, I reached the clear conclusion that we were certainly not dealing with an apolitical act here—as the official account believed, but with far-right terrorism in the form of a "lone wolf" attack. Later, I even found out about virtual US media links between Munich and New Mexico, via a gaming platform which apparently aroused no suspicion, which official security services had completely overlooked and were not aware of. Other cases from different countries highlight the new challenges we face. This is why the author, in order that his objective meets with resonance, differentiates this complex phenomenon as far as possible, clarifying it during my examination and in this way initiating a discussion on possible counterstrategies. Politicians and political machinations, security services and officials, but also society are confronted by this challenge to an equal extent. In the case of Munich, it took the authorities more than three years to acknowledge that the attacks there were politically motivated (*and the nature of these motivations*).

And this topic continues to be highly relevant. On 9th October 2019, Germany was shaken by a lone wolf attack carried out by Stephan Balliet in broad daylight. The 27 year-old German carried out a copy-cat assault to Christchurch but failed with his attempted attack on a Jewish synagogue full of people in Halle/Saxony Anhalt. The loner addressed "his fans" via livestream on this date but got more and more nervous whilst carrying out his murderous deed. He killed two people at random and shouted repeatedly about how he was "a loser". His actions were clearly politically motivated. Balliet justified his action with anti-Semitism, with a fight against the "Zionist Occupation Government" (ZOG), but also through his hatred of feminism and Islam. Linked deeply to expressions used in gaming, a new debate on the "gamification of right-wing terrorism" has commenced. The dilettantism or lack of commitment during implementation also highlighted on the other hand, what the actions in Norway and Christchurch had achieved.

Tallinn, Estonia Florian Hartleb
October 2019

Contents

1 **Right-Wing Terrorism. Still an Underestimated Threat**   1
   1.1   The Current Threat of Terrorist Attacks by Single Actors   1
   1.2   Emotionally Charged—The Question of "Why"   6
   1.3   Right-Wing Terrorism Is Neglected in Public Perception   7
   1.4   The National Socialist Underground (NSU) as an Early Warning   10
   1.5   Why We Must Stand up to Lone Wolves   13
   1.6   The Current Situation: Errors of Judgement by Politicians and Officials   15
   1.7   Hypotheses   24
   References   26

2 **What Is a "Lone Wolf"?**   29
   2.1   A Phantom?   29
   2.2   Forms of Terror   32
   2.3   A Look Back in History   34
   2.4   Assassination Attempts on Representatives of Democratic States   37
   2.5   Theory and Origins of Lone Wolf Terrorism   41
   2.6   Profile and Nature of the Lone Wolf   44
   2.7   Political Motives and Personal Ideology of Grievances   47
   2.8   Killing Sprees, Running Amok and Terror—The Difference Is Important   49

2.9	Lone Wolves and Islamic Terrorists	52
2.10	"Battle Mode" as a Principle	55
References		59

3 Offenders and Terrorism. Ideology, Motives, Objectives — 63

3.1	Isolated and Disappointed: Frank Steffen, Thomas Mair, Luca Traini	66
3.2	Failures, Megalomaniacs and Dangerous: Franz Fuchs, John Ausonius, Anders Breivik, Brenton Tarrant	73
3.3	Uprooted and Radical: Peter Mangs, Pavlo Lapshyn, David Sonboly	92
3.4	Young and Fascist: David Copeland, Pekko Auvinen and Anton Petterson	106
3.5	Significance of Observing Individuals for the Overall Picture	110
References		120

4 Radicalisation in Our Midst and in Virtual Rooms and Spaces — 123

4.1	Terror as a Portrayal of Developments in Society	123
4.2	Internationalisation of the Radical Right	127
4.3	Virtual Worlds	131
4.4	Boom Time for Conspiracy Theories	136
4.5	Reich Citizens [Reichsbürger]—Merely "Paper Terrorists?"	138
4.6	Identitarians and the Christchurch Terrorist	141
4.7	Consequences	146
References		147

5 Counter-Strategies and Prevention — 149

5.1	Rethinking Required by Security Officials	151
5.2	Virtual Platform as a Source of Danger	155
5.3	Searching for a Trail in the Social Environment	165
References		171

6 Conclusions — 173
References — 179

Index — 181

1

Right-Wing Terrorism. Still an Underestimated Threat

1.1 The Current Threat of Terrorist Attacks by Single Actors

A famous old Chinese proverb, attributed to the war theorist Sun Tzu, states: "Kill one, terrify 10,000."[1] A modern terrorist would even say in the global age and following 11 September 2001: "Kill one, terrify 10 or even 100 million." And also: We no longer need an organised group to generate this terror, more or less the DNA of terrorism. One lone individual suffices nowadays. Global media discovered this on 22 July 2011: After many years of planning, the Norwegian far-right extremist Anders Behring Breivik murdered 77 people according to a diabolical choreography, with many young people numbered amongst the victims. Initial "knee-jerk", reflex-like and premature assessments pondered whether the work of al-Qaeda could be observed in this cold-bloodedness. In the meantime, the question has arisen of whether we should not use two different scales of measurement, as the threat of right-wing terrorism was underestimated for a long time and attention remained fixed entirely on Islamic terrorism.[2]

However, it quickly transpired that a single actor was at work here. Breivik was not known to the police before this, had neither any relevant registrations nor any previous convictions. Before staging his attacks, Breivik tweeted a single message revealing the destructive power lone wolves possess: "One person

---

[1] Quoted in Paul Wilkinson: Terrorism and the Liberal State, London 1977, p. 48.
[2] Cf. Trevor Aaronson: Terrorism's double standard. Violent far-right extremists are rarely prosecuted as terrorists, in: The Intercept dated 23 March 2019, https://theintercept.com/2019/03/23/domestic-terrorism-fbi-prosecutions/.

with a belief is equal to the force of 100,000 with merely interests." Former US President Barack Obama demonstrated that he was downright far-sighted in this regard following Breivik's assaults. In August 2011, he stated that the threat of "lone wolves", terrorist single actors, is greater than that of organised groups, such as those who carried out the terrorist attacks on 11 September 2001 for example. Obama stated: "The risk we are presently confronted with, is that of the lone wolf terrorist, someone with a single weapon, who is in a position to carry out a massacre on a large scale, as we witnessed in Norway a short time ago."[3]

A single actor extinguished 51 human lives in Christchurch, New Zealand on 15 March 2019 and seriously injured dozens more. A large number of these were praying Muslims, as the assailant targeted Islamic locations in the city, and two mosques in particular. The perpetrator, the 29-year-old Australian Brenton Tarrant achieved his goals just as he had imagined he would: With an emphasis on global notoriety. 17 unbearable minutes were broadcast live on Facebook. Tarrant underpinned the live broadcast of the assault with a song from war-time Bosnian Serbs, who had fought against the Muslim-dominated army in Bosnia-Herzegovina during the 1990s in the wars in Yugoslavia. The song "Karadžić, lead your Serbs" glorified the Serbian leader during those times, Radovan Karadžić, who was sentenced by the UN Tribunal for his part in the massacre of Srebrenica amongst other things; and in this context is considered to be a martyr. An inhabitant of New Zealand was sentenced to 21 months in prison in June 2019, for broadcasting his terrorist video on the Internet. The court considered that a "hate crime" had been committed. The offender, a 44-year-old businessman even inserted crosshairs and numbered the victims.[4]

It is, therefore, easy to see a correlation between the "lone wolves" Breivik and Tarrant, as the German magazine „Der Spiegel" stated in a story on its front page following the event in Christchurch. This applies in particular to issuing and broadcasting a "manifesto" on the Internet to accompany the assaults: "Both fabricated an amalgam of theorems scorning human beings in order to justify their murders. Compiling these into so-called manifestos,

---

[3] Barack Obama: "Obama says "lone wolf terrorist" biggest US threat", in: *Reuters.com* of 17 August 2011, https://www.reuters.com/article/us-usa-obama-security/obama-says-lone-wolf-terrorist-biggest-u-s-threat-idUSTRE77F6XI20110816.

[4] BBC news, 21 June 2019, New Zealand man jailed for 21 months for sharing Christchurch shooting video, https://www.bbc.com/news/world-asia-48671837.

which now permeate digital channels and are becoming the Bible for potential new assassins. Tarrant refers to Breivik in his declarations and uses a similar form of expression and layout to the latter."[5] Tarrant regrets his deeds equally as little. Similar to his role model, he professes he is not guilty. The courts should be misused as propaganda media and for self-portrayal.

A prima facie paradox: Tarrant not only travelled extensively around Europe. Like his Norwegian predecessor, he bound himself to existing currents in Europe, likewise considering himself to be a "white supremacist", as a self-appointed freedom fighter against supposed Muslim infiltration. Norway and New Zealand are particularly peace-loving regions of the world free from conflict, both free from the threat of terrorism up until now. Accordingly, people there were basically not prepared for such types of attack. Uncomfortable questions were asked in New Zealand as once they were in Norway, along the lines of whether society had missed warning signals.[6] But in Norway, the public was shaken again on 10 August 2019 by an attack on a mosque in Oslo. The 21-year-old Norwegian shooter, identified as Philip Manshaus, acted as a white supremacist. One person was injured, and the gunman's stepsister was later found dead in their family home.

Therefore, we may also argue these were postnational terrorists, considering the West to be threatened by decadence and Islamisation. In other words: invaders from foreign cultures were plundering Europe. This narrative also exists in other regions of the world: An assailant referred to Christchurch in El Paso on the Mexican border in the USA. On 3 August 2019, he murdered 20 people in a shopping centre there, predominantly Hispanics with seven of them Mexican. The 21-year-old Patrick Crusius considered his assault a response to the "Hispanic invasion of Texas." Travelling there specifically for the attacks, residing in Allen, ca. 660 miles away. Justifying his attacks with the following statement: "I am simply defending my country from cultural and ethnic replacement brought on by an invasion." Like Tarrant, he also presented his manifesto on the platform "8chan".

Enemies of a democratic system of values and social order have for a long time concerned themselves not just with words, for example with exchanges in virtual rooms, but with deeds. In order for concrete, perfidiously planned events to be carried out by singular, so-called lone wolves. These events also

---

[5] Jörg Diehl amongst others: Ego-Shooter, in: Der Spiegel (cover), No. 13, 23 March 2019, pp. 12–19, here p. 13.
[6] See Eleanor Ainge Roy/Michael McGowan: New Zealand asks: how was the threat from the far right missed, in: The Guardian of 20 March 2019, https://www.theguardian.com/world/2019/mar/21/new-zealand-asks-how-was-the-threat-from-the-far-right-missed.

occurred in isolated cases even before the virtual era. As the case of the Austrian letter bomber Franz Fuchs attested for example, who created fear and terror with his letter bombs during the 1990s. But the case of the "homegrown" terrorist with all its severity was scarcely handled systematically and slipped into oblivion again.[7] This initially received comprehensive scientific treatment in English[8] in 2018 and is also covered in this book.

The new dimension of terrorism was ignored by political decision-makers, investigators and secret service authorities as well as experts on terrorism for a long time and was filed away as attacks by crazy individual assailants. This tendency still persists today. Right-wing extremist and/or xenophobic acts of violence directed against foreigners, curiously enough are still considered by security officials and other observers to be emotional and hate-filled, with little planning and organisation. Politically motivated multiple offenders, with an extreme right-wing view of the world, cropping up in scientific and journalistic treatises as "also-rans".[9] The findings of the terrorism expert Jeffrey D. Simon were in contrast to this, that "Lone Wolf Terrorists can be more creative and innovative than terrorist groups:" "Lone Wolves tend to think outside the box, since that is how they live, as loners and outsiders not constrained or obligated to follow what might be considered socially accepted norms of behaviour."[10]

Terrorism through lone assailants, without an organisation pulling the strings in the background—up until now we had thought we were only aware of this phenomenon from other regions of the world, described using the metaphor Lone Wolf, from Afghanistan, Iraq or from the conflict in Israel, where radical Palestinians unleash targeted knife attacks. Yet whether we wish to accept the fact or not: in the meantime, acts of terrorism have also occurred in Europe, even using buses and trucks. And the background for these need not always be political. Yet the destructive force of the individual is evident for all these terrible acts.

It is high time we recognise and acknowledge these excesses of force from single actors as an acute threat. The insight is appropriate, that this threat

---

[7] Fuchs was not included in the renowned standard reference work by Law, Randall D. (ed.): The Routledge History of Terrorism, Oxon/New York 2015.
[8] See Paul Schliefsteiner: Austria's Homegrown Lone Actor Terrorist: Franz Fuchs and the Letter Bomb Campaign of the 1990s, in: Journal for Intelligence, Propaganda and Security Studies, 12 (2018) 1, pp. 67–92.
[9] Cf. Uwe Backes: Rechtsextremistische Gewalt in Europa, in: Gerhard Hirscher/Eckhard Jesse (ed.): *Extremismus in Deutschland*, Baden-Baden 2013, p. 43.
[10] Jeffrey D. Simon: The Alphabet Bomber. A Lone Wolf Terrorist ahead of his time, Nebraska 2019, p. 172. This book covers the lone-wolf Muharem Kurbegovic, forgotten today, the so-called "Alphabet Bomber". This native Yugoslav, possessing specialist training as an engineer, exploded a bomb at Los Angeles airport on 6 August 1974. Three died. And further attacks followed.

was simply not characterised sufficiently up until now, that right-wing acts of terrorism are almost always stripped of any political demands.[11] We were not ready for this type of risk up until now, still connecting terrorism with rigid networks and structures as well as with careful planning, requiring a high degree of operational intelligence. We apparently do not believe one single person acting alone can radicalise himself to such an extent without joining a group directly; and can then set off down the road of destruction under the pretext of being a political fanatic under his own direction—as *ultima ratio* [*as a last resort*]. It often appears incomprehensible for officials, that such a perpetrator has no prior criminal convictions, that he may be a so-called "Clean-Face perpetrator,"[12] that is someone who is supposedly integrated into society and who does not have any prior criminal record with the police.

This book provides evidence to the contrary and for the first time gives a well-founded and detailed insight into the characteristics, motivations and radicalisation processes of so-called right-wing extremist, lone wolf perpetrators. The classification "single actor" in these cases merely represents planning the concrete event. It does not negate the fact, that the respective fixation with violence and ideology of offenders has causes, that their acts may be a consequence of communicating and interacting with kindred spirits, and that the actors feel they are motivated, in view of the growing hostility towards foreigners in society and the accompanying discourse associated with it. Their deeds are by no means spontaneous actions: but at first glance, a lot just does not seem to fit into place.

Approaching the subject matter can only take place via mosaic-like tesserae, and we are left with a diffuse sense of discomfort. Public safety is at risk in Western democracies, where up until now the principle applied, that by and large people had a good quality of life and enjoyed living here. The politically motivated commitment of the perpetrator feeds off of hackneyed, outdated racist ideas, feelings of superiority and a wish to eliminate people. We observe that we are confronted by people who wish to kill for the white race, who correlate their view of the world with Adolf Hitler's and see a route for overcoming their personal grievances through terrorism, and for expressing their hatred with force. Their basic motive is a militant hatred of foreigners: in the first instance, they wish to hurt an ethnic minority in their

---

[11] See as an exception Daniel Koehler: *Right-Wing Terrorism in the twenty-first Century. The 'National Socialist Underground' and the history of terror from the Far-Right in Germany*, London/New York 2017.
[12] Musharbash, Yassin: *Die neue al-Qaida. Innenansichten eines lernenden Netzwerks*, Cologne 2006, p. 211.

own country to the core and by proxy society as a whole. It is precisely their choice of victims which differentiates right-wing terrorists from other forms of terrorism—from left-wing terrorism, which is directed against symbols of capitalism and the "big-wig state" and from Islamic fundamentalism, which sets its sights on the West and "followers of other religions."

1.2 Emotionally Charged—The Question of "Why"

The researcher of risk, Nassim Nicholas Taleb cuts straight to the chase with my own motivation to write this book in his global bestseller: "We wish to not merely just survive uncertainty, not merely just escape again. We wish to survive uncertainty completely unharmed and what is more – like a certain class of belligerent Roman stoic – to have the last word. The question is: How will we succeed not only to comprehend what we cannot see, cannot explain, taming it, dominating it, perhaps even subduing it?".[13] A strategic and international competency will be required if we wish to succeed with this—and in good time. After all, terrorism finalises a meticulously prepared act. Its apparent unpredictability stirs up our enlightened system of values.

People who can no longer be reasoned within a civil and harmonious manner, wish to do the Western society they live in one last disservice. Whenever people kill for lust or revenge, simply randomly, we call them murderers or say they are running amok (*in a killing frenzy* or *a killing spree*). Murderers killing people according to a plan, based on political convictions, connected to heroic self-aggrandisement, are called terrorists. We ask ourselves instinctively: How could this happen, that an obviously sick idea has been realised? What subtext are such deeds based upon? Are we dealing with a destructive or a revolutionary impulse? Can any traces be found in the social setting? Generally: What could society have done in order to prevent it? Why did the mechanisms of an early-warning system not take hold in the social context? Why did security officials not intervene in good time? At the same time the camera, often craving the sensational, shows the extent of despair and destruction.[14] This corresponds to the mentality of gaping onlookers in society, based on curiosity for the sensational. We already speak cynically of "Terrortainment" in the media. Reporting on terrorism has traits of media hysteria, with strong

---

[13] Nassim Nicholas Taleb: *Anti-Fragilität. Anleitung für eine Welt, die wir nicht verstehen*, Munich 2014, p. 21.
[14] Cf. Michael König: *Poetik des Terrors. Politisch motivierte Gewalt in der Gegenwartsliteratur*, Bielefeld 2015, p. 9.

commercial traits. In other words: "Terrorism is an emotionally-charged and fashionable subject."[15]

Why does terrorism appal us so greatly? After all, the probability of falling victim to an act of terrorism is still small. There are a number of approaches to explain this:

- We divide people up into either "entirely normal" or "emotionally disturbed". Extremes fascinate us in particular.
- We enjoy puzzling over implications in the social environment, sensing decadence and moral degeneration.
- Discussing political motivation captivates us, generally concerning the subtext, clearly hidden behind deeds planned well in advance.
- We scrutinise the emphasis on personal grievance and excessive political radicalisation in the perpetrator.
- We mourn the victims, whose lives were arbitrarily and abruptly cut short.
- We think of an appropriate commemoration, reflect on the question of an appropriate culture of remembrance.
- It becomes clear, that the State and Society are not perfect, and that they must recognise the warning signals earlier in order to prevent such acts in future.
- We discuss whether the public reactions as a first step were appropriate for the severity of the occasion, and whether preventative measures have been applied in the longer term, as our next step.

The degree and type of terrorism say something about the current state of our society. Perhaps the special attraction is based precisely on decoding the message behind it and developing a counter-strategy.

1.3 Right-Wing Terrorism Is Neglected in Public Perception

In the eyes of the public, Islamic Fundamentalists play the central role as a threat today and dominate reporting as regards terrorism. Al-Qaeda and IS appeal explicitly to perpetrating Lone Wolf Terrorist acts and acknowledge corresponding assaults—irrespective of whether connections really existed. Much has been written regarding the motive, radicalisation processes and the

---

[15] Peter Waldmann: *Terrorismus, Provokation der Macht*, Munich 1998, p. 9.

danger for our liberal society emanating from Islamic terrorists, and at great length, which is also entirely justified.

Right-wing terrorists, such as the National Socialist Underground (NSU) in Germany, on the other hand, appear to be a footnote. A public, sustained, debate has not been carried out by the same means. There are studies on hand, according to which single actors with right-wing extremist leanings have killed more people than those with Islamic motives. Yet Islamic Fundamentalism is the centre of attention, as it represents a larger threat context.[16]

A new dimension was presented to the global public on 22 July 2011, as peaceful Norway received a blow to its very core. Exactly 5 years later, on 22 July 2016, a similar pattern of right-wing terrorism recurred in Munich: the meticulous planning, expedited in the virtual sphere, the targeted choice of victims, the same assault weapon of a Glock 17 and the racist reference. The Indian intellectual Pankaj Mishra was not alone in realising the clear parallels here. He considers "Heirs of Nihilism" and "related spirits" to be at work. Breivik was "the first mass murderer spawned by the Internet [...]. For his part, he inspired the German-Iranian teenager."[17] The teenager concerned here was 18-year-old David Sonboly, called Ali Sonboly Hamedani at birth in Munich and whilst growing up there. This act of violence turned everything in Germany on its head. Everything about him seemed to be so unusual, that he apparently evaded any classification. The officials were simply not prepared for this type of terrorism and did not consider the decisive details during their investigations.

In order to look into the case of "Sonboly" more closely and its significance, we must also observe what terrorism in general contributes in this day and age. There are overlaps between the groups of assailants, but also large differences, which cannot be disregarded. Terrorist attacks are calculated to attract maximum attention in real time—including rash judgements and hysterical reactions. These components unleash a special effect in the era of Facebook, Twitter etc. This includes the possibility of subsequent representation in literature or in film, and a media narrative is produced. A judgement made as far back as 40 years ago is equally as valid today: "Communication

---

[16]The Royal United Services Institute (RUSI) based in London, a think tank for security questions, reached such a result for the period from 2000 to the end of 2014 on the basis of a Global Terrorism Database. Cf. RUSI: *Final Report Lone Actor Terrorism*, London 2016, https://rusi.org/sites/default/files/201604_clat_final_report.pdf.

Indeed, as experts verify, the statistics on Lone Wolf terrorism must be enjoyed with care. Cf. Mark S. Hamm/Ramón Spaaij: "Key Issues and Research Agendas in Lone Wolf Terrorism", in: *Studies in Conflict & Terrorism*, 38(2015) 3, p. 173.

[17]Pankaj Mishra: *Das Zeitalter des Zorns. Eine Geschichte der Gegenwart*, Frankfurt on Main 2017, p. 319.

is an essential constituent part of the terrorist's act of violence: The terrorist achieves nothing alone, publicity on the other hand everything."[18] Said differently: publicity is the oxygen of terrorists.

There is no doubt: The phenomenon of terror is en vogue and reached a global scale a long time ago. If an assault takes place, political decision-makers express solidarity with and empathy for one another, promising to stand shoulder to shoulder in a "fight against terrorism". Whoever speaks of terrorism today, has the global event of 11 September 2001 in mind, thinks of the most terrifying events for example in Brussels or Paris, where terrorist networks made brutal strikes. Or of the "annus horribilis" (*year of horror*) in 2016, when attacks using a truck on the most magnificent boulevard in Nice and at a Christmas market in Berlin, abruptly and without warning despatched innocent people to their death. In the meantime, these events have contributed towards an Islamic background being assumed to be behind every attack, virtually as a reflex reaction. One can assume that immediately after every strike populists crops up, assuming an assault on the West by "Islam", in order to capitalise on the simplified rhetoric of indignation.

All of this takes place in a context, wherewith reference to a quote from William Shakespeare's "Hamlet" the statement is heard everywhere, that time is out of joint. The hero of the drama the Prince of Denmark, slips ever increasingly into self-pity, until he finally seals his own fate. Are we likewise now on this same path? The sociologist Ulrich Beck coined the phrase "World Risk Society" in his global bestseller, in which the search for a lost security sets the tone. Accordingly, risks are not just real and present, but are stage-managed and exploited for political ends. With the result that anxiety and fear become the dominant emotions in life.[19] This is especially true for terrorists: "They succeed in landing a double blow, firstly through physical force and then via our brains. The first blow initially attracts all the attention, the second one on the other hand often remains undetected."[20]

An important aspect in today's emotionally charged debate on the new dimension of terror has almost come to an end: Contrary to the current excitement, terrorism in Western Europe is nothing new. In the twentieth century, waves of terrorism descended on Europe again and again from the 1970s until the middle of the 1990s. Global databases show that terrorism is on the increase worldwide, however, not in Europe. Researchers at the University of Maryland in the USA have attempted to record global terrorist

---

[18] Sepp Binder: *Terrorismus. Herausforderung und Antwort*, Bonn 1978, p. 55.
[19] Cf. Ulrich Beck: *Weltrisikogesellschaft. Auf der Suche nach der verlorenen Sicherheit*, Frankfurt/Main 2007.
[20] Cf. Gerd Gigerenzer: *Risiko. Wie man die richtigen Entscheidungen trifft*, Munich 2013, p. 22f.

attacks since 1970. Terrorist attacks are included in their "Global Terrorism Database" with one precondition: A non-governmental organisation as the protagonist must intentionally exercise force against people or objects, or at least threaten to do so, in order to achieve political, religious or social goals.[21]

There is or there were a multitude or terrorist or separatist organisations: the IRA (*Irish Republican Army*) in Northern Ireland, proclaiming to be Catholic, the Basque separatist Euskadi Ta Askatasuna (ETA—Basque language for the Baqsue Homeland and Liberty), the left-wing extremist Red Army Faction (RAF) in the Federal Republic of Germany, the communist Red Brigades, the neo-fascist Ordine Nuovo in Italy as well as many other non-European terrorist cells. These groups questioned the structures of their respective countries and were in part actively or secretly supported by the populace. A look at the 1970s and 1980s shows that there were even more victims being mourned at that time than nowadays.[22] Terrorist attacks by the IRA alone amassed at least 3,500 human victims over 30 years. Right-wing terrorism plays a comparatively modest role in the consideration of terrorism during the post war years of the twentieth century. This has now suddenly changed, particularly as the "success" of terrorism is not measured by the number of victims killed, maimed or injured. The attention which a terrorist attack receives is one important and valid criterion.

1.4 The National Socialist Underground (NSU) as an Early Warning

The undetected actions of the National Socialist Underground (NSU) may serve as the start of a new dimension of right-wing terrorism in Germany. Murders by the small NSU cell were however dismissed for years as apolitical criminality, and the surviving dependents of victims were even suspected. Three far-right extremists Uwe Mundlos, Uwe Böhnhardt and Beate Zschäpe lived in the shadows for at least 13 years, from 1998 to 2011, and murdered at least ten people during this period—nine migrants and a female police officer. The only surviving person, Beate Zschäpe, was sentenced to lifelong imprisonment in July 2018 after a trial lasting more than 5 years. Her far-right extremist views were proven, likewise her significant contribution to the assaults. Apparently the trio primarily foresaw the face-to-face murder

---

[21] Cf. University of Maryland: *Global Terrorism Index 2017*. Institute for Economics & Peace, https://reliefweb.int/sites/reliefweb.int/files/resources/Global%20Terrorism%20Index%202017%20%284%29.pdf.
[22] Cf. ibid.

of foreigners, according to the motto "actions not words". Over and above this, numerous bank robberies and attacks using explosives were able to be attributed to the terrorists. There were no letters claiming responsibility. In a film which was unearthed later, the criminals make fun of their crimes in a scornful and cynical manner, and also spoke of a "network of comrades".[23] The German security agencies and secret services looked on, albeit watching carefully, without acting. There were no early-warning indications of right-wing terrorism, although this was maintained by politicians. The Home Secretary of the Federal Republic of Germany at that time, Hans-Peter Friedrich praised the intelligence services only a few months before the NSU became public knowledge as an "indispensable early-warning system," "performing good and valuable work."[24]

The intelligence service's report stated: "In 2010 we were not able to determine any far-right terrorist structures either."[25] Whilst the murderous trio had a large support network throughout the whole of Germany, numbering up to 200 people, who provided weapons and apartments, for example, helping them out logistically and financially. The murders were carried out throughout the whole of Germany, from Rostock via Dortmund down to Munich. Therefore, it would be inappropriate to speak of an isolated terrorist trio. The domestic intelligence services painted an extremely unhappy picture. A massive loss of trust in the establishment arose after it became public knowledge that files had been destroyed, computer files had been manipulated by officials, especially in some of the Intelligence Service's regional state offices.[26]

The NSU terrorists were apparently influenced by the single actor John Ausonius, who had to take the stand in a trial in 2018 for a murder in Frankfurt 26 years earlier. The Swede born as Wolfgang Alexander John Zaugg with German-Swiss roots had attracted attention at the start of the 1990s because of a series of murders of immigrants in Sweden. The Swedish media called him "Laserman", as he used a laser aiming device installed on a sawn-off rifle

---

[23] The 15 min long video consists of sequences from the cartoon series "The Pink Panther", in which original exposures of victims and sites of attacks as well as television extracts and newspaper cuttings were pasted over the series of attacks. By using the Pink Panther cartoon figure, the assailants are celebrated, victims and investigative authorities are ridiculed. There is a threat at the end, announcing further attacks. This is carried out with a promise typical for the closing credits of the series "Today is not just any day, I will return, no question". The DVDs were clearly stored for several years in the NSU activists' apartment building and should have been sent at a specified time to certain institutions, media outlets and organisations (cf. Petra Bernhardt: "Terrorbilder", in: *Aus Politik und Zeitgeschichte*, 66 (2016) 24–25, p. 8).
[24] Cf. with Olaf Sundermeyer original documents: *Rechter Terror in Deutschland*, Munich 2012, p. 253.
[25] German Federal Ministry of the Interior (ed.): *Verfassungsschutzbericht 2010*, Berlin 2011.
[26] Cf. Olaf Sundermeyer: *Rechter Terror in Deutschland*, Munich 2012, p. 253.

for some of his attacks. The German secret services classified him in 2012 as a "possible blueprint for the NSU", when it finally took note of the German terrorist cell. The female in charge of the right-wing extremist department of German homeland secret services reported "clear parallels" between the two series of racist attacks—these had by no means been exhausted by the fact the victims were immigrants selected at random. The Federal Prosecutor's Office instigated investigation proceedings against Ausonius on account of this. Striking parallels existed[27]: Like him, Uwe Mundlos and Uwe Böhnhardt often shot victims who were not known to them directly in the head at close range. They financed their lifestyles with bank robberies. But why should the terrorist trio from Zwickau of all things have taken a Swedish serial killer as their role model? The intelligence services had a theory here too: They could have read of his racist attacks in the writings of the globally active far-right extremist Blood & Honour network. The so-called C18 field manual (also known as the Blood & Honour Field Manual) appeared in the early years of the new millennium under the pseudonym "Max Hammer" (the Norwegian neo-National Socialist Erik Blücher was behind this). It tells us amongst other things, that "Aryan people must die fighting."[28] In one chapter, John Ausonius is mentioned in glowing terms.[29] Like the NSU, Ausonius left no letters of acknowledgement behind—a calculated move? An address list discovered refers to the closely intermeshed relationship to Blood & Honour.

It is not only here that provocation by far-right extremist terrorist single actors extending beyond national boundaries is in evidence, independent of any organisations whatsoever. The NSU, a small cell with three protagonists, is not included in this. However, their drive was similar: Fuelled by a hatred of ethnic minorities, they wished to make statements against immigrant communities—in a perversion of the Do It Yourself principle. Membership of a party, brotherhood or any other grouping is far and away no longer necessary nowadays, attending "regular party get-togethers" has become outdated. Likewise, the image of cliques of youths with sparse means, fuelled by alcohol does not apply either, making foreigners, immigrants or ethnic minorities scapegoats for their own situation, mutually stimulating one another to set off together and in the truest sense of the word to strike home. Like-minded people have been able to find one another on social media for a long time,

---

[27] Cf. Ulrich Schmidt: „Blaupause „Laserman"", in: *taz* dated 5 September 2012, http://www.taz.de/Vorbild-des-Terrornazi-Trios/!5084793.
[28] Max Hammer: *Blood & Honour Field Manual*, (no source of origin), p. 29, https://archive.org/details/Blood_Honour_Field_Manual_Max_Hammer.
[29] Ibid. p. 21.

in chats and chatrooms for example with partners in violent video games or on the dark net. They can easily erase their trails when doing so by using encoding services or fake accounts.

1.5 Why We Must Stand up to Lone Wolves

Far-right terrorism is presenting a new face in Western democracies. We have been able to detect the Lone Wolf phenomenon in many countries over recent decades, and also right in the midst of Western democracies. Such cases occurred more frequently in the USA, but also in Germany, Austria, Great Britain, Norway, Sweden, Italy and Finland. Experts even spoke of an "age of lone wolf terrorists,"[30] We find ourselves in the middle of a new wave of terrorism. The four previous waves[31] have been followed by a fifth one[32]:

- 1st wave: anarchistic terrorism (at the end of the 19th and start of the twentieth century): attacks on numerous heads of state and governments in monarchies (Russia and Europe)
- 2nd wave: anti-colonial waves of violence (from the 1920s), for example in Indochina, Algeria and several South American countries
- 3rd wave: left-wing extremist motivated terrorism in countries such as Italy, Germany, Spain (second half of the twentieth century)
- 4th wave: Islamic terrorism (from 1979,[33] above all in the twenty-first century) with no limits to violence, propelled by the terrorist organisations al-Qaeda and IS.
- 5th wave: Lone Wolf terrorism with new opportunities through the Internet in the USA and Europe (different ideological inspiration).

The tabloid press also concerns themselves with the subject of lone wolf terrorism in an opinionated manner, with the German Bild newspaper talking

---

[30] According to Mark S. Hamm/Ramón Spaaij: *The Age of Lone Wolf Terrorism*, New York 2017.
[31] Cf. David C. Rapoport: "The Four Waves of Modern Terrorism", in: Audrey Kurth Cronin/James M. Ludes (ed.): *Attacking Terrorism: Elements of a Grand Strategy*, Washington D. C. 2004, pp. 46–73.
[32] Cf. Jeffrey D. Simon: "Technological and Lone Operator Terrorism: Prospects for a Fifth Wave of Global Terrorism", in: Jean Rosenfeld (ed.): *Terrorism, Identity, and Legitimacy: The Four Waves Theory and Political Violence*, 2011, pp. 44–65; Sebastian Gräfe: *Rechtsterrorismus in der Bundesrepublik Deutschland*, Baden-Baden 2017, pp. 76f.
[33] During an attack by a group of armed Sunni fundamentalists on the Great Mosque in Mecca, the Holy place in Islam, almost one thousand people lost their lives in 1979. The high number was due to the special celebration for the turn of the century according the Islamic method of counting the passage of time.

about the "most dangerous terrorist phenomenon in the world".[34] Precisely because no larger organisation is behind it, no large "scene" can be made out of it and so the media, politicians and officials struggle greatly when assessing it. The dilemma in dealing with this type of terrorism has its basis in fixating perpetrators. Victims become shadows, and their members are quickly forgotten. Perhaps this is precisely the reason security officials in Germany, for instance, warn of possible glorification.[35] One lone individual acting criminally—or rather even barbarically—should not move to occupy the centre of attention.

This book seeks to initiate an examination of the new right-wing terrorism which has been needed for a long time, terrorism which definitely was not imported, but came about in our very midst. I will reveal how a type of perpetrator has been formed from the new technical as well as digital opportunities, which up until now has scarcely been perceived. I argue using concrete cases, for example using my expertise as an expert witness for the City of Munich in the case of a terrorist attack on 22 July 2016. Later I discovered via media in the USA, that this perpetrator in Munich was networked with a perpetrator in New Mexico via the gaming platform "Steam". This shows that single actors with far-right extremist motivations have long since departed from the terrain of national states and now set themselves up in a global dimension.

We should not fall victim to rhetoric of reassurance and appeasement, according to which this phenomenon is unfathomable or even marginal. I should like to delve into it in this book and at the same time describe opportunities for us to avoid this danger. Terrorism does not bear down on us like a natural catastrophe, this is not an earthquake or an erupting volcano. On the other hand, the risk of being the victim of a car crash (precisely if the driver is sending an SMS text), has a far greater probability. The reaction to terrorism has the effect of being a balancing act between fatalism (according to the motto: we must get used to terrorism, we should sooner hush it up) and paranoia (according to the motto: terrorism destroys the humanitarian basis of our coexistence). However, we should not allow ourselves to succumb to panic mongering. Populists and the tabloid press help fuel this image; however, many drivers of public opinion too, according to which we must reckon with terrorism everywhere. That is dubious: Far sooner we are concerned with an objective debate, with no zeal or lust for sensationalism.

---

[34]Viktoria Dümer: „Bild erklärt die „einsamen Wölfe". Das gefährlichste Terrorphänomen der Welt", in: *Bild.de* dated 20 October 2015, https://www.bild.de/politik/ausland/terroranschlag/einsame-woelfe-was-macht-sie-so-gefaehrlich-43064650.bild.html.

[35]The Bavarian Intelligence Services office wrote to me in a letter of 22 September 2017 following my request. The term "lone wolf" was a "choice of words inspiring heroism".

Our aim must be to develop an early-warning system and to detect warning signs.

Therefore, we must flag up the destructive connection between the individual person and background conditions in society. Only then will we be able to find strategies for dealing with the new racist hatred which occurs, which I should like to introduce in the last part of my book. There is a lot at stake. We are dealing with maintaining freedom and upholding order in our society, which individuals are seeking to undermine. We are not only addressing the role of the State here, which must think up a new concept for a fortified democracy. The key can also be found in civil society itself, to brace itself against brutalisation and barbarisation. We also need integrated prevention—and must all pull together in order to be stronger than the "Propaganda of the deed." This also includes taking psychological disorders seriously and allowing them to be included in our consideration of this phenomenon, especially as they were a taboo for society for a long time and still are. There is no doubt: Whoever executes his evil deed after lengthy planning, often carries deep frustration around inside, and—what is more—psychological or mental disorders. Racist ideas are then suitable as the perfect catch-all, in order to make other people responsible for our internal misery or for acting out chauvinistic feelings.

1.6 The Current Situation: Errors of Judgement by Politicians and Officials

This was also the case with David Sonboly. He unleashed his deed exactly 5 years after Breivik's cold-blooded murders. He changed his name for the second time 11 weeks prior to his act, from Ali to David. He wished to operate as a German prior to striking out. On 22 July 2016, an apparently normal Friday evening in summertime, the City of Munich spent hours in an apocalyptic state of emergency—along with the involvement of a global audience. At a highly symbolic spot in the heart of the city, the Olympia Shopping Centre, people succumbed to mass hysteria and panic. Some 2,600 security personnel were deployed in one of the largest ad hoc deployments in recent decades. Buses and tram services stopped running, television stations and online media vied to outdo one another via Live Ticker with speculations hungry for sensationalism and also through other phantom sites of crimes and further offenders. Social media above all unleashed their own internal dynamic. At the end of a documentary initially broadcast by Bayrischer Rundfunk on 18 July

2018, the journalist Martin Bernkopf who had been reporting live for the station at that time, reported: "All of us together created this terrorism. People who posted on Facebook. Ourselves, the media. The police, who did not say: 'No, this is not a terrorist attack', to a certain extent too. The word terrorism is dangerous and triggered the entire hysteria."[36] Speculation concerning an Islamic background followed quickly, on CNN too, for example. Reporting by the German broadcaster ARD commenced whilst it had still not been established how many victims there were and how many assailants were possibly involved.[37]

Virtual rumour mills went so far as reporting further attacks at other locations in Munich city centre. And thus, an erroneous tweet from a young man was distributed for over an hour, that shots had been fired in the large square Karlsplatz/Stachus. This information dominated various television and radio stations. Thereupon, taxis were instructed by their bases to avoid the area. As a consequence, the same information channel started spreading a large amount of misinformation concerning the whereabouts and the number of assailants.[38] Mistakes of this kind additionally raised the level of attention for the deed which was already dramatic in itself. Nine people, eight young people and one mother fell victim to the actions of an individual assailant, five further people were in part seriously injured by shots. Several dozen people injured themselves whilst escaping and in the panic which ensued. Eyewitnesses forced to observe the shooting in close proximity were traumatised. The terrible deed had a personal reference for many people, which should not be left unmentioned.

As an official expert witness for the City of Munich in this case, I explained that the 18-year-old German-Iranian had intended migrants to be victims of his rigid far-right extremist view of the world, and that he had acted entirely alone. He wished to be more "German" than the Germans, hated immigrants, although an immigrant himself. He had been planning his deeds for more than a year. Authorities considered him to "sooner (be) a mentally deranged avenger based on his self-image," but not however a "terrorist combatant", to paraphrase the Bavarian State Office for Intelligence Services.[39]

---

[36] Cf. Bayerischer Rundfunk *Munich – Stadt in Angst*, directed by Stefan Eberlein, initially broadcast 18 July 2018.

[37] *Focus.de*: „Amoklauf in München. Zuschauer kritisieren ARD-Mann Roth für Berichterstattung", 24 July 2017, https://www.focus.de/kultur/kino_tv/nach-bluttat-in-muenchen-zuschauer-kritisieren-ard-mann-roth-fuer-berichterstattung_id_5756468.html.

[38] Cf. Robert Kahr/Frank Robertz/Ruben Wickenhäuser: „Mediale Inszenierung von Amok und Terror", in: *Aus Politik und Zeitgeschichte* 67 (2017) 4, p. 35.

[39] Bavarian State Office for Intelligence Services: *Vorläufige Erstbewertung vom 10. August 2016*, Munich.

The unanimous verdict was: His terrible act had not been politically motivated. Revenge, not political motivation had supposedly "acted to trigger the deed."[40] Officials wrote in their closing report: "We must not assume the act was politically motivated."[41] Criticism of the officials' assessment elicits precisely this determination of a "prime motive".

Should it really be true there is no right-wing terrorism in Bavaria—the Free State of Bavaria has traditionally been proud of its supposed pioneering role in the fight against extremism and terrorism, especially after the NSU debacle? The terrorist cell has numerous connections in the Free State, where five murders were committed. As a consequence, the Intelligence Services wished for example to work towards rectifying these faults. In Sonboly's case the authorities do not detect terrorism, and this was apparently unshakably so, but rather an apolitical act of violence, the result of supposed bullying at school, which the perpetrator "subsequently expanded".[42] The Bavarian Intelligence Services assessed the case internally, set the course for the interpretational sovereignty on a spree killing, and ignored it in their official reports. Whoever looks through official communiqués for 2016 under right-wing extremism and for far-right terrorism, will find nothing—as though the attacks in the Bavarian state capital had never occurred. By hook or by crook, the evil deed was by all accounts not supposed to have been right-wing terrorism, David Sonboly, as the *Frankfurter Allgemeine Zeitung* writes, appears to have "slipped through as a far-right extremist." The journalist Patrick Bahners downright scoffed at the assessment of the Bavarian State Office for Intelligence Services: "They talk of, borrowing from the realms of far-right extremism' as with a postgraduate student citing theories on grounds of prestige, which he has not entirely understood. The 'internalisation' of the right-wing ideology is missing. David S. had ‚not managed' to adopt an ideology whilst still in the run-up or like Breivik to develop his own ideology."[43] Obviously

---

[40] Bavarian Ministry of the Interior (July 2017): Reply to the written question from the member of the state parliament Katharina Schulze (Fraction of the Greens in the Parliament) dated April 2017, p. 4, https://www.bayern.landtag.de/www/ElanTextAblage_WP17/Drucksachen/Schriftliche%20Anfragen/17_0017018.pdf.

[41] Cf. With original documentation Heiner Effern: „Tödlicher Hass eines Rassisten", in: *Süddeutsche Zeitung* of 7/8 October 2017, p. 79.

[42] Quoting according to spree killing researcher Britta Bannenberg, who here nevertheless detects a killing frenzy, according to: Martin Bernstein: „Das war ein rassistischer Ansatz", in: *Süddeutsche Zeitung* dated 18 June 2018, p. 43. Sonboly was sooner the offender than a victim. This is what a one-time friend said, that Sonboly had hacked into his old Facebook account: "He knew my e-mail addresses and my password. Then he wrote to my friends and told them I was gay."

[43] Patrick Bahners: „Als Rechtsextremist durchgefallen", in: *Frankfurter Allgemeine Zeitung* dated 9 October 2017, http://www.faz.net/aktuell/feuilleton/kommentar-als-rechtsextremist-durchgefallen-15237076.html.

according to this logic, only such people become ideologists, who have completed a course of study or have an elaborate manner of expression as was the case with the RAF.

The political side was able to adopt this view seamlessly, with ease. The Bavarian Minister for the Interior Joachim Herrmann stated after completing his investigations: "To speak of a right-wing extremist act, would then seem to go a little far."[44] His press conference reflected the capitulation before solid, schematically as well as scientifically specified assessment criteria. On request Herrmann spoke of the fact that "everyone [must] decide for themselves, whether to classify the deed as right-wing extremism."[45] In order to justify not classifying this assault as far-right extremism, he stated that Sonboly had never been part of a far-right extremist organisation.[46] This argument, however, is derived from heavily antiquated understanding, which in an era distinguished by virtual interactions and Lone Wolf terrorism has long since no longer been in keeping with the times and has become obsolete. Two years later he now at least acknowledged a "racist approach".[47] This changes nothing, that the course had been set in the wrong direction, likewise with his incorrect assessment, which lingers. It is astonishing that immediately following it and up until the end of investigations, the deed apparently was irrevocably interpreted along the lines of an apolitical killing spree—especially as Herrmann himself had already acknowledged David S.' extreme right-wing view of the world.[48] Therefore, recognising a reverse in the evaluation is questionable here.

The "profiler" Alexander Horn also created the narrative of a "spree killing", as head of the Office for Operational Case Analysis (OFA), Inspectorate 115 of Munich Police Headquarters. He is considered to be a super-detective, as one of the most successful officers for criminal manhunts. His assertion that a "previous bullying incident at school should be the main cause of an act of revenge on society" should have the desired effect, and the political background could be faded out. In conclusion, we are able to say about David Sonboly: "A mentally and emotionally disturbed young man, who fell victim to bullying and physical abuse, and in this way experienced insults

---

[44]Quotation from ZDF *heute journal*, broadcast on 12 July 2017.
[45]Quoted according to ARD *Fakt*: „München-Attentat: Warum viele Hintergründe im Dunkeln bleiben", Report: Christian Bergmann/Marcus Weller, broadcast on 22 August 2017.
[46]Cf. Joachim Herrmann: „Bei der Polizei gibt es Baustellen", in: *Der Spiegel* 32/2017, pp. 42–44.
[47]Quoted according to Martin Bernstein: „Das war ein rassistischer Ansatz", in: *Süddeutsche Zeitung* dated 18 June 2018, p. 43.
[48]Cited according to *Frankfurter Allgemeine Zeitung* of 28 July 2016: „Herrmann bestätigt Hinweise auf rechtsextremistisches Weltbild", http://www.faz.net/aktuell/politik/inland/herrmann-bestaetigt-rassistisches-weltbild-von-muenchen-amoklaeufer-14361209.html.

harmful to his self-image, and started developing revenge fantasies."[49] Following this line of argument, Islamic attacks may not be classified as terrorist acts, if the assailants have not displayed extensive signs of ideologization.

Still, a change in thinking has taken place in the meantime, through my expert's report presented in October 2017 as part of an expert discussion with the State Criminal Investigations Office and Munich Public Prosecutor's Office, which transpired following a painstaking study of thousands of pages of investigation files lasting several months.[50] And that, although up until now only a brief extract, a condensed version of it had been published. The body of evidence is too overwhelming. Officials in the Federal Office of Justice spoke for the first time of an extremist assault in February 2018 and made a hardship payment to surviving dependents and people who had suffered injuries.[51] In addition, there was an entirely new turn of events, which I stumbled upon during my international research for this book. In April 2018, I was astounded when I came across a freely accessible article in US media revealing entirely new contacts with Sonboly, and which I immediately passed on to the Bavarian State Criminal Police Office [*Bayerisches Landeskriminalamt (BLKA)*]. The officials apparently knew nothing of the freely accessible information or at least told me as much. In this way I informed myself, astonished at the apparent disinterest, and investigative journalists about these freely accessible facts, which after further research suggested the existence of spiritual twins with similar views of the world and intentions to carry out assaults.

One of these journalists was Christian Bergmann, who amongst other things works for the German public sector broadcaster, "ARD Fakt". He quickly discovered: Sonboly was part of a virtual network of potential mass murderers along with a person from Germany with a similar outlook. William Atchison acted as the key figure for this, a 21-year-old who carried out an attack on a school in Aztec, New Mexico in December 2017, murdering two students and killing himself as intended. The two were in contact online,

---

[49] Alexander Horn: Amoklauf von David Sonboly, Ergebnis der Fallanalyse, München, internal document, 15 December 2016.

[50] Cf. Florian Hartleb: *Rechtsextremistisch motivierter Einsamer-Wolf-Terrorismus statt Amoklauf. Eine notwendige Neubewertung der Morde am Olympiaeinkaufszentrum München. Gutachten für die Stadt München im Zuge einer Expertenanhörung*, Munich, October 2017. (A short version can be viewed at https://www.muenchen.de/rathaus/Stadtpolitik/Fachstelle-fuer-Demokratie/Kampagnen/Expertengespr-ch--Hintergr-nde-und-Folgen-des-OEZ-Attentats-.html.) There is a somewhat longer version in *Kriminalistik* 12/2017, p. 715–722.

[51] Federal Office of Justice, press release: „Bundesamt für Justiz zahlt Härteleistungen zugunsten der Opfer der Tat am Münchener Olympia-Einkaufszentrum", Berlin, 14 March 2018, https://www.bundesjustizamt.de/DE/Presse/Archiv/2018/20180314.html?nn=3449818.

communicating via the platform "Steam", as a sheriff stated for the record.[52] They exchanged far-right extremist and racist subject matter on a gaming platform in a forum called "Anti Refugee Club", including phantasies about killing sprees and frenzied attacks as well as global homicide lists. Atchison celebrated the assailant following David Sonboly's murderous rampage in Munich's Olympia Shopping Centre. This North American, a professed racist, ensured that Sonboly was immortalised as a hero in a virtual "ancestral" portrait gallery which resembles Wikipedia (he was specially appointed as an "honorary gamer" on Steam).[53] There is nothing astonishing about this: Single actors are praised and inflated in such forums in spite of demonstrably being socially disturbed.

It was easy to follow the chat clubs on the gaming platform Steam, to design and construct the former propaganda forums (like a club, which had explicitly turned against refugees) and to chat with former chat partners.[54] The Munich Public Prosecutor Office's surprise at this new development was astonishing. Repeated applications for evidence were made to Steam during the proceedings against the arms dealer who sold Sonboly the weapon for his assault, which were all declined. Nevertheless, there was concrete information from one witness. It is piquant that investigations in the case of David S. officially closed in March 2017, all traces having been checked thoroughly according to statements from officials. A good 60 investigators from the Olympia Shopping Centre Special Commission evaluated around 1,750 pieces of information and inspected more than 1,000 files.[55] Nevertheless, the virtual network remained undetected.

Equally as tricky: The Federal Criminal Police Office (BKA) knew from 9 December 2017, that is before my discovery, of the connection between Atchison and Sonboly. According to the BKA's own information, the Bavarian State Criminal Police Office (LKA Bayern), however, was not informed about it until 14 June 2018,[56] although it was in charge of the investigation.

---

[52] Cf. *Farmington Daily Times*: "Aztec school shooter reached out to other school shooters, planned killings online", 20 April 2018, https://www.daily-times.com/story/news/crime/2018/04/17/aztec-high-school-shooting-investigation-william-atchison/513013002/.

[53] Cf. Entry „Munich Massacre", https://encyclopediadramatica.rs/Munich_Massacre.

[54] Cf. ARD *Fakt*, broadcast dated 15 May 2018, Report: Christian Bergmann, https://www.mdr.de/investigativ/ermittlungsfehler-oez-attentat-muenchen-100.html (retrieved on 25 May 2018).

[55] According to Martin Bernstein/Susi Wimmer: „Freunde von David S. nun in der Psychiatrie", in: *Süddeutsche Zeitung* dated 28 July 2016, https://www.sueddeutsche.de/muenchen/nach-amoklauf-in-muenchen-freunde-von-david-s-nun-in-der-psychiatrie-1.3099158.

[56] Cf. Response by the federal government (Federal Ministry of the Interior, Building and Community) to the request from the German Member of Parliament Martina Renner (The Left) dated 27 June 2018, Verbindungen des Attentäters vom Olympia-Einkaufszentrum in München in die USA, BT Drucksache 19/2246, Response to Question 82.

The failure to pass this on, along with the lack of a reconciliation of information is astonishing, although The Federal Criminal Police Office (BKA) certainly "accompanied and supported" the Bavarian police responsible "at the request of the Bavarian Police responsible in their headquarters. This included coordinating and monitoring the exchange of the criminal police force's information with forces in foreign countries".[57] This internal failure by officials also exposed the myth of the supposedly so accurate German administration. And therefore, the question now arose in public of whether this proposition of a frenzied killing could continue to be upheld in public or whether the assault must not be considered an outpouring from a virtual terrorist network.[58]

A delayed courtesy expert's report[59] for the Bavarian Federal Criminal Police Office as client was supposed to save the narrative before and during this development in the case. The researcher of frenzied killings, Britta Bannenberg went so far as explicitly not classifying David S. as a far-right extremist. Some trouble of the heart suffered years before was supposed to have been the trigger for his attack—a new motive for the crime with an abstruse effect, difficult to understand.[60] Her analysis contains the following passage: "The perpetrator was not active either on extreme right-wing websites or in relevant forums, nor had he sought any contact whatsoever with far-right groups, simply because he never intended to perpetrate a group assault. His personality had always been that of a loner and his planning for the assault had accordingly been directed towards a single actor's attack. But merely allocating the subject to far-right extremism would clearly have been too short-sighted."[61]

---

[57] Cf. ibid.
[58] Cf. Alexander Kain: „Amoklauf oder Tat eines virtuellen Terror-Netzwerks?", in: Passauer Neue Presse dated 16 May 2018, p. 3.
[59] The statement speaks for this a little: "It cannot be denied that the anniversary of the date of the attack in Norway was chosen as the date for his assault (22.7.2011)" (Britta Bannenberg: Expert Report for the case David S. for the Bavarian State Criminal Police Office, Gießen, February 2018). This has the effect as though something has been denied, which is undeniable.
[60] As had already been reported in a public speech, see Gießener Anzeiger, 12 November 2017, p. 14, http://www.giessener-anzeiger.de/lokales/stadt-giessen/nachrichten-giessen/giessen-teilnehmer-informieren-sich-ueber-den-aktuellen-forschungsstand-zum-thema-amoklauf_18310878.htm.
[61] Cf. Britta Bannenberg: „Gutachten zum Fall von David S. für das Bayerische Landeskriminalamt", Gießen, February 2018, p. 64. cf. Ralph Hub too for criticism of the Expert Report: „Rechtsextrem oder nicht? Streit um Todesschützen", in: Abendzeitung dated 9/10 June 2018, p. 6. Criticism likewise rained down in the Süddeutsche Zeitung: "Experts will perhaps still be talking about the scientific merits of Bannenberg's expert's report. She describes the perpetrator's thoughts in a few places, as though she knew them. 'The fact he asked the police officer to shoot him, concerned his fear of suffering pain and of possibly surviving.' This is always the case. 'Whatever empathy may be lacking for the victims, the cowardly perpetrators' feelings of self-pity are all the more distinctive.'" (Ronen Steinke: „Der große Streit über David S.", in: Süddeutsche Zeitung dated 8 June 2018, p. 47).

The irritations increased once again with the Expert's Report. They ensured that the Bavarian State government had to re-think their previous assessments as the result of a unanimous decision by the Ministry of the Interior in the Bavarian Parliament.[62] However, an ethos of little enlightenment continued to predominate in accordance with a piecemeal strategy. The Bavarian State government asked Parliament for patience and a postponement,[63] prolonging submission of a final report with sparse information. The new insights of the trail to the USA appeared to make an assessment impossible: "In spite of the fundamental obligation under constitutional law to fulfil requests for information from the Bavarian State Parliament, after carefully weighing up the interests concerned in this particular case, the interests of the parliament in information are secondary here to the justified interests in implementing investigations under criminal law [...] As insights from investigations by US officials of William A. could possibly be of relevance to evaluating the motive of David S., but a response from the US officials has still not been received, at present a final evaluation of the motive and backgrounds is not possible [...] As reporting, which at the moment must disregard the complex William A. lacking sufficient insights of their own at present, which could only partially satisfy the recognisable interest for information from Members of the Bavarian Parliament, I therefore request your tacit consent, that reporting on this subject matter be completed once investigations with regard to William A. and David S. have been concluded [...]."[64] Only in October 2019, the police admitted that the Munich attacks also had political motives: "The radical right and racist view of the perpetrator should not be ignored."[65] So it

---

[62] Application with printed matter number 17/22714, resolved on 13 June 2018 by the Committee for the Interior in the Bavarian Parliament.

[63] There were individual requests from the ranks of the Bavarian Parliament over a period of more than two years for example by the delegates Florian Ritter (Social Democrats), Katharina Schulze (Green) and Claudia Stamm (Independent). The responses were in part delayed or dismissed on formal grounds. The overall context has not yet been discussed in the State Parliament, and not in specialist committees either. In the meantime, the CSU faction had agreed to the requests. Nevertheless, there has scarcely been any enlightenment on the part of the State Parliament, and also no admission of having made any mistakes. This applies to the Ministry of the Interior in particular. The Member of the Bavarian Parliament Claudia Stamm organised a specialist discussion and organised a press conference in June 2018 in light of the new revelations, the latter with the author in attendance. In general, however we are able to record there was a poorly coordinated, scarcely interested as well as a poor strategic response by the Opposition.

[64] Communication from the Bavarian Ministry of the Interior to the Bavarian Parliament on 3 July 2018 (Response to the resolution of the Bavarian State Government dated 12 December 2017 concerning a murderous attack of 22 July 2016 at the Olympia Shopping Centre in Munich—Motives and Background of the assailant David S.).

[65] Bavarian Ministry of the Interior: Final report in the case of the Munich attacks, Munich, 24th October 2019, p. 15.

took the authorities including the Bavarian minister for interior Joachim Herrmann more than 3 years to acknowledge the lone wolf terrorism (without using the term).

The entire affair in the "Sonboly" case is highly explosive. It is also the starting point for taking a good look at the Lone Wolf phenomenon in this book, which has been considered far too seldom up until now. One would probably have stumbled into a hornet's nest and have been able to prevent the attacks in Munich and Aztec if obvious indications had been followed up, both on the American as well as the German side. Suspected terrorists used the platform Steam to communicate unhindered, and at the same time to play games and stoke themselves up. At the latest by now, it is clear that such attacks have had an international range for a long time. Virtual contacts via TeamSpeak, Chats etc. made this entirely possible. The trails to the USA nevertheless were not followed up, no official request to the FBI etc. was made. However, investigators stated that all chatroom contacts by David S. had been thoroughly evaluated. How did we reach this obvious discrepancy? Once again a lack of cooperation between officials and a lack of sensibility for right-wing terrorism was evident, also in the aftermath.

The BKA referred to the fact prior to the attacks by David S. in the report „Gefährdungslage Politisch motivierte Kriminalität – rechts" (or politically motivated offences as official statements reveal and with added right-wing motives), that attacks and serial murders such as those by the NSU could lead to copy-cat crimes. Isolated terrorist actions by self-radicalised single actors as well as the formation of small groups of terrorists would need to be taken into consideration.[66] Nevertheless, the assault by David Sonboly was considered an "apolitical killing spree," sealed by the prerogative of interpretation of Bavaria's officials in this case. Perhaps the misinterpretation has something to do with the circumstance which appeared strange, of the assailant originally from Iran being proud of his "Aryan roots" (the "earliest Aryans" supposedly originate from Iran) and developing xenophobia (*or a hatred of strangers*) towards different migratory backgrounds. With the consequence that the case for traditional concepts of standards and norms came undone and had become a "political issue"[67] even before the trail to the US was revealed. At any rate, it was not obvious for a long time how seriously the assailant was

---

[66] Cf. Michail Logvinov: „Terrorismusrelevante Indikatoren und Gefahrenfaktoren im Rechtsextremismus", in: *Totalitarismus und Demokratie*, 10 (2013) 2, p. 267f.

[67] Nina Job: „Nicht politisch motiviert – das darf bezweifelt werden", in: *Abendzeitung* of 22 July 2017, http://www.abendzeitung-muenchen.de/inhalt.amoklauf-am-oez-nicht-politisch-motiviert-das-darf-bezweifelt-werden.4672c2f9-63cf-44bb-8609-53b4c079d73f.html.

driven by political, right-wing extremist views. Whilst with Islamic perpetrators the ideology is a central declaratory basis for far-right perpetrators, racist convictions are often dismissed as a secondary aspect. This case does not fit the picture up until today. The established researcher of terrorism and extremists Karin Priester goes so far as to make the following presumption in her book „Warum Europäer in den Heiligen Krieg ziehen. Der Dschihadismus als rechtsradikale Jugendbewegung", in which she evaluates the curriculums vitae of over 500 Muslim socialised or converted jihadis from five Western European countries: "The 18-year-old frenzied killer Ali David Sonboly could clearly not join the jihad simply because he hated Turks and Arabs and felt himself racially superior to them."[68]

1.7 Hypotheses

An understanding of the actions of this terrorist is essential here, in order to learn for the future and to be able to take preventative measures. This also applies to the extensive ideological justification of the attack—the historian of ideas Barbara Zehnpfennig demonstrated that as early as in Adolf Hitler's „Mein Kampf", we were not actually concerned with mental and spiritual confusion, but were dealing with a logical thought process in itself, which first of all manifested itself theoretically, and was then realised practically.[69] Obviously, the security officials made a big deal of acknowledging the new risk from right-leaning single actors.

Terrorists are people, not monsters or robots. Suddenly they surface. Apparently disturbed single actors, who wish to leave a memorial even if only a posthumous one. They actually do not act pathologically like frenzied killers (I will go into the difference in detail below), but justify their terrifying deeds with pamphlets, letters or videos claiming responsibility, manifestos, confessions or wills and legacies. On the part of the public, on the other hand, speechlessness sets in at first. There is a psychological trick in portraying the actors as "sick" and as "foreigners". It is too painful to discover that terrorism grows in our midst, develops in quiet little rooms and then explosively unleashes its powerful effect—on innocent people, who are in the wrong place at the wrong time. Terrorism is a cultural challenge, placing the might and power of civilisation in question. Whoever reduces terrorists to

---

[68] Karin Priester: *Warum Europäer in den Krieg ziehen. Der Dschihadismus als rechtsradikale Jugendbewegung*, Frankfurt on Main 2017, p. 267.
[69] Cf. Barbara Zehnpfennig: *Hitlers „Mein Kampf". Eine Interpretation*, Munich 2006.

one-dimensional psychopaths or produces analogies to cinematic villains can hardly develop suitable anti-terrorist strategies.

Right-wing terrorism feeds precisely off the fact that one ethnic group derives a superiority against another and wishes to push this through using militant means, in order to set a marker for the public, as an example to others. The debate about migrants which is intensifying, especially for refugees, should sooner increase the relevance of the subject.

The British Member of Parliament Helen Joanne "Jo" Cox, who was committing herself for refugees to be accepted, was murdered by a socially isolated far-right extremist in June 2016, shortly before the Brexit Referendum. And in February 2018 the Italian Luca Traini fired shots at African migrants out of racial hatred in Macerata/Central Italy. Western societies are divided as to why conspiracy theories are experiencing a boom, not only in the field of terrorist attacks. Considerable parts of the population have estranged themselves for the long-term from the Centre of society. We can already gauge this solely from the fact that right-wing populist and extremist groups are succeeding, conspiracy theories are rife in filter bubbles and echo chambers, and obscure movements receive massive popularity. I am not merely interested here in arbitrary or glorified accounts and tallying up criminal acts, but in recognising patterns, parallels and current developments.

My book intends to present ten hypotheses and provide evidence for these:

- Politics, officialdom, media and society are not prepared for the new challenge of terrorism from individuals. The image still predominates that groups and networks are behind terrorist attacks.
- Right-wing terrorism in general is chronically neglected on the basis of on left-wing terrorism in the second half of the 20th century and Islamic terrorism in the 21st century. Right-wing terrorism is still greatly underestimated by all parties involved, in spite of the "shadows of the past."
- Terrorism organised in groups should be consigned to the past: The opportunities for obtaining information and possibilities to communicate have been simplified in the virtual era, the Internet affords potential lone wolves the opportunity to comply with their need for a larger group without being in contact personally, and to learn the theory and practice of terrorism autodidactically, self-taught.
- Lone Wolves are part of a globalised right-wing terrorism, a virtual network in which potential perpetrators connect with one another. They chat on platforms which are not suspicious, play games and exchange plans for attacks with one another. The central as well as fatal radicalisation process takes place there in a small minority of these people.

- Lone Wolf terrorism is a male phenomenon. Usually it concerns young people during a difficult phase of adolescence, but which also includes men who consider themselves to be social failures during their middle-age.
- Investigations continue to run along national lines, which in view of the threatening situation and virtual communication is no longer current and up to date. Field analyses have needed to be adjusted and extended for a long time, in order to prevent attacks.
- Killing sprees and frenzied attacks based on troubles of the heart or bullying at school can clearly be distinguished from Lone Wolf terrorism by the political dimension of the terrible deed. Mental illness should not detract from the radical right-wing body of thought.
- A right-wing terrorist proceeding as an individual acts in a calculated manner when choosing his victims. He focusses on ethnic minorities and in particular on people who devote themselves to an open society.
- There are no practicable laws to appropriately punish right-wing terrorism by individuals. The reason for this is that criminal law does not cover attacks based on convictions and considers terrorism a group phenomenon.
- Preventative measures are still completely inadequate. They refer too heavily to possible and actual personality disorders which are present and leave the political realisation process to one side.

References

1. Backes, U. (2013). Rechtsextremistische Gewalt in Europa. In G. Hirscher & E. Jesse (Eds.), *Extremismus in Deutschland* (pp. 43–62). Baden-Baden.
2. Beck, U. (2007). *Weltrisikogesellschaft. Auf der Suche nach der verlorenen Sicherheit*. Frankfurt/Main.
3. Bernhardt, P. (2016). Terrorbilder. *Aus Politik und Zeitgeschichte, 66*(24–25), 3–10.
4. Binder, S. (1978). *Terrorismus. Herausforderung und Antwort*. Bonn.
5. German Federal Ministry of the Interior (Ed.). (2011). *Verfassungsschutzbericht 2010*. Berlin.
6. Gigerenzer, G. (2013). *Risiko. Wie man die richtigen Entscheidungen trifft*. Munich.
7. Gräfe, S. (2017). *Rechtsterrorismus in der Bundesrepublik Deutschland*. Baden-Baden.
8. Hamm, M. S., & Spaaij, R. (2015). Key issues and research agendas in lone wolf terrorism. *Studies in Conflict & Terrorism, 38*(3), 167–178.
9. Hamm, M. S., & Spaaij, R. (2017). *The age of lone wolf terrorism*. New York.

10. Kahr, R., Robertz, F., & Wickenhäuser, R. (2017). Mediale Inszenierung von Amok und Terror. *Aus Politik und Zeitgeschichte, 67*(4), 33–38.
11. Koehler, D. (2017). *Right-wing terrorism in the 21st century. The 'National Socialist Underground' and the history of terror from the far-right in Germany.* London/New York.
12. König, M. (2015). *Poetik des Terrors. Politisch motivierte Gewalt in der Gegenwartsliteratur.* Bielefeld.
13. Law, R. D. (Ed.). (2015). *The Routledge history of terrorism.* Oxon/New York.
14. Logvinov, M. (2013). Terrorismusrelevante Indikatoren und Gefahrenfaktoren im Rechtsextremismus. *Totalitarismus und Demokratie, 10*(2), 265–300.
15. Musharbash, Y. (2006). *Die neue al-Qaida. Innenansichten eines lernenden Netzwerks.* Cologne.
16. Priester, K. (2017). *Warum Europäer in den Krieg ziehen. Der Dschihadismus als rechtsradikale Jugendbewegung.* Frankfurt on Main.
17. Rapoport, D. C. (2004). The four waves of modern terrorism. In A. K. Cronin & J. M. Ludes (Eds.), *Attacking terrorism: Elements of a grand strategy* (pp. 46–73). Washington D. C.
18. Schliefsteiner, P. (2018). Austria's homegrown lone actor terrorist: Franz Fuchs and the letter bomb campaign of the 1990s. *Journal for Intelligence, Propaganda and Security Studies, 12*(1), 67–92.
19. Simon, J. D. (2011). Technological and lone operator terrorism: Prospects for a fifth wave of global terrorism. In J. Rosenfeld (Ed.), *Terrorism, identity, and legitimacy: The four waves theory and political violence* (pp. 44–65).
20. Simon, J. D. (2019). *The alphabet bomber. A lone wolf terrorist ahead of his time.* Nebraska.
21. Sundermeyer, O. (2012). *Rechter Terror in Deutschland.* Munich.
22. Taleb, N. N. (2014). *Anti-Fragilität. Anleitung für eine Welt, die wir nicht verstehen.* Munich.
23. The Royal United Services Institute (RUSI). (2016). *Final report lone actor terrorism.* London.
24. University of Maryland. (2017). *Global terrorism index 2017.* Institute for Economics & Peace. https://reliefweb.int/sites/reliefweb.int/files/resources/Global%20Terrorism%20Index%202017%20%284%29.pdf.
25. Waldmann, P. (1998). *Terrorismus, Provokation der Macht.* Munich.
26. Wilkinson, P. (1977). *Terrorism and the liberal state.* London.
27. Zehnpfennig, B. (2006). *Hitlers „Mein Kampf". Eine Interpretation.* Munich.

2

What Is a "Lone Wolf"?

2.1 A Phantom?

Terrorism as such is already a "complicated, eclectic phenomenon."[1] It can be defined as "an anxiety-inspiring method of repeated violent action."[2] Different governments, institutions, scholars and journalists have their own criteria when it comes to deciding how to label violence which is linked to political, religious, social, and other causes. Approaching the lone wolf is more demanding.[3] Let us leave the normal cases aside and move across to exceptions. The high degree of organisation required attested to terrorism, connected with sect-like structures, does not appear to include the lone wolf. Said differently: "Up until now, we always had *collective* or *corporative* protagonists in mind with terrorists and their victims."[4]

The expert on terrorism Peter Waldmann exemplifies this with the operative intelligence required, which he does not believe an individual person is capable of. This covers methodical preparation for targeted attacks, under difficult conditions in the underground and calculating the shock effect.[5] The "Terrorist" is considered to be a person who is ideologically driven and

---

[1] Cf. Hendrik Hegemann/Martin Kahl: *Terrorismus und Terrorismusbekämpfung. Eine Einführung*, Wiesbaden 2018, p. 5.
[2] Joseph J. Easson/Alex P. Schmid: 250-plus Academic, Governmental and Intergovernmental Definitions of Terrorism, in: Alex P. Schmid (ed.): The Routledge Handbook of Terrorism Research, London/New York 2011, pp. 99–157, here p. 129.
[3] Jeffrey D. Simon: *Lone Wolf Terrorism. Understanding The Growing Threat*, New York 2016, pp. 259–266.
[4] Thomas Kron: *Reflexiver Terrorismus*, Weilerswist 2015, p. 423.
[5] Cf. *Peter Waldmann*: Determinanten des Terrorismus, Weilerswist 2005, p. 15.

© Springer Nature Switzerland AG 2020
F. Hartleb, *Lone Wolves*,
https://doi.org/10.1007/978-3-030-36153-2_2

is connected to a rigid, organised structure dividing the work up with a high degree of group coherence. This is our image of ringleaders, instigators and sympathisers once commonplace, which sought to gain understanding through campaigns (hunger strikes etc.), providing "reinforcements" (stolen cars, weapons, false passports) and hiding places.[6] Terrorism includes disappearing from social life, on grounds alone of not being conspicuous, not "giving oneself away."

The term Lone Wolf terrorist is not under dispute, from time to time it is dismissed as a myth or fable.[7] A particular need for justification appears to exist, precisely in the European context for using the term. Apparently, there are no "Lone Wolves".[8] It is not astonishing that lone perpetrators are frequently excluded. Purely on statistical grounds, they appear to be a "*quantité négligeable*", to represent a negligent parameter. Scientific involvement with this continues to eke out a shadowy existence. This is recognised in a conclusion by the experts Mark S. Hamm and Rámon Spaaij which states: "To say that lone wolf terrorism is a neglected field of research is an understatement."[9] In other words, as Jeffrey D. Simon points out: "For a long time, lone wolves were ignored by policymakers, intelligence officials, and terrorism experts. Even today, despite the prevalence of lone wolf attacks throughout the world, the idea that the individual terrorist can be as dangerous as large-scale terrorist organizations is still a difficult concept for some people to accept."[10]

The last count of cases of lone wolf terrorist was years ago, it was carried out even before the turning point of IS terrorism and before Breivík. It came to the conclusion that not even two percent of all terrorist attacks were down to lone wolves, although even at that time the frequency of cases in the USA was conspicuous.[11] Individual terrorism occupies a marginal role, if it is mentioned at all in the public debate as well as in textbooks on the subject of terrorism and violence. A look at the research archives in the Library of Congress in Washington D.C. provides us with an explanation: Inputting "terrorism" yields 32,552 results, for "lone wolf terrorism" the number is exactly 312. This means that attention is directed to the phenomenon of the lone wolf in

---

[6]Cf. Hans Joachim Schneider: *Kriminologie der Gewalt*, Stuttgart/Leipzig 1994, p. 175.
[7]According to Peter A. Neumann: *Der Terror ist unter uns. Dschihadismus und Radikalisierung in Europa*, Berlin 2016, p. 181.
[8]According to Pauline Garaude: „Einsame Wölfe gibt es nicht", in: *Die Weltwoche* of 30 May 2015.
[9]Cf. Mark S. Hamm/Ramón Spaaij: The Age of Lone Wolf Terrorism, New York 2017, p. 13.
[10]Jeffrey D. Simon: *Lone Wolf Terrorism. Understanding The Growing Threat*, New York 2016, Preface: IX.
[11]According to a broad assessment by Ramón Spaaij: *Understanding Lone Wolf Terrorism. Global Patterns, Motivations and Prevention*, amongst other things 2012.

less than 1% of all literature, articles, sources, etc. Moreover, the term "amok" provides even fewer hits, only 292.[12]

Theodore ("Ted") John Kaczynski, an American mathematician and bomber is considered up until today to be the reference point and a kind of "prototype" for lone wolf terrorism. He is supposed to have sent 16 letter bombs to different people in the USA in the period from 1978 to 1995, killing 3 people and injuring a further 23. Before his identity was revealed, the FBI classified him using the code name "Unabomber" (*university and airline bomber*), as the bombs were predominantly sent to university professors and directors of airline companies. The terrorist lived from 1970 in the mountains in Montana in a small self-built wooden cabin. In 1995, Kaczynski sent an anonymous, 35,000 word manifesto titled *Industrial Society and its Future* to different addresses with an offer to stop the bomb attacks, if this text was printed in a renowned newspaper. His intention was to show that the Industrial Revolution and its consequences had left an absolute disadvantage behind for mankind. Although this critic of civilisation criticised left-wing political powers ("leftism") to an equal extent to the supposed dominant role of the blacks, he could not be attributed to any right-wing extremism.[13] He complained personally of rejection in social relationships. The "New York Times" and the "Washington Post" printed his manifesto on 19 September 1995, in order to obtain information about the assailant. Once the copy had been printed in the newspapers, Ted's younger brother David recognised his brother's style of writing in it and informed the authorities after making a few enquiries. Kaczynski set out in his manifesto, the reasons he wished mankind would overcome the mechanisation of society as quickly as possible. And so, the terrorist lived for two and a half decades in strict seclusion and nevertheless terrorised his surroundings. In the end, he fell victim to his vanity, for in spite of living in isolation, he wished publicity.[14] Today very likely, he would have used the Internet instead to post the manifesto online earlier in his terrorist career, despite his distaste for technology.[15] Gabriel Weimann, long-serving and renowned expert on terrorism at the University in Haifa has a strong desire to research this. Although an alarming increase is apparent in the field of lone wolf terrorism, there is still a gaping hole between the perceived threat and the almost exclusive fixation by experts on terrorists based

---

[12] Search of 31 July 2017.
[13] Cf. Nash, Jay Robert : "Terrorism in the 20th century. A narrative Encyclopedia from the Anarchists through the Westermen to the Unabomber", New York 1995, pp. 275–282.
[14] Cf. Ramón Spaaij: *Understanding Lone Wolf Terrorism. Global Patterns, Motivations and Prevention*, Heidelberg et al., 2012.
[15] According to Jeffrey D. Simon: The Alphabet Bomber. A Lone Wolf Terrorist ahead of his time, Nebraska 2019, p. 163.

in groups. This requires a change of thinking, precisely with a view to the virtual era.[16]

Many myths often grow around a lone wolf. They too strive for fame and recognition like every terrorist, although in reality they sit alone in their apartment. However much they should like to be alone, we should not forget that they are very clearly part of a larger community of like-minded people—real or virtual or part of both spheres.[17] A profile of "lone wolf" assailants published by the FBI employee Kathleen M. Puckett in 1999 came to the conclusion that lone wolves would very clearly like to be part of a larger group. They hope to obtain prestige and power, posthumously at least. Due to their inability to maintain stable social relationships, however, this has proven impossible in the long term. Instead of this, the lone wolf seeks refuge in an ideology which cannot reject him, the way another person may do in a group. He becomes a "true believer", a blind, fanatical believer. He focuses all his negative energy into his ideology of hatred.[18] And so the lone wolf may be considered as a phenomenon, embedded in a societal context and has become a child of our time.

2.2 Forms of Terror

Violent ideas are behind terrorism: proclaiming a fight for freedom, a social revolution, separatism or a racist brand symbol towards an ethnic grouping. This all concerns an action group, connected on an emotional level by a joint, if also often vague target. Solidarity with one another allows them to get involved in and submerge themselves in illegality. They may also mutually support one another in a group bonded together for better or for worse, convinced they are able to launch their attack under a common banner. Even the introverted and independent lone wolf is caught up no matter the sect by the pull of the supposed historical battle, experiencing camaraderie within

---

[16] Cf. Gabriel Weimann: "Lone Wolves in the Cyberspace", in: *Journal of Terrorism Research*, 3 (2012) 2, pp. 75–90.

[17] Cf. Jeffrey Kaplan/Heléne Lööw/Lena Malkki: "Introduction", in: Ditto. (eds.): *Lone Wolf and Autonomous Cell Terrorism*, London/New York 2015, pp. 1–12, here p. 4.

[18] According to Kathleen M. Puckett/Therry D. Turchie: The American Terrorist. The FBI's War On Homegrown Terror, New York 2007, p. 239 und 270 f. This extract explains the blind following, from the support for totalitarian systems. The standard work about this was written by the social psychologist Eric Hoffer: The True Believer, New York City 1951. This book is topical again today, for example to explain the support of the "angry white man" for Donald Trump in the years 2015/2016 during his nomination and above all the election battle.

the group and an entirely new form of recognition. Group dynamic processes unfold their effect. Legitimation and manipulation of totalitarian terror regimes feed off the importance of collectivism, as they typically represent National Socialist and Stalinist ideas. They are able to rally a convinced group of supporters behind them based on tyranny charged with propaganda, who are prepared to subjugate themselves to the movement's objectives without reservation, even at the expense of their own life. We can still find a representative of such a state and societal structure in North Korea today.

From time to time it is difficult to decide when we are dealing with terrorism. Therefore, we will try to define its characteristics, before we come to individual terrorism. Terrorism distinguishes itself through inhumane, perfidious and propaganda actions, designed to achieve political objectives. Louise Richardson, who has dealt with this phenomenon for years at Harvard University amongst other places, talks of the three R's, revenge, renown and reaction, according to which "substate actors" act, when meeting out terror. Terrorists take supposed or alleged harm as a pretext which must be revenged. They seek to achieve a shining cloud and aura of fame, paired with greatness and prestige. Their aim, of course, is to be idolised, embraced by a community. Their actions are supposed to demonstrate strengths, which is why they wish to provoke a reaction from the state for example. With this understanding, Islamic terrorists conjure up a war between the Islamic and Western Worlds. This is how they demonstrate their power, and their ability to kindle or end worldwide conflict at will.[19]

Terrorists need by no means at all have carried out lengthy political work, for example in parties or in other organisations, before carrying out their deed. Their drive nevertheless always feeds off political motivation, as is also expressed for example through letters of acknowledgement or their choice of victims. In short, terrorism means despatching innocent people to their deaths out of political motives. When doing this, executors of violence aim to obtain a media presence and the widest possible effect during the deeds and the perception of these. In the final analysis, they wish to deliver bad tidings to the public and by so doing to evoke secret sympathy, disgust or deterrence. The recipients of this message descend into panic and assume that a large number of people must be at work, in order to carry out such types of terrible act.

In point of fact, political socialisation often takes place in a group; and operational intelligence must be gleaned painstakingly. And so, with terrorism we think of organisations arranged in a hierarchy. The Red Army Faction

---

[19]Cf. Louise Richardson: *Was Terroristen wollen. Die Ursachen der Gewalt und wie wir sie bekämpfen können*, Frankfurt on Main/New York 2007, pp. 126–141.

(RAF) for example consisted of the so-called command level, independent "combat units" as well as militant associates. A certain professionalisation, therefore, appears to be required—connected to conspirators' meetings and planning the deed. Terrorist groups often submerge into the underground through confrontations with security officials, inspiring myths and legends.

Can terrorist behaviour be explained satisfactorily? Especially where the actor is no longer alive, at the end of the day we can only continue to speculate what triggered the terrifying act, and whether a cause can actually be determined at all.[20] Questions force their way to the surface regarding lone wolves, by this point at the latest: Can self-recruitment, connected with self-radicalisation actually take place? Can one individual person commit a terrorist act anyway, and can they apparently get by without a group identity? Is it possible after all, for one individual to act entirely without a remit, in the context of an action situated outside the command structure of a terrorist organisation?

2.3 A Look Back in History

Against this background, it is worth casting a look back over the history of terror. The word "terror" has its origins in the French Revolution or in the rule of terror following it (*la grande terreur*) from 1793 to 1794, symbolised by the instrument for executing the death penalty, the guillotine. It referred to a thoroughly organised and thoroughly orchestrated state violence. This image resonates up until today, that terror emanates from an elite group formed within a society, particularly as many terrorist movements felt attracted by the belief that a radical breach in society was possible.

The point of departure for many types of terrorism, in particular also for lone wolf terrorism, can already be located prior to the twentieth century: anarchism in Czarist Russia concerning the aristocrat Michail Alexandrowitsch Bakunin (1814–1876). He travelled throughout Europe inspired by thoughts of social revolution, in order to act in a supporting role wherever civil disobedience developed. He was "almost omnipresent in the crisis pressure cookers of Europe," admittedly without actually achieving anything.[21] Therefore, the concept of the *Propaganda of the deed* developed in this context, covering a mixture of violence and communication, proving itself to be

---

[20]Louise Richardson: Was Terroristen wollen. Die Ursachen der Gewalt und wie wir sie bekämpfen können, Frankfurt on Main/New York 2007, p. 81.
[21]Cf. Jürgen Osterhammel: *Die Verwandlung der Welt. Eine Geschichte des 19. Jahrhunderts*, Munich 2009, p. 799.

as influential as it was dangerous. Terror was inspired by this in Czarist Russia in particular. So-called "utopian socialists" believed, Russia could succeed in achieving socialism directly by circumventing capitalism through a peasants' revolt. They wished to achieve their goals predominantly through the propaganda of the deed. As long as the ground had not yet been prepared for the final coup d'état, a structured, hierarchical large organisation did not need to act either, but an individual or a small group could make the desperate situation of the poorest known by means of acts of violence. An escalation strategy was pursued here, which expressly included planned murders. Lenin on the other hand rejected terror by individuals. When he was 17 years of age, his older brother Alexander became a supporter of the Utopian Socialists and was sentenced because of an assassination attempt on the Czar. This event seems to have left its mark on him. Lenin envisaged more effective routes to changing the portents: Full-time revolutionaries, who prepared themselves professionally, in order to count on the growing dissatisfaction of the populace, and by so doing able to build up a real bastion of power.[22] The anarchistic violence corresponded to a world order in which the lower echelons eked out a wretched existence and suppression by the state reigned. Radicalisation then came about as a consequence of violence and its interpretation in ideological frameworks.

There was a series of bloody assassination attempts on representatives of the state around the turn of the century. Countless groups and individual people were active in Europe and the United States, committing assassination attempts on prominent personalities. Amongst others, victims included Empress Elisabeth of Austria in 1898, King Umberto I of Italy in 1900, the President of the USA William McKinley in 1901 and Spanish Prime Minister José Canelejas in 1912.[23]

Such an act of violence was also perpetrated in Germany following the First World War and the November Revolution of 1918 in Germany—times distinguished by uncertainty and chaos—The first democratic Bavarian Prime Minister Kurt Eisner was murdered on his way to the Bavarian Parliament on 21 February 1919. The unpopular Eisner actually wanted to announce his resignation that very day. Two employees accompanied him; two policemen walked ahead of him as bodyguards. The assassin, Count Arco-Valley, was lying in wait in the entrance area of the Bavarian State Parliament,

---

[22] Cf. Louise Richardson: *Was Terroristen wollen. Die Ursachen der Gewalt und wie wir sie bekämpfen können*, Frankfurt on Main/New York 2007, p. 65.
[23] Richard Bach Jensen: The Pre-1914 Anarchist "Lone Wolf" Terrorist and Governmental Responses, in: Jeffrey Kaplan/Heléne Lööw/Leena Malkki (eds.): *Lone Wolf and Autonomous Cell Terrorism*, London/New York 2015, pp. 86–94.

approached Eisner from behind and shot him twice in the neck. Eisner died on the spot. The bodyguards fired at the assassin, who was seriously injured but survived. As it turned out, he was acting out of ethnic anti-Semitic motives. He perceived Eisner to be a Bolshevik and a Jew, who had committed treason against the Fatherland.[24] Count Arco-Valley can be considered a prototype of the lone wolf. The assassin sympathised with the anti-Semitic Thule Society, but did not belong to any terrorist organisation.

Individual perpetrators of right-wing terror during the fascist era were members of clandestine societies or hierarchical terrorist groups. There was one case, Paul Gorguloff, a Russian white emigrant and president of the so-called Russian Nationalist Fascists. As we know from other cases mentioned later in this book, this is entirely typical and a part of the self-aggrandisement, which is precisely that which distinguishes the single actor. Gorguloff, a former soldier in the Czarist army, was dissatisfied with the Bolshevik revolution and the fact that Western countries were not able to defeat Bolshevism. He also had some psychological problems. Gorguloff lived in Czechoslovakia in the 1920s. In 1930, he prepared for the unsuccessful assassination attempt on the Czechoslovakian president, Tomas Garrigue Masaryk. In 1932, Gorguloff assassinated the French president, Paul Doumer, for which he was sentenced to death.[25] From a modern perspective, there was a broad spectrum of lone wolves who executed acts of terror with the passage of time: Anarchistic revolutionaries, religious fanatics such as Islamic Fundamentalists, radical environmental and animal welfare activists, homophobes, racist supporters of "white supremacy"[26] and right-wing terrorists in general.

Left-wing extremist (anarchistic) lone actors are hardly discussed any longer, as only a few examples can be unearthed in the twenty-first century. Two cases in the USA are worthy of a mention. Both assassins hated Donald Trump and supported the left-wing candidate Bernie Sanders. James T. Hodgkinson, a 66 year-old, carried out an attack on a group of Republican delegates at a baseball game in 2017. Four people suffered bullet wounds, and the assailant was killed. Hodgkinson posted on Facebook shortly before his deeds: "Trump is a Traitor. Trump Has Destroyed Our Democracy. It's

---

[24] Cf. Sven Felix Kellerhoff: „Rechtsterrorismus – Es begann im Jahr 1919", in: *Die Welt*, 14 November 2011, https://www.welt.de/kultur/history/article13716280/Rechtsterrorismus-Es-begann-im-Jahr-1919.html.

[25] Miroslav Mareš/Richard Stojar: Extreme right perpetrators, in: Michael Fredholm (ed.): Understanding Lone Actor Terrorism. Past experience, future outlook, and response strategies, London/New York, 2016, pp. 66–86, here p. 66.

[26] This term means "white supremacy" and means a racist ideology, which has its origin in slavery during colonial times. The large landowners were not only concerned with the difference between "black" and "white", but also with the manifestation of a power relationship which from time to time was executed brutally.

Time to Destroy Trump & Co."²⁷ The 24-year-old named Connor Betts who shot nine people in Dayton, Ohio (including his own sister) in August 2019, shared extreme left-wing tweets, which for example called for destroying American Immigration officials' vehicles. Apart from this, Betts declared on Twitter that he was a Satanist and used Hashtag #HailSatan in numerous tweets.²⁸

2.4 Assassination Attempts on Representatives of Democratic States

We discuss right-wing terrorism by single actors as a phenomenon active within Western democracies. This is also true for other regions of the world. The Israeli Prime Minister Yitzhak Rabin was murdered by a lone wolf on 4 November 1995. *The assassin Yigal Amir, a law student, considered the existence of the State of Israel was at risk, especially due to the Oslo Peace Process and secret agreements between the Palestinian Liberation Organisation (PLO) and Israel.*²⁹

Time and again we return to revolutionary situations for radical change, with assassination attempts on politicians, as the murder of the Bavarian Prime Minister Kurt Eisner after the First World War shows. Right-wing terrorism was experiencing a boom time in the Weimar Republic, which was still in its formative years, with soldiers and young mercenaries from the Free Corps as protagonists. In principal, however, such types of attacks can also be carried out in authoritarian or even totalitarian states.³⁰ Several assassination attempts were made unsuccessfully against Adolf Hitler, amongst other things by the single actor Georg Elser, in the Münchener Bürgerbräukeller

---

[27] CNN Suspect in congressional shooting was Bernie Sanders supporter, strongly anti-Trump, 15 June 2017. https://edition.cnn.com/2017/06/14/homepage2/james-hodgkinson-profile/index.html?fbclid=IwAR2zbAsLXwu0szWRLsCGFxCo1RHdAsAwh1OdrRDk6dIa9O2LdUeFsZXbWHU; Washington Post, Emerging portrait of shooting suspect James T. Hodgkinson, 14th June 2017, https://www.washingtonpost.com/local/public-safety/law-enforcement-officials-identify-shooter-at-congressional-ballgame-as-illinois-man/2017/06/14/ba6439f4-510f-11e7-91eb-9611861a988f_story.html.

[28] CNN news: Dayton shooter had an obsession with violence and mass shootings, police say, 7 August 2019, https://edition.cnn.com/2019/08/05/us/connor-betts-dayton-shooting-profile/index.html.

[29] Jeffrey D. Simon: *Lone Wolf Terrorism. Understanding The Growing Threat*, New York 2016, pp. 171–176.

[30] The murder of the tyrant in ancient Rome is a historical figure, such as the murder of Julius Caesar by Marcus Brutus in 44. B.C. Hardly anyone cannot know of this Act, with the last words of the dictator stabbed 23 times "You too, my son?" cf. Meier, Mischa : (K)ein Tyrannenmord: Der Tod des Iulius Caesar 44 v. Chr., in: Georg Schild/Anton Schindling (eds.): Politische Morde in der Geschichte. Von der Antike bis zur Gegenwart, Paderborn amongst others 2012, pp. 11–36.

beer hall in Munich on 8 November 1939, with his bombs exploding just a few minutes too late. Prominent members of the NS Party were the target, seated around a speakers' rostrum. Elser, who was a trained carpenter and had been a member of the Red Front Fighting Alliance (*RFB*) from 1928 to 1929, the fighting arm of the Communist Party of Germany (*KPD*), was a staunch opponent of National Socialists. In this way, Elser was a classic lone wolf with political motives—he turned himself against the NS State as well as against war.[31]

Politicians in democratic countries are perfect targets for mentally deranged assailants; however, these are not always politically motivated. Mentally ill people react to polarising political debates from time to time with violent outbursts. Assailants may be suffering from delusions or may feel hatred out of base motives.[32] Lee Harvey Oswald, who assassinated President John F. Kennedy on 22 November 1963 was likewise murdered shortly after his attack, so there has been room for numerous speculations lasting up until today, and plots and large-scale conspiracy theories remain. Oswald denied committing the deed; he cannot be classified as a terrorist because of his lack of a propaganda background. Even the murder of JFK's brother Robert F. Kennedy in San Francisco in 1968 remains puzzling, although in this case, the assassin survived. Sirhan Bishara Sirhan entangled himself in several contradictions in his "justification" of the assassination. According to witness statements he stated immediately after the attack: "I did it for my country!" Supposedly, the victim's alleged pro-Israeli politics were a thorn in his side. Clearly, an envy which had grown into hatred played a role here above all. The assassin is now behind bars in prison. A lone wolf murdered the younger brother Robert Kennedy in the night from 4 to 5 June 1968. Robert was standing in the presidential election campaign and had good prospects. The assassin, Sirhan Bishara Sirhan, was Palestinian by birth and a refugee. Immediately after his arrest following the shooting, Sirhan told his captors that he had made the decision to kill Kennedy only three weeks earlier. He had heard a speech delivered by the candidate during a visit to a synagogue on the radio, in which Kennedy promised to arm Israel with dozens of warplanes, calling it the lesson he'd learned from the Six Day War one year earlier.[33]

---

[31] Cf. Peter Steinbach/Johannes Tuchel: *Georg Elser. Der Hitler-Attentäter*, Berlin 2010.

[32] Cf. Sven Felix Kellerhoff: Warum irre Attentäter so oft Politiker attackieren, in: Die Welt of 17 June 2016, https://www.welt.de/geschichte/article156310936/Warum-irre-Attentaeter-so-oft-Politiker-attackieren.html called up on 23 April 2018).

[33] Nettanel Slyomovics: Why Sirhan Sirhan, a Jerusalem-born Palestinian, Shot Bobby Kennedy, in Haretz.com, 24 May 2018, https://www.haaretz.com/us-news/.premium.MAGAZINE-palestinian-terrorist-or-american-psycho-what-motivated-rfk-s-killer-1.6116114.

The direction of impact of such terrorism lies in the direction of democratic values, which it fights against and ethnic minorities, which it hates. The emerging populist right-wing politician Pim Fortuyn from the Netherlands was murdered during the election campaign for the parliamentary election in 2002. Volkert van der Graaf, the assassin, was considered to be a militant environmental campaigner and animal activist and had a direct political motive, which is why he can be considered to be a lone wolf. He said, he had spent a lot of time preparing for his deed on his own and that he wished to protect Muslims—Fortuyn had been selected as a target, as he was known for his anti-Islamic sentiments.

The idea of a "Propaganda of the deed" as a type of recipe for the inspired single actor is, therefore, not a product of the virtual era, but is "as old as terrorism" itself.[34] It marks a departure from the belief that an uprising, rebellion or even a revolution distinguishes itself through the power of the masses. The fire of violent terror, according to this underlying thought, can also be unleashed by individuals.[35] This was displayed in Germany, when the President of Kassel Parliament, Walter Lübcke was murdered by being shot in the head at close range on the patio of his own home in the night from 1 to 2 June 2019. It transpired that his assassin had a far-right extremist background, and later also that he was functioning as a single actor. And therefore, this was the first assassination enacted against a German politician by far-right extremists since 1945. The assassin Stephan Ernst had a far-right extremist past. At the age of 19, he had almost killed a foreigner in a toilet at a railway station in Wiesbaden. In 1993, he failed in his attempt to launch an attack on occupants of a home for asylum seekers. He built a pipe bomb with his own hands. The assailant moved in the sphere of members of militant groups such as Combat 18. "Combat 18" is based on a similar network to the so-called "National Socialist Underground" and propagates terror emanating from separate cells with no central structure. Ernst was also a member of the right-wing extremist NPD Hessen (National Democratic Party Germany).

For over 10 years he lived inconspicuously with his family, a wife and two children, in a terraced house and disappeared from security officials' radar. He appeared to have been re-socialised. He worked as a shift worker although his employer apparently knew nothing of his past. He also joined a gun club in 2010. He did not possess a gun permit. The discussion of refugees in 2015/2016 appeared to have radicalised him again. Stephan E.

---

[34] According to Peter A. Neumann: *Der Terror ist unter uns. Dschihadismus und Radikalisierung in Europa*, Berlin 2016, p. 183.
[35] Cf. Louise Richardson: *Was Terroristen wollen. Die Ursachen der Gewalt und wie wir sie bekämpfen können*, Frankfurt on Main/New York 2007, p. 61.

spent his time in relevant extreme right-wing forums. The trigger was probably a statement from the 65-year-old CDU politician Walter Lübcke, who had once belonged to the Hessian State Parliament, at a town hall meeting in a neighbouring town to Kassel on 14 October 2015, which Stephan Ernst attended in person. Lübcke's office needed to create space for up to 14,000 refugees during these hectic times. As Parliamentary President, Lübcke travelled around the government district of Kassel in person to different towns, explaining the situation. He supported Federal Chancellor Angela Merkel's Welcome Culture Policy. At this said town hall meeting things clearly got very heated. There were shouts from the audience such as "Go home" and "Useless Politicians". Lübcke found himself forced into making a statement: "And whoever does not support these values can leave this country at any time, if they do not agree with this." This was the freedom of every German. The video later circulated on social media and was distributed in relevant circles. Stephan E. stated that he had already been thinking about an assassination attempt against Lübcke for some time and had preoccupied himself with this. It had not been a spontaneous decision. The town hall meeting had played a significant role for him. And he left traces on the Internet: He is supposed to have written inflammatory comments under his username of "Game Over" for example on the video platform YouTube. "Either this government resigns shortly, or people will die", Stephan E. posted on the net. Why no-body noticed this post by a violent right-wing assailant with a number of previous convictions and followed the matter up, remains worthy of discussion. And so clearly the victim, Walter Lübcke was made to pay for a single sentence with his life. The perpetrator was a classic lone wolf. Yet the man only acted alone at first glance—internally he was carried along by the convictions he shared with other lone wolves.[36] Uncomfortable debates are on the cards, as Walter Lübcke was already included on an NSU address list (along with his home address), which nevertheless listed 10,000 people. The German Director of Public Prosecutions took up the investigation.[37]

Stephan Ernst appeared in the files of the NSU lawsuit, as he was active in the thoroughly vibrant right-wing extremist scene in Kassel. And Halit Yozgat, a German with Turkish origins was murdered there in his Internet café in Kassel in 2006—like Walter Lübcke, shot in the head. He was supposedly the ninth and, therefore, the last victim of the series of NSU murders. Andreas

---

[36] Cf. Matthias Bartsch amongst others: Die Hinrichtung, in: Der Spiegel, No. 26 of 22 June 2019, pp. 14–23.
[37] Deutsche Welle, Walter Lübcke murder raises spectre of neo-Nazi terrorism, 17 June 2019, https://www.dw.com/en/walter-l%C3%BCbcke-murder-raises-specter-of-neo-nazi-terrorism/a-49238157.

Temme, an agent working for the German domestic intelligence service (Verfassungsschutz) was in this Internet café at the time. Temme maintains he did not see the murder take place. Lübcke's supposed assassin Stephan Ernst had a relationship—at least indirectly—with Temme. He knew the Neo-National Socialist informant for the German domestic intelligence services Benjamin Gärtner, whom Temme had telephoned shortly before Halit Yozgat was murdered. Benjamin Gärtner had confirmed that he knew Stephan Ernst in February 2016, as a witness before the NSU investigation committee of the Hessian State Parliament. He was mentioned as an example of a violent neo-Nazi in Kassel by representatives of the left-wing faction in a request for evidence. All in all, we are certain: The German domestic intelligence services must concern themselves with similar questions, which cropped up during the course of the debate on the NSU and were the subject of numerous parliamentary investigations.

2.5 Theory and Origins of Lone Wolf Terrorism

The term lone wolf dates back to Tom Metzger, a one-time member of the Ku Klux Klan. He published "*Laws for the Lone Wolf*" on his website in the middle of the 1990s. This states: "I am prepared for the war ahead. I will be ready, when the red line is crossed [...] I am the underground combatant, and independent. I am in your neighbourhood, in schools, in police departments, bars, coffee shops, shopping centres etc., and I am 'The Lone Wolf'."[38]

The American William L. Pierce (1933–2002) can be considered to be a mentor for the movement called into life by Metzger. He wrote the best-known texts on the recent history of National Socialism under the pseudonym Andrew Macdonald. Highly talented, with a Ph.D. and once an Assistant Professor of Physics, he ended his university career in order to dedicate himself to right-wing extremist activities. His *The Turner Diaries* published in 1978 are considered to be the "far-right extremist bible", an important propaganda work, which cultivates feelings of white supremacy in a militant manner.[39] Timothy James McVeigh, the assailant in Oklahoma in 1995, is one of those who read the book. It can be obtained free of charge on the Internet and inspired numerous right-wing terrorists in Europe too, lone

---

[38] Quoted according to Jason Burke: "The myth of the "lone wolf"-terrorist", in: *The Guardian* of 30 March 2017, https://www.theguardian.com/news/2017/mar/30/myth-lone-wolf-terrorist.

[39] Cf. J. M. Berger: The Turner Legacy, International Centre for Counter-Terrorism—The Hague, 2016, p. 1, https://icct.nl/wp-content/uploads/2016/09/ICCT-Berger-The-Turner-Legacy-September2016-2.pdf).

wolves such as Breivik among them. The novel deals with Earl Turner, who organised the fight against the system and foreign infiltration in a "cell". An "Aryan" world would follow on from a nuclear civil war. The novel's plot in this way is only a smoke screen for the instructions to unfold a "Race war".

The second novel, likewise fictional, *Hunter* ("*Jaeger*" in German) appeared in 1989. It is about the 40-year-old right-wing terrorist with the meaningful name Oscar Yaeger, a Vietnam veteran, Engineer and Advisor to the Ministry of Defence. First of all, he was a so-called part-time terrorist, but Yaeger radicalised himself more and more as the book goes on. Later he built up a "cell", in order to carry out illegal activities. However, the protagonist himself remained outside of any organisation. As a single actor, as a lone wolf, he shoots people from his car, murdering politicians and well-known personalities. Well over 100 people fall victim to him. Yaeger also enjoys his triumph to the full together with his girlfriend after the attacks, and so is not entirely isolated (the detail that Yaeger has a girlfriend will still turn out to be relevant, as lone wolves in general do not have a partner). He considers "the white race" to be superior and defends himself against decadence which he attaches to dumbing down, drug taking and homosexuality. And he recruits copy-cats, to whom he, however, attributes dilettantism and amateurism.

William L. Pierce maintained many contacts to right-wing extremist factions in Europe. He wrote a greeting for example for the NPD (National Democratic Party of Germany). In the commemorative publication appearing for the Party's 35th anniversary in 1999, Pierce proclaimed war on "capitalists": "Nationalists in Germany, in Europe and also in America stand shoulder-to-shoulder against a common enemy of all nations, international big business, which is trying to sound the death knell for all historically evolved nations in favour of a multicultural 'melting pot'. Our fight against efforts at world domination and economic imperialism of multinational conglomerates will be hard and full of sacrifices."[40] Moreover Pierce had a close acquaintanceship with another "mentor" of the right, Louis Beam. Beam was born in Texas in 1946, and as a Ku Klux Klan activist coined the phrase *Leaderless Resistance* („Führerloser Widerstand") in an essay at the start of the 1980s. Leaderless Resistance omits any central command structure, on the other hand placing its faith in small mobile groups with a high degree of autonomy in planning and flexibility. The system propagated is based on cells, which in spite of the necessity for a common objective, operate independently of one another. This also applies to the targets of their assassination attempts, which are carried out at different locations.

---

[40]William Pierce: „Grußwort", in: Holger Apfel (ed.): *Alles Große steht im Sturm. Tradition und Zukunft einer nationalen Partei*, Stuttgart 1999, no page.

Leaderless Resistance was also a response to the problem of not being able to set-up a powerful organisation by themselves. Beam reacted to his own inability to build up structures and remain unknown to the American federal police, the FBI. He saw a strategic solution for carrying out racially motivated attacks in one-man phantom cells. Beam wrote in his text composed in 1983 and published in 1992: "The question is naturally asked of how 'Phantom cells' or individuals can cooperate with one another, if there is no communication between them or with a central directive [...] It is the individual's responsibility to adopt the necessary skills and to acquire the information needed [...] There is no mistaking here, that Leaderless Resistance must lead to small, even one-man cells of resistance."[41] And in this way, there is a preamble for lone wolf tactics.

The classification *Lone Wolf terrorism,* which Metzger used for the first time, was quickly adopted by US officials and was popularised. The FBI founded a so-called "Operation Lone Wolf" in 1998, directed against small groups of white racists on the West Coast of America. Before this, US security officials used expressions such as *Freelancers, homegrown, cleanskin* or simply *unaffiliated.*[42] The notion of this type of terrorism quickly spilled over to Europe, which is also based on the organisational weakness of this scenario.[43] The "lone wolf tactics" were distributed in relevant circles, for example in the British Combat 18 (C-18).[44] This neo-National Socialist faction was founded by British militant right-wing extremists in 1992. Their parent organisation Blood & Honour obtained a degree of recognition above all through extreme right-wing concerts and recordings, but also invoked attacks on migrants and political opponents. Neo-National Socialists ready for violence are connected to each other across Europe in C-18.

We find the lines in Combat 18s *National Socialist Political Soldiers Handbook*: "The most efficient route is to operate alone and not speak with anyone about your plans—the 'lone wolf' tactics. These tactics are the safest variant up until now, as you are not dependent on anyone for successfully implementing your plan. If your undertaking should fail for any reason at all, then the fault is yours alone. If it passes off successfully, your courage speaks for you." Clearly, NSU small cell terrorists were also inspired by this

---

[41] Louis Beam: "Leaderless Resistance", in: *The seditionist,* 6/1992, http://www.louisbeam.com/leaderless.htm (author's own translation).
[42] Ibid.
[43] Cf. Sebastian Gräfe: „Leaderless Resistance and Lone Wolves. Rechtsextreme Theoretiker aus den USA und deren Einfluss in Europa", in: Eckhard Jesse/Roland Sturm (eds.): *Demokratie in Deutschland und Europa,* Berlin 2015, pp. 307–321.
[44] The number 18 stands for the initials of Adolf Hitler according to the Latin alphabet.

approach. Moreover, Combat 18 delivered numerous presentations in publications, from instructions for making bombs right through to ideas of who to direct assassination attempts against.

The German homeland intelligence services already made reference to the fact that C-18 enjoyed high recognition in Germany amongst right-wing extremists prepared for violence in 2004, even although—allegedly—at this time no terrorist activities emanated from them.[45] Ironically—or far sooner tragically the German domestic intelligence services referred in the same publication to discovering pipe bombs in Jena in 1997, which were found in the "residential premises" of Uwe Böhnhardt, Uwe Mundlos and Beate Zschäpe—therefore, long before the trio embarked on their series of murders. At the time of the study by officials in 2004, five people had already been murdered. However, "no further indications of additional militant actions by refugees" were revealed, according to the inappropriate final conclusion at that time.[46]

The German domestic intelligence services also explicitly considered lone wolf terrorism in this report. Regarding a foiled attack with firearms on a military training area in Stetten/Baden-Württemberg, it stated: "The former professional soldier who had left following differences displayed his sympathy for Adolf Hitler and for National Socialism." The German domestic intelligence services issued the following warning: "We must reckon with this 'lone wolf' type of assailant at any time in the field of right-wing extremism/terrorism. Such assailants can scarcely be detected in the run-up by security officials, as they (…) did not appear either to be members of extremist right-wing organisations or to be individual extremist right-wing agitators up until their attack."[47] In the end, however, the German domestic intelligence services associated "part-time terrorism" with this,[48] that is a form of terrorism, in which the assailant hides behind the facade of being a law-abiding citizen.

2.6 Profile and Nature of the Lone Wolf

A preliminary profile of a lone wolf can be drawn up with the help of historical allocation: Unlike with other terrorist violence, he is not concerned with following collective goals, but with fulfilling personal fantasies of violence and revenge.

---

[45] Cf. German domestic intelligence services (Verfassungsschutz): Gefahr eines bewaffneten Kampfes deutscher Rechtsextremisten. Entwicklungen von 1997 bis Mitte 2004, Cologne 2004, p. 29 f.
[46] Ibid. p. 15 f.
[47] Ibid. p. 24 f.
[48] Ibid. p. 46.

2 What Is a "Lone Wolf"? 45

The lone wolf acts alone when carrying out his attack, at least without associate actors. Apparently, he is not in a position or does not have the inclination to build up an organisation of people with similar outlooks or to recruit accomplices for his murderous plans. Lone wolf terrorism according to the general definition[49] means intended acts, which can be committed by people, who

1. operate as individuals
2. profess they act on grounds of political convictions
3. do not belong to an organised terror group or terrorist network
4. act without the direct influence of a leader or any kind of command structure or obedience hierarchy
5. provide propaganda and communicative distribution of extremist ideology themselves.

Therefore, according to Raffaello Pantucci's definition lone wolves are "individuals who, while appearing to carry out their actions alone and without any physical outside instigation, in fact demonstrate some contact with operational extremists."[50] The latter refers to the Internet. The relationship with far-right cultures may be on different levels. Some might make further distinction between "'loners', who have vicarious relationships with wider far-right cultures; 'lone actors' who have long-lasting, two-way relationship with far-right cultures; and 'small groups', clusters of activists who develop into self-directed, autonomous cells".[51] The differentiation, however, is scarcely convincing, as small cells precisely (such as for example the NSU) are excluded from the general definition of a lone wolf.

A widely circulated misunderstanding in the discussion of lone wolves must be prevented right away: The criteria mentioned merely refer to our consideration of the deed. For the assassination attempt is executed by an individual person, without other people being included or involved. So-called packs such as the NSU, that is small groups consisting of two or three people, are excluded by this definition. Naturally lone wolves *do not* operate in a vacuum: During the preparation phase they are *directly* supported by people who involuntarily help implement the deed (such as arms dealers, for example)

---

[49] Cf. Ramón Spaaij: "The Enigma of Lone Wolf Terrorism. An Assessment", in: *Studies in Conflict & Terrorism*, 33 (2010), pp. 854–870.
[50] Raffaello Pantucci: A Typology of Lone Wolves: Preliminary Analysis of Lone Islamist Terrorists, International Centre for the Study of Radicalization and Political Violence, London 2011, pp 19 f.
[51] Paul Jackson: Beyond the "Lone Wolf": Lone Actor Terrorism and the Far-Right in Europe, in: Aristotle Kallis/Sara Zeiger/Bilgehan Öztürk: Violent Radicalisation and the Far-Right Extremism in Europe, Ankara 2018, pp. 38–53, here p. 39.

and *indirectly* by people, who provide "inspiration" (such as a mentor on the Internet, previous terrorists or even frenzied spree killers, or likewise ideologies such as National Socialism or Islamic Fundamentalism, with its promise of salvation for actors committing suicide and corresponding instructions).

From time to time it is not always clear whether an actor is really acting alone. The American Timothy James McVeigh for example does not fall under the definition of a lone wolf terrorist, although he is repeatedly apostrophised as such.[52] McVeigh had a co-actor, who helped him decisively with his preparations and knew all about them. Gundolf Köhler, the bomber in Munich who killed 12 people along with himself on 26 September 1980 during the Oktoberfest beer festival by exploding a bomb and injured more than 200 others, some of them seriously, had emerged from the far-right extremist student environment. For a while he had maintained contact with the "Hoffmann Paramilitary Group" (*Wehrsportgruppe Hoffmann*) which was prohibited in January 1980—a collaboration of hundreds of militant right-wing extremists, who dressed in uniforms with symbols similar to the SS and had declared war on the Left as well as on Democracy—and took part in military exercises, which is why his acting as a single actor remains questionable up until today. The paramilitary group distinguished themselves precisely by integrating young people into organisational discipline. Its impact was underestimated in an era in which all eyes were turned towards the threat from the Left. A parallel to the situation today can be drawn from this, in which Islamic terrorism is described as being the central source of the fire—and terror from the Right is neglected.

The term *Lone Wolf* allows inevitable associations with the animal world. Every lifeform which forms a society actually tends towards group life, but also pays a price for this in each case. Associations are formed in many groups in the animal kingdom, in which intelligent behaviour definitely plays a role: with bees, parrots, dolphins, gorillas and chimpanzees likewise as with wolves.[53] Wolves although predators and not cuddly toys, are also animals which live socially, living in union in a wolfpack and with their own hunting ground and able to fend for themselves.

Wolves usually stand for "masculine characteristics", especially for a lust for assaults and recklessness. There are fixed hierarchies within the pack. Only the highest-ranking males and females mate with one another. In times of crisis, high-ranking adults and pups have the first claim to food. Hunting in a pack, however, usually leads to the ability to kill larger prey. For example, a

---

[52] For example, from Jeffrey D. Simon: *Lone Wolf Terrorism. Understanding The Growing Threat*, New York 2016.
[53] Cf. Steven Pinker: *Wie das Denken im Kopf entsteht*, Frankfurt/Main 2011, p. 243.

group can capture an elk by acting together, whilst a lone wolf could scarcely manage this. But lone wolves are dangerous too: A single wolf acting alone can massacre sheep. Nevertheless, the lone wolf is generally a rather pitiful figure—he dances out of line and has been expelled from the pack. He is a synonym for a stray, an outsider, an eccentric loner, a loner, an individual, underdog or a lone combatant. He is in crass contrast to a team player or the leader of the pack. The analogy to the animal world is, therefore, really suitable for this type of actor.

2.7 Political Motives and Personal Ideology of Grievances

We assume there are strong identification moments with terrorism, for example of solidarity effects for comrades in arms who have died. And so, for example after the suicide of the first generation of the RAF in prison in Stammheim, the second generation came into being. The reference, in this case, is considered as a real group. For single actors, the group may merely be an abstract and fictious parameter. He likewise has no direct "battle comrades" or close reference person, however, like the group terrorist he has an ideology, which he himself "carves into shape" according to his personal needs, in particular his own frustrations: the *personal ideology of grievances*. The lone wolf communicates with his surroundings in this way, at least perceiving influences and impressions. The following three levels play a role here:

(1) *ideologically conditioned sympathies* through societal attitudes and trends
(2) "*media contacts*" through chats, research and publications from right-wing extremist websites and conspiracy theories on the Internet
(3) *personal connections,* contacts to appropriate organisations and "people with similar outlooks"

We must examine the radicalisation process in more detail in order to understand individual terrorism. Peter A. Neumann, who is considered an expert above all with regard to Islamic terrorism, is of the following opinion: "Radicalisation usually takes place in a social environment, via cliques, mates and pals, charismatic leaders. Only a very small number of terrorists are so-called lone wolves."[54] And so Neumann assumes that people are conditioned to become terrorists through social pressure and convictions. In this way he

---

[54]Peter A. Neumann: „Kaum ein Terrorist ist ein einsamer Wolf", in: n-tv.de of 14 October 2016, http://www.n-tv.de/politik/Kaum-ein-Terrorist-ist-ein-einsamer-Wolf-article18854546.html.

disregards the condition, that mental instability is a decisive driving force for terrorism—including the opportunity or even the desire, to sacrifice his own life for this.

There is typically a triggering event for every form of terrorism at a personal level. Such a type of key moment is classified as a *Trigger*—an English expression, which is also used for a camera's shutter release or for firing a gun for example. In political science, a trigger in the context of terrorism is defined as follows: "'Triggers', which lead to political terrorist organisations coming into being or elicit larger terrorist organisations, are events like the well-known drops which lead to a barrel overflowing." This can easily be understood in the case of the RAF for example. Events such as the shooting of demonstrator Benno Ohnesorg by a policeman in 1967 or the attempted murder of the 1968 icon and guiding light Rudi Dutschke led to boundaries around violence dissolving, and to a high motivation to act as well and make a contribution as a terrorist.[55] However, what is the disturbing event, what is the trigger for a single actor, who has no exact reference to an organisation, who gets by effectively without institutional support? Can such a person manage at all, can any "One Person Cells" exist at all?

It is an additional help here to understand the levels of motivation and radicalisation. The expert on threat management, Jens Hoffmann describes this very clearly: Lone wolves fall into the category of the "Violent True Believer"—likewise, they should "not be mistaken for political activists, who express their grievance in the context of an existing legislative order, or for extremists, who whilst they break the law, do not, however, use severe or potentially deadly force. In contrast for example to the serious targeted and directed acts of violence in workplaces or schools in a terrorist context, *Violent True Believers* do not usually act outside their subjectively experienced sphere of insults. Likewise, a revenge motive does not usually play a primary role in the origin of the act. Far sooner people or institutions are attacked, in order to achieve a higher level of goal, wherein an ideology or religion provides justification for the deed."[56]

Precisely for this reason, it would not be expedient, to exclude the political motive when considering a deed, to allocate revenge or insult as a trigger for the deed or to cite the actor's mental confusion. The trigger lies in political

---

[55] Cf. Wolfgang Kraushaar: „Einleitung. Zur Topologie des RAF-Terrorismus", in: Wolfgang Kraushaar (ed.): *Die RAF und der linke Terrorismus*, Hamburg 2006, p. 26f.

[56] Jens Hoffmann: „Bedrohungsmanagement und psychologische Aspekte der Radikalisierung", in: Nils Böckler/Jens Hoffmann (eds.): *Radikalisierung und terroristische Gewalt*, Frankfurt on Main 2017, p. 279.

motives. We go into individual radicalisation processes in more detail In the third chapter.

2.8 Killing Sprees, Running Amok and Terror—The Difference Is Important

The etymological origin of the term amok lies in the Malay word "amuk", which means "angry" or "berserk". Running amok has its origin with the people of the Malay archipelago. Two forms of running amok were distinguished from the first reports in the 14th and 15th centuries: war-like running amok (*spree killing*) in groups and individual running amok by one single person. The form mentioned first was a battle tactic of Malay fighters, who charged their opponents without regard for their own survival with killing in mind whilst shouting the war cry "Amok".[57] Accordingly, the term amok distinguishes "a spontaneous and unforeseen mad frenzy."[58] The World Health Organisation (WHO) today understands by the phrase linked to this of running amok "an arbitrary, apparently unprovoked episode of murderous or serious destructive behaviour (towards others)."[59]

Not only the vernacular often mixes up terrorist attacks and people running amok. On the surface, they may have certain commonalities: Terrorists as well as people running amok, for whatsoever reasons at all, carry out cruel and terrible deeds which effectively drum up publicity. Nevertheless, we do not speak here of a mind game, without any direct reference to purpose or practice. What distinguishes terrorists from people running amok is the direction they target: Whilst terrorists wish to gain publicity with their deeds, in order to placate political demands in the end (and to change society according to their preconceptions), objectives of people running amok can sooner be found on a personal level. Terrorists and people running amok even differ in their choice of victims. Whilst terrorists attack civilians who are not involved according to the direction they are targeting, in order to spread terror, most people running amok sooner restrict themselves to a circle close to them in a certain way, which should usually be impressed by the acts or deeds.

---

[57]Cf. Judith Thier: "Amok", in: *Kriminologielexikon online*, http://www.krimlex.de/artikel.php?BUCHSTABE=&KL_ID=221.
[58]According to Britta Bannenberg: "Amok", in: Christian Gudehus/Michaela Christ (eds.): *Gewalt. Ein interdisziplinäres Handbuch*, Stuttgart/Weimar 2013, p. 99.
[59]Cited after Markus C. Schulte von Drach: „Rache der gestörten Persönlichkeit", in: *Süddeutsche Zeitung*, 22 May 2010, http://www.sueddeutsche.de/leben/die-psyche-der-amoklaeufer-rache-der-gestoerten-persoenlichkeit-1.863414.

Most people running amok (*spree or frenzied killers*)—as opposed to terrorists—cannot be attributed any rationality in the spirit of a suitable choice of means for achieving this (or other) goals. Placing terrorism and running amok on a par is, therefore, inappropriate at any rate.[60] And so for example, the social scientist and social psychologist Richard Albrecht sees purely an emotional impulse in running amok: "Running amok [...] means, that a person in a furious disinhibition, so to speak in a blind rage, attacks everyone whom he coincidentally comes into contact with, without them apparently opposing him as though intoxicated and/or kills them, until the actor himself gives up, collapses, kills himself or is killed by other parties."[61] Political motivation does not play any role here.

It is often simply difficult for the observer to distinguish whether a political message should be deduced or not. A lot depends on this, which is why an allocation should not be made without thinking. An apt assessment by the Swiss journalist Eric Gujer, an expert on foreign intelligence, put his finger on the problem with his statement: "The dividing line between clearly motivated political violence and pathological running amok cannot always be drawn clearly [...] The evaluation of whether one considers murders to be terrorism or sheer madness is not only academic in nature. How the courts and society deal with these deeds depends on this evaluation, and how they can cope with the shock."[62] Arbnor Segashi also emphasises how important a definition is for the victims, who had lost his little sister Armela through David Sonboly's terrifying deeds: "Generally, one spoke in public of someone running amok, and therefore we also perceive this to be the case. But now after inspecting the files, it is perhaps important to investigate the totality and to enquire whether this was someone running amok at all."[63]

Amok or an assassination attempt—this makes a big difference in the political evaluation. Someone who runs amok is considered to be mentally ill—the causes can, therefore, also be determined in the personal sphere. A debate on possible missed opportunities and immediate measures in the form of responses by the State, and also by society can scarcely be avoided in the case of terrorism. From time to time the classification gets mixed up.

---

[60] Cf. Torsten Preuß: *Terrorismus und Innere Sicherheit. Eine Untersuchung der politischen Reaktionen in Deutschland auf die Anschläge des 11. September 2001*, Dissertation, Universität Leipzig, 2012, p. 42, http://www.qucosa.de/fileadmin/data/qucosa/documents/8861/20120602_Torsten_Preu%C3%9F_Terrorismus_und_Innere_Sicherheit.pdf.

[61] Richard Albrecht: „Nur ein „Amokläufer"? – Sozialpsychologische Zeitdiagnose nach „Erfurt"", in: *Recht und Politik*, 28 (2002) 3, p. 143.

[62] Eric Gujer: „Terrorismus und Wahn", in: *Neue Zürcher Zeitung*, 28/29 April 2012, p. 1.

[63] Cited after ARD *Fakt*: „München-Attentat: Warum viele Hintergründe im Dunkeln bleiben", Report: Christian Bergmann/Marcus Weller, broadcast on 22 August 2017, 21.45 h.

Typically, in an ideal case terrorism and running amok can be distinguished as follows:

Terrorism	Amok
Sending a political message is to the fore (publicity)	Personal level in connection with a general hatred of people is decisive (publicity)
Inspiration through an ideology ("broadcasting commission")	Ideology is insignificant ("Insult or offence commission")
Rationality in choice of victims (for example ethnic minorities, people in public life)	Arbitrary (from time to time close surroundings as well as the former school)
Intended outcome: Heroic death/suicide/living underground	Suicidal intentions ("murder-suicide")
Considered approach when carrying the deed out	"blind rage", pathological
Letters of acknowledgement (where present) also with political statements	Farewell letter with a reference to one's own insults and a personal hatred of the world and people in general
Long-tern objectives: copy-cat deeds, a desire for political change, destabilisation of the political system is intended	Sooner "a terrifying moment" in the foreground, one's own singular-final settlement with the world

School assassins wish one last "super show" as a superlative for revenge, in order to practically create a reality or fantasy TV show. When doing so they actually proceed in a disinhibited manner, not in a cool and calculated one. Right-wing terrorists on the other hand regard themselves as saviours or as liberators of the "Fatherland", wishing to set an example under the banner of racism and against political conditions which they detest. Precisely determined ethnic factions are a thorn in their side, a multicultural society is an abomination to them. They plan their deeds meticulously, from the ideological justification right through to their choice of victims. Whoever presents deeds as pathologized and the actors as mentally ill, runs the risk of belittling the responsibility of actors for their actions. Social characterizations recede into the background, likewise the questions of which factors actually made the actors "ill." One example from recent times is the attack in El Paso in Texas in August 2019. A manifesto "justifies" the deeds through "superalienation." The choice of victims targeted Hispanics and Mexicans. Investigators do not actually categorise the attack in El Paso as a mentally deranged person running amok due to the political background, but as a terrorist assassination attempt motivated by right-wing radicals.

2.9 Lone Wolves and Islamic Terrorists

The new wave of lone wolves within right-wing terrorism and Islamic terrorism has a lot to do with online platforms, websites, blogs and chatrooms, in which extremism is well and truly cultivated. Al-Qaeda started a recruitment drive a few years ago, as a change of strategy in order to win over young people in Western countries to the idea of suicide bombing attacks[64] in the course of their being weakened.

Terrorists with extreme right-wing and Islamic motivations have a number of commonalities throughout:

- acknowledgement of a higher authority (a strong leader such as Adolf Hitler or God).
- using violence against ethnic minorities or non-believers.
- fundamental contempt for human beings.
- claiming a higher purpose.

There are signs that extreme right-wing and Islamic terrorist attacks are strongly on the increase at present. Global databases bear testimony to this. A lot of things tell us that a spiral of violence has been set in motion.[65] Every terrorist risks life and limb, must count on being shot, if he has not taken his own life first. Right-wing terrorists can also commit suicide. However, in Islamic terrorism suicide bears a religious signature, promising redemption in the hereafter. There are main connecting threads which understand the terrorist attack to be a spiritual act. In other words: The suicide cannot be considered without the assassination attempt and vice versa. A suicide-assassin converts himself into a walking bomb, using his body for one final act. He considers his religion, Islam to be a promise of eternity, the Koran to be a handbook for his suicide-assassination attempt.[66] We have often heard the Arab cry being issued at the end, of *Allahu Akbar*.

The opinion prevails with the advent of international Islamic terrorism, that logistical competence, meticulous preparation as well as transnational networks from a group must be behind terrorist attacks. This was displayed in an especially drastic manner on 11 September 2001 ['9/11']. Apparently, a fundamental change of strategy has emerged since then. For years, the talk has

---

[64] Cf. Gabriel Weimann: Terrorism in Cyberspace, Chapter 3 "Lone Wolves in Cyberspace", Washington D. C. 2015, pp. 63–75.
[65] Cf. Julia Ebner: The Rage. The Vicious Circle of Islamist and Far-Right Extremism, London 2017.
[66] Cf. Wolfgang Kraushaar: „Einleitung. Zur Topologie des RAF-Terrorismus," in: Wolfgang Kraushaar (ed.): *Die RAF und der linke Terrorismus*, Hamburg 2006, pp. 16–17.

already been time and again of Islamic terrorist organisations, first of all al-Qaeda and then the so-called Islamic State started calling for acts, small cells or even individuals were supposed to commit. This was a kind of emergency quick fix for al-Qaeda at one time, after the USA had increased pressure on the organisation, for example destroying training camps in Afghanistan and Pakistan. The single actors were considered a "welcome 'extra'"[67] for IS along with fighting in Syria and Iraq.

The influx of refugees into Europa, especially to Germany in the context of an at times uncontrollable immigration provided IS an opportunity to smuggle in terrorists, in a targeted manner under the guise of being refugees. The Foreign Intelligence Service of Germany (*Bundesnachrichtendienst*) reported that targeted behavioural training was carried out, for example for the asylum process.[68] The territorial losses of the IS in the meantime have been enormous, many of their ringleaders are dead. This is precisely why the credo appears to continue to assert itself, of striking out alone.

The following still holds: IS is currently writing a screenplay for terror in Europe—whether for knife attacks on trains or attacks using trucks. Terrorists are concerned with setting up a supranational caliphate, but also with hitting the West. Numerous legends and myths exist regarding their organisational strengths: "Individual people or factions can join them worldwide, and moreover simply through rhetorical references to the parent organisation and without requiring operative instruction from them."[69] IS has become a "participation event" for a very small number of fanaticised Muslims or lone wolves. Whether the assassins are ultimately motivated by convictions, whether they are even Muslim believers at all—all this has no longer been of any significance to IS leadership for a long time. It invokes attacks and assassinations at will and attributes the deeds to themselves. The actors train themselves related to their own personal grievance ideology, possibly via videos. The arm of terror may extend right into the children's nursery.

And so, we can ascertain that two typological forms of Islamic terrorism exist, in principle

- the terrorist network, which struck out for example in January and November 2015 in Paris and just a few months later in Brussels in March 2016.

---

[67] Peter A. Neumann: *Der Terror ist unter uns. Dschihadismus und Radikalisierung in Europa*, Berlin 2016, p. 187.
[68] Cf. Manuel Bewarder/Florian Flade: „IS schult Kämpfer, damit Sie mit Asyl umgehen können", in: Die Welt of 13 November 2016, https://www.welt.de/politik/deutschland/article159451941/IS-schult-Kaempfer-damit-sie-Asyl-beantragen-koennen.html.
[69] Masala, Carlo: Weltunordnung. Die globalen Krisen und das Versagen des Westens, Munich 2016, p. 126.

- the single actor or so-called lone wolf. This manifestation is clearly popular at present, as it instigates concrete copy-cats.

The tendency to be a single actor becomes apparent, as with right-wing terrorism. And one other parallel is conspicuous: Even with Islamic lone wolf terrorism, officials apparently take a long time to react to it. The murderous Islamic terrorist attack by the Tunisian Anis Amri, 24 years of age at the time of his act, in Berlin on 19 December 2016 marked a "turning point" for a state under rule of law. Twelve people died, more than 60 were injured, some seriously. The assailant was able to flee abroad and was finally shot by police in Milan following an international manhunt, during a routine check of his papers. His perfidious attack with a stolen truck was described in detail in the IS glossy magazine *Rumiyah*.[70] In their issue of November 2016, and therefore prior to the murderous attack, the magazine published an article across several pages with the symptomatic title: "Just Terror Tactics." We do not know whether Amri was aware of this. In any case, another connection is clear in view of the terrorist logic, namely, the copy-cat effect: The previous summer, on 14 July 2016 a Jihadist originally from Tunisia sat behind the wheel of a truck on the most magnificent boulevard in Nice and killed 86 people. Amri was the opposite of a blank page; the investigators' files cover thousands of pages, also due to astute collecting by various officials. The result is actually devastating, and not worthy of a functioning state under rule of law: Amri had spent 18 months in Germany, committing numerous offences from obtaining benefits payments through deception through to being a commercial-scale drugs dealer; he hid from view in the Salafist network in various towns throughout Germany, had at least 14 identities and nonetheless only spent one day in prison.

At the moment a debate is underway, of what part IS played in lone wolf terrorism coming into being: an empty jacket or mantle, and so merely a label, or the instigator as a network for operationalisation? Above all, the question of self-radicalisation is left hanging in space; however, unclear this term may also be. However, it is possible through the Internet at any rate, for someone to train themselves to be a terrorist on their own. Will merely a chat or an IS video even suffice here? A more refined, graduated typology for actors exists under the impact of these difficult demarcations—with the

---

[70]"Rumiyah" is The Arabic name for the city of Rome. The centre of the Catholic Church is considered the main enemy.

encouragement of finally being able to understand terrorism better in the digital era[71]:

- *"genuine" lone wolves*: no communication whatsoever with Jihadi networks (either online or in person)
- *"virtual, loosely connected" lone wolves*: There is evidence of connecting via chatrooms or other digital channels. However, no direct instruction is given
- *"virtually instructed" lone wolves*: A planner in the Middle East or Far East, for example, gives concrete instructions and orders, and in this way helps with "operationalisation" (targets for murderous attacks, technical assistance), and ensures that the assailant is "immortalised" by claiming responsibility
- *practically trained lone wolves*: trained by IS or other organisations (*foreign fighters*), for example smuggled into Europe as so-called refugees with their remit or orders.

There is evidence of numerous virtual and real reference points for Amri. He had regular contact with IS combatants via chatrooms over a lengthy period. It remains open, whether he was only connected up virtually or was instructed with a view to the concrete deed. He also recorded a video prior to his murderous assault, in which he confessed to being IS, which was published on their website immediately.

Terror networks also fall back on lone wolves whenever their own organisation is weakened, as was the case with IS, whenever they suffer heavy losses of personnel and territory. Single actors do not "cost" them anything and can be used for propaganda purposes.[72] The question of a large-scale organisation no longer has any significance for right-wing terrorism. Some actors, however, nurture the thought, they maintain a continuity to National Socialism.

2.10 "Battle Mode" as a Principle

As was the case with "Amri", lone wolves have the tendency for having mental problems. However, it is also evident here, that it would be selling our study short to merely concentrate on the personal realm. These kinds of people are "in battle mode". In such cases, the ideology is not merely a jacket or cloak

---

[71] Cf. Daveed Gartenstein-Ross/Nathaniel Barr: "The Myth of Lone-Wolf Terrorism. The Attacks in Europe and Digital Extremism," in: *Foreign Affairs*, July 2016.
[72] Cf. Daniel Byman: "How to Hunt a Lone Wolf. Countering Terrorists Who Act on Their Own", in: *Foreign Affairs*, 2/2017, p. 101.

('*a mantle*'). At least this is the opinion of the renowned psychiatrist Nahlah Saimeh, who reports on well-known criminal cases as an expert witness. She is of the opinion that it is to the greatest extent coincidental, which radical movement someone becomes affiliated with. This also depends on the region the actor socialises in.[73] It remains uncontested, that there are boom times for ideologies as we witnessed in the twentieth century, the era of extremes—in this case, two totalitarianisms conditioned and cross-fertilised one another, National Socialism and Stalinism. Nevertheless, it would be wrong to assume, that it is almost inconsequential and a coincidence, which ideology one affiliates oneself to. The connecting element for the appeal at that time of Islamic as well as of right-wing extremist ideologies is the battle mode, the mixture of personal and political grievances, misogyny and the belief in a utopian social order.

What is relevant for the drive of the desire to create a fait accompli is there are definitely similarities between right-wing terrorists and single actors with Islamic motivations. The award-winning Norwegian journalist Åsne Seierstad, who concerned herself intensively with Breivik and two sisters who affiliated themselves to IS sees a similar motivation: "Both wish to kill tolerant liberals and/or non-believers. Both unify a hatred of women, exaggerated thoughts of martyrdom and a thirst for power. Both argued with an excessive sense of honour. Both were striving through terrorist means for a polarisation of democratic societies, from which the shades of liberal grey tones forming opinions should recede more and more. Right-wing terrorism and Islam are, if you wish perfect enemies which mutually build one another up."[74] Both ideologies are unified in their tactic of marching on towards their deed alone in an improved manner.

Lone wolf terrorism is a male phenomenon. Right-wing actors are happy to regard themselves as ready for anything, resolute "combatants", entirely in the tradition of fascist or National Socialist fighting alliances, who regard violence as a ritual act. The objective is the eternal fight (Fig. 2.1).

Michael Kühnen, an icon of militant right-wing extremism in latter days of the "old Federal Republic," alluded to this in his pamphlet *Die zweite Revolution. Kampf und Glaube,* published in 1979: "The fight is our lifeblood. It is healthy and natural, to seek one's pleasure in the fight and in proving one's manhood."[75] What was true then is still true for right-wing extremists today:

---

[73] Cf. Nahlah Saimeh: *Ich bringe Dich um! Hass und Gewalt in unserer Gesellschaft,* Salzburg/Munich 2017, p. 190.

[74] Åsne Seierstad: „Rechtsterror und Islamismus machen sich gegenseitig stark" (Interview), in: Der Standard of 3 March 2018.

[75] Quoted after Bernhard Rabert: Links- und Rechtsterrorismus in der Bundesrepublik Deutschland von 1970 bis heute, Munich 1995, p. 309.

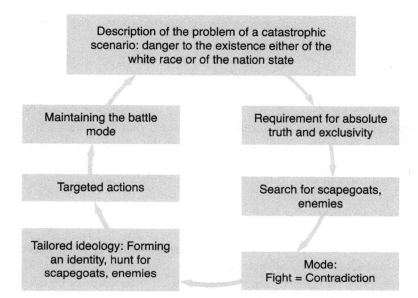

Fig. 2.1 Circle of the right-wing extremist fight, based on Uwe Backes et al. 2014 (Based on relevant texts of songs in the right-wing extremist and terrorism scene, Uwe Backes et al.: Rechts motivierte Mehrfach- und Intensivtäter in Sachsen, Göttingen 2014, p. 243.)

It appears that all the classical gender stereotypes apply with all the associated clichés: crude phantasies of violence, admiring cinematic and action heroes as well as the inability to build up social ties, in connected with an excessive use of computer games. Women are not admired, but are hated or are treated badly, as is the case with IS. There is usually neither a real nor a virtual relationship to them. The image of women is laden with complexes. Women appear unobtainable, they become objects of hatred, as they show no interest in misfits. On the other hand, there are hardly any cases in which women became single actors themselves. This is in part due to the ideological mantle, as right-wing ideology regards the role of women as that of a wife, caregiver and mother. Striking out independently or alone would be in contradiction to this.[76]

The expert on terrorism Peter A. Neumann draws attention in very general terms, to the usual misconceptions when dealing with lone wolves with an

---

[76] See Hanna Runeborg: Targeting herself. Female lone actors, in: Michael Fredholm (ed.): Understanding Lone Actor Terrorism. Past experience, future outlook, and response strategies, London/New York, 2016, pp. 136–159.

Islamic orientation[77], which can also be transferred to lone wolves motivated by right-wing terrorism:

- *The myth of inability to be at fault due to a psychosis*

Actors are portrayed as "mentally deranged", precisely in media reporting. Moreover, this still does not mean by any means that a psychosis, i.e. a loss of reality is present—with the consequence of the inability to be at fault. If for example, clear political or religious messages can be detected and deeds are planned meticulously, this almost sounds like exculpation.

- *The myth of lighting fast "blitz" or "turbo" radicalisation*

With the most recent impression of solo terrorism having been planned or at least inspired by IS, from time to time the impression arises that the actor had so-to-speak radicalised himself overnight. In the majority of cases with this type of single actor, there is evidence both of contact to the Salafist scene, relevant exchanges in chatrooms and general traces in virtual arenas as well as lengthy preparations for the deed: "That radicalisation processes can be accelerated through online influences, even when this is only seldom the single cause, in the meantime is the consensus [...] Yet it is unlikely, even with the help of the Internet, that a jihadist murderer will emerge from a well-integrated refugee, who—to the best of our knowledge—does not suffer from a psychosis or severe psychological problem."[78] For the murderer driving the truck in Berlin, Anis Amri, this is understandable. Soon after his arrival, he submerged himself in the Salafist scene. Doors were opened for him. He could be considered a potential terrorist in the name of his belief at the latest in February 2016, when he was flirting with his role as an IS combatant. There are few signs of deradicalisation, which he has been linked with due to his commercial-scale drug-dealing and his very worldly lifestyle. We see here that clearly excessive demands are being placed on the state by such phenomena. The security services and secret services thought they had averted the terrorist danger of an Amis Amri through banishing criminality. This assumption turned out to be a fatal fallacy. It also shows that the political motivation is not taken seriously enough. This also applies to right-wing perpetrators.

---

[77]Cf. Peter A. Neumann: *Der Terror ist unter uns. Dschihadismus und Radikalisierung in Europa*, Berlin 2016, pp. 191–196 and 257–261.
[78]Cf. ibid. p. 260.

References

1. Albrecht, R. (2002). Nur ein "Amokläufer"?—Sozialpsychologische Zeitdiagnose nach "Erfurt". *Recht und Politik, 38*(3), 143–152.
2. Backes, U., et al. (2014). *Rechts motivierte Mehrfach- und Intensivtäter in Sachsen.* Göttingen.
3. Bannenberg, B. (2013). Amok. In C. Gudehus, M. Christ (Eds.), *Gewalt. Ein interdisziplinäres Handbuch* (pp. 99–104). Stuttgart/Weimar.
4. Berger, J. M. (2016). *The Turner Legacy* (p. 1). International Centre for Counter-Terrorism, The Hague. https://icct.nl/wp-content/uploads/2016/09/ICCT-Berger-The-Turner-Legacy-September2016-2.pdf
5. Byman, D. (2017). How to hunt a lone wolf. Countering terrorists who act on their own. In *Foreign Affairs* (vol. 2, p. 101). https://www.brookings.edu/opinions/how-to-hunt-a-lone-wolf-countering-terrorists-who-act-on-their-own/
6. Ebner, J. (2017). *The Rage. The Vicious Circle of Islamist and Far-Right Extremism.* London.
7. Gartenstein-Ross, D., & Barr, N. (2016). The myth of lone-wolf terrorism. The attacks in Europe and digital extremism. In *Foreign Affairs*, July.
8. Easson, J. J., & Schmid A. P. (2011). 250-plus academic, governmental and intergovernmental definitions of terrorism. In A. P. Schmid (Ed.), *The Routledge Handbook of Terrorism Research* (pp. 99–157). London/New York.
9. German Domestic Intelligence Services (Verfassungsschutz). (2004). *Gefahr eines bewaffneten Kampfes deutscher Rechtsextremisten. Entwicklungen von 1997 bis Mitte 2004.* Cologne.
10. Gräfe, S. (2015): Leaderless resistance and lone wolves [Rechtsextreme Theoretiker aus den USA und deren Einfluss in Europa]. In E. Jesse & R. Sturm (Eds.), *Demokratie in Deutschland und Europa* (pp. 307–321). Berlin.
11. Hamm, M. S., & Spaaij, R. (2017). *The Age of Lone Wolf Terrorism.* New York.
12. Hegemann, H., & Kahl, M. (2018). *Terrorismus und Terrorismusbekämpfung.* Wiesbaden: Eine Einführung.
13. Hoffer, E. (1951). *The True Believer.* New York City.
14. Hoffmann, J. (2017). Bedrohungsmanagement und psychologische Aspekte der Radikalisierung. In N. Böckler & J. Hoffmann (Eds.), *Radikalisierung und terroristische Gewalt* (pp. 277–298). Frankfurt/Main.
15. Jackson, P. (2018). Beyond the „Lone Wolf": Lone actor terrorism and the far-right in Europe. In A. Kallis, S. Zeiger, & B. Öztürk (Eds.), *Violent radicalisation and the far-right extremism in Europe* (pp. 38–53). Ankara.
16. Kaplan, J., Lööw, H., & Malkki, L. (2015). Introduction. In Ditto. (Eds.), *Lone wolf and autonomous cell terrorism* (pp. 1–12). London/New York.
17. Kraushaar, W. (2006). Einleitung. Zur Topologie des RAF-Terrorismus. In W. Kraushaar (Ed.), *Die RAF und der linke Terrorismus* (pp. 13–61). Hamburg.
18. Kron, T. (2015). *Reflexiver Terrorismus.* Weilerswist.

19. Krumwiede, H. (2004). Ursachen des Terrorismus. In P. Waldmann (Ed.), *Determinanten des Terrorismus* (pp. 29–84). Weilerswist.
20. Mareš, M., & Stojar, R. (2016). Extreme right perpetrators. In M. Fredholm (Ed.), *Understanding lone actor terrorism. Past experience, future outlook, and response strategies* (pp. 66–86). London/New York.
21. Masala, C. (2016). *Weltunordnung. Die globalen Krisen und das Versagen des Westens.* Munich.
22. Meier, M. (2012). (K)ein Tyrannenmord: Der Tod des Iulius Caesar 44 v. Chr. In G. Schild & A. Schindling (Eds.), *Politische Morde in der Geschichte. Von der Antike bis zur Gegenwart* (pp. 11–36), Paderborn et al. 2012.
23. Nash, J. R. (1995). *Terrorism in the 20th century. A narrative encyclopedia from the anarchists through the Westermen to the Unabomber.* New York.
24. Neumann, P. A. (2016). *Der Terror ist unter uns. Dschihadismus und Radikalisierung in Europa.* Berlin.
25. Osterhammel, J. (2009). *Die Verwandlung der Welt. Eine Geschichte des 19. Jahrhunderts.* Munich.
26. Pantucci, R. (2011). *A typology of lone wolves: Preliminary analysis of lone islamist terrorists, international centre for the study of radicalization and political violence.* London.
27. Pinker, S. (2011). *Wie das Denken im Kopf entsteht.* Frankfurt/Main.
28. Preuß, T. (2012). *Terrorismus und Innere Sicherheit. Eine Untersuchung der politischen Reaktionen in Deutschland auf die Anschläge des 11 September 2001*, Dissertation, University of Leipzig.
29. Puckett, K. M., & Turchie T. D. (2007). *The American terrorist. The FBI's war on homegrown terror.* New York.
30. Rabert, B. (1995). *Links- und Rechtsterrorismus in der Bundesrepublik Deutschland von 1970 bis heute.* Munich.
31. Richardson, L. (2007). *Was Terroristen wollen. Die Ursachen der Gewalt und wie wir sie bekämpfen können.* Frankfurt on Main/New York.
32. Runeborg, H. (2016): Targeting herself. Female lone actors. In M. Fredholm (Ed.), *Understanding lone actor terrorism. Past experience, future outlook, and response strategies* (pp. 136–159). London/New York.
33. Saimeh, N. (2017). *Ich bringe Dich um! Hass und Gewalt in unserer Gesellschaft.* Salzburg/Munich.
34. Schneider, H. J. (1994). *Kriminologie der Gewalt.* Stuttgart/Leipzig.
35. Simon, J. D. (2016). *Lone wolf terrorism. Understanding the growing threat.* New York.
36. Simon, J. D. (2019). *The alphabet bomber. A lone wolf terrorist ahead of his time.* Nebraska.
37. Spaaij, R. (2012). *Understanding lone wolf terrorism. Global patterns, motivations and prevention*, amongst other things.
38. Spaaij, R. (2010). The enigma of lone wolf terrorism. An assessment. *Studies in Conflict & Terrorism, 33*(9), 854–870.
39. Steinbach, P., & Tuchel J. (2010). *Georg Elser. Der Hitler-Attentäter.* Berlin.

40. Waldmann, P. (2005). *Determinanten des Terrorismus.* Weilerswist.
41. Weimann, G. (2012). Lone wolves in the cyberspace. *Journal of Terrorism Research, 3*(2), 75–90.
42. Weimann, G. (2015). *Terrorism in cyberspace.* Washington DC.

3

Offenders and Terrorism. Ideology, Motives, Objectives

Lone wolf terrorism motivated by right-wing extremism is a real problem, which allows itself to be conclusively delineated from other types of terror, frenzied and spree killings (amok). Lone wolves by no means act out of emotion, do not act madly or irrationally, but—completely the opposite—act after thorough planning and out of political motives. They speak of freedom or redemption, declare a race war or consider themselves to be at war with immigrants and refugees. Their ideologically justified hatred of ethnic minorities spurs them on. Their search for a strike against society turns these introverted, absent-minded, often not taken to be "the full shilling" actors into extroverted, strongly focussed offenders by conviction, whether for one singular bestial act or a series of malicious murders. All of this clearly distinguishes them from terrorist organisations, left-wing and Islamic single actors as well as from people running amok.

Our society today provides a political climate in which a radical right-wing lone wolf terrorist can easily develop along with the opportunities on the Internet.

We must not overestimate the danger of such deeds occurring, but we must also not ignore it and under no circumstances may we negate it. At present, however, this appears to still be the case in the majority of instances. Therefore, the predominant consideration is that we are simply dealing with highly peculiar and unusual individuals, who "could no longer be helped," as they would not take the hand extended to them in familial and social environments. We are often told that we are really powerless against deranged lone actors. Like the legendary, mysterious Kaspar Hauser in Germany in times gone by, simply originating from a different world, scarcely able to be fathomed by citizens or police. Yet such considerations release society from all guilt—with fatal consequences for victims, their dependents, criminal prosecution services and offering no defence. A liberal society, however, should precisely not concern itself with alienation tendencies, particularly if they are of a violent nature. We are concerned here with the effects of teaching and instruction: Nevertheless, we are concerned with an international phenomenon, which several countries in Europe have been and are confronted by, and probably also will be in future. The following chapter must, therefore, shed light on the assailant's perspective whilst including personal and political socialisation, which unfortunately is always in the forefront when considering terrorism.

Each case of individual terrorism is riddled with peculiarities and cannot be forced exactly into a tight, rigid framework, corresponding to the nature of terrorism in general. After all, terrorism is "a strange category of violence."[1] Even in the case of the RAF we discussed puzzling justifications in letters of acknowledgement, and the allocation of anti-capitalist and Marxist ideas. There simply is no rigid, fixed template; nevertheless, analysing individual cases and comparing them helps improve detection. The cases are not conclusive here. The danger of right-wing terrorism from far right lone actors in the USA did not just start with the shooting in El Paso, in August 2019. We already mentioned the case of Timothy McVeigh, who carried out the so-called Oklahoma Bombing on 19 April 1995. 168 people lost their lives and 853 people were injured. McVeigh, a white supremacist had a co-conspirator, however, which is why he should not be included in the category "lone wolf".

A lone wolf terrorist who wished to make a stand against the "spread of socialist norms" into traditional American society, namely abortion and homosexuality, was behind the bomb attack on the Centennial Olympic Park in Atlanta during the Olympic Games in Atlanta in 1996. Two people died and more than one hundred were wounded by the attack. The person behind the attack was Eric Rudolph, born in Merit Island, Florida in 1965, who was elusive and could not be caught at first. Rudolph continued his violent campaign over the next 2 years, with a bombing at an abortion clinic in Atlanta in January 1997, injuring six people. Then 1 month later he bombed a gay night club in Atlanta where five people were wounded. This was followed by a bombing at an abortion clinic in Birmingham, Alabama in January 1998, killing one person and injuring another. More than 5 years later, Rudolph was still in hiding despite the best efforts of the FBI and other law enforcement

---

[1] According to Steven Pinker: Gewalt. Eine neue Geschichte der Menschheit, Frankfurt/Main 2011, p. 511.

agencies. It seems that he used some strategies he had learned during a short period of service in the US army. He was not captured until 2002, hiding in the mountains of North Carolina and was sentenced to lifelong imprisonment in 2005. Rudolph was part of the militant anti-abortion movement, but his convictions were connected with extreme right-wing beliefs.[2]

Another case was the United States Memorial Shooting, carried out in 2009. The perpetrator James von Brunn may be considered an atypical lone wolf terrorist due to his age. He was 88 years of age at the time he carried out the deed. He was a white supremacist, anti-Semitic and a holocaust denier. He had a website and wrote the relevant, self-publicising book "Killing the Best Gentiles" praising Adolf Hitler. He was in contact with a few activists operating in the extreme right-wing subculture, but still acted alone. The actor started shooting in the museum building, killing Stephen T. Johns, an African American security guard. He was shot and wounded himself by another security guard. Von Brunn died in a federal penitentiary in 2010.[3]

The actual size of the new threat becomes clear, if we examine examples from the recent past in more detail, which up until now were only considered to be part of radical right-wing terror. In addition, an effort should be made here to find common denominators between the actors. Profiles of actors can be drawn up by this means, dangers and starting points for radicalisation can be restricted and as a result of this we can obtain important information on opportunities to prevent these events. It should be apparent to the reader that all the deeds coming into question were perpetrated by men. Whilst there are female members of terror organisations or small cells from time to time, there does not appear to be a single case of female single actors amongst lone wolves.

Individuals do not have a mark of Cain on their forehead where it is written, they will become terrorists. Yet we should still like to know: Is it possible to determine a terrorist personality? Are there moments in the course of one's life which lead to radicalisation, for example within the family unit, at school or at work, or are we dealing with "socially autistic people" when considering actors, who may draw their motivation from the fact they are not able to form a relationship with a partner? Can we detect societal influences? Can a process of radicalisation be detected, which we would still have been able to intervene in? How politicised are actors and what are their objectives? The

---

[2] See Gus Martin: Understanding Terrorism: Challenges, Perspectives and Issues, Los Angeles 2013, pp. 418–419; Jeffrey D. Simon: *Lone Wolf Terrorism. Understanding The Growing Threat*, New York 2016, pp. 59–64.

[3] Miroslav Mareš/Richard Stojar: Extreme right perpetrators, in: Michael Fredholm (ed.): Understanding Lone Actor Terrorism. Past experience, future outlook, and response strategies, London/New York 2016, pp. 66–86, here p. 71.

title of one book ponders: "Who becomes a terrorist and why?".[4] The following chapter should now clear these questions up, in which we work out actors' characteristics and analyse them.

3.1 Isolated and Disappointed: Frank Steffen, Thomas Mair, Luca Traini

The most widespread image of the lone wolf is certainly that of the "invisible actor", or terrorists disappointed by life. There is a type of actor, whom often not even his neighbours know, and this really is the case, with examples including Frank Steffen, Thomas Mair or Luca Traini. This type of actor contests their life deeply bowed. His own family do not even think he was able to achieve very much, if anything at all. He has more or less withdrawn from any social life, voluntarily or feeling compelled to do so. The best he can achieve is being an also-ran, and that only for the short-term too. He shuts himself away following bad experiences and turns his back on the world. This aloof person has never experienced love; he is not able to maintain a relationship with a partner. He leads a hermit's existence, shutting himself off inside his own four walls. However, this does not stop him developing fantasies of hatred and violence towards other ethnic groups, internalising extremist right-wing thoughts and becoming a terrorist. On the other hand, the virtual world does not play a highly significant role in his radicalisation process. Friends in chatrooms are just as scarce as in real life. The Internet at best serves as a way to whilst away time for him and as a source of information, for example for informing himself about potential victims. The secret, yet in this way more distinguished hatred in the notorious loner continues to grow and grow. Ethnic groups become surfaces to project onto and scapegoats for the independent, apparently unavoidable dilemma, of not being able to construct a regular social life or professional, working life or a career. His friends from former times which were in any case sparsely numbered make detours to avoid this disappointed person, particularly if he becomes noticeable through radical changes and in this way withdraws off to one side. The lone wolf, isolated from society lives for years with a clenched fist in his pocket—until the longing in him emerges to break out of the vicious circle of loneliness and not being heeded, and become someone who is able to manage for himself.

Frank Steffen was considered a "successful" drop out. And by so doing he represents a group of lone wolves who became conspicuous and from time

---

[4] Rex Hudson: Who becomes a terrorist and why?, Washington D.C. 2018.

to time were even receiving medical treatment, not that we were able to help them or to recognise the danger or the fact that they should have been taken seriously.

Steffen stabbed the mayoral candidate Henriette Reker at an election event in Cologne, using a monstrous Rambo-like hunting knife he had ordered from an online dealer, on 17 October 2015. He admitted later, he wished to render his deed "more theatrical" in this way.[5] The assassination attempt was not carried out through emotion, first of all he even asked his victim for a rose. Henriette Reker survived the attack with severe injuries. The muscular actor, with all his hair shaved off was concerned with a xenophobic motive and did not agree with Reker's policy on refugees, wishing to instil a sense of fear in refugee hostels. He considered himself to be a martyr here: "I wanted to kill her, in order to do Germany and the police a favour." He also wanted to meet the "lunatic Chancellor", who still only wished to look after "these refugees". He is supposed to have explained to police, the German government had committed high-treason and could no longer protect their women and children. The outcome would be everyone would need to live in a society distinguished by Muslim traits. Every German was obliged to take steps against this "terror regime". This man who had carried out an act of violence and had prior criminal convictions stylised himself as a "true defender of the nation,"[6] clearly without being linked to this society in any way and by attacking an elected representative. Frank Steffen said during the investigations, that he was "no Nazi", but a "rebel with conservative values." At the same time, he was provocative by wishing to have a new "right-wing" defence counsel in court.

In the period before his deed, the single actor was heavily immersed in sombre online games, where he gained attention through his hate messages and confrontations with others. Whilst doing so, he listened to extreme right-wing music, for example from the groups „Division Germania" and „Stahlgewitter". As a child he had been subjected to traumatic experiences, which certainly influenced him: At 4 years of age he had been discovered dishevelled in his parents' apartment, after they simply left him there. He was placed in a foster home, moved out at the age of 19 and broke off all contact. As a young man he was often involved in fights, became involved in the extreme right-wing subculture—for example in the area involving the Freiheitliche Arbeiterpartei (*Free German Workers' Party*), which was banned in 1995 by

---

[5]Cf. with original documentation Anna Neifer/Simon Wörpel: „Frank S., der Rechtsradikale", research amongst others with ZDF *Frontal*, 17 October 2016, https://correctiv.org/blog/ruhr/artikel/2016/10/17/reker-attentat-festplatte-frank-s-doch-ein-nazi/.
[6]Ibid.

the Federal Constitutional Court on the basis of their consubstantiality with the NSDAP (*National Socialist Party*). And thus, Frank Steffen took part in a march held in memory of Hitler's representative Rudolf Hess, for example. He had the name of his Skinhead Brigade tattooed on his stomach in Old German lettering. After a variety of suspended sentences because of causing bodily harm, he was finally sentenced to 3 years behind bars. Upon his release, he clearly straightened himself out. He left his extreme right-wing contacts alone and wished to reintegrate himself into society.

He worked as a painter and spray-painter, but frequently rubbed his superiors up the wrong way, and frequently changed his place of work. In the end he became unemployed. He amassed a mountain of debt and withdrew more and more.[7] In isolation, new as well as old hatred welled up inside him, under the impression of being a political debate. He watched Germany's "Welcome Culture" being introduced in the autumn of 2015 in a furious state, which was clearly the "trigger" for the intended deed which he had been planning for a long time, to take his revenge on Society which had treated him badly and preferred other people.

In spite of all his mental dispositions, an expert witness declared him to be fully criminally liable following his attack. Whilst he had a paranoid–narcissistic personality disorder, he was not suffering from a psychotic illness or delusions. The political motive also played a certain role; however, he was not assessed as being a lone wolf terrorist: Frank S. wished to create a climate of fear and to influence politics, we read in the grounds for the judgement. He did not consider the federal government entitled to allow refugees to enter the country. To the contrary, he wished to deliver an "extreme and brutal message."[8] This blatant political consciousness, however, speaks in favour of evaluating him as a prima facie lone wolf terrorist.

Steffen acted in a calculated and by no means uncontrolled manner. He knew what he was trying to affect through his deed. After attempting to integrate himself, he clearly slipped back into his old manner of thinking, which had lain dormant inside him. The debate on refugees suited him as a vehicle, for compensating his own dissatisfaction and putting his destructive stamp on it himself with an act of violence. By attempting to assassinate the Lady Mayoress, he obviously felt he had the opportunity to achieve certain notoriety. He was assured of public attention 1 day before the election.

---

[7] Cf. Ibid.
[8] Cf. for the case of Armin Pfahl-Traughber: „Das "Lone-Wolf"-Phänomen im Rechtsterrorismus in Deutschland und Schweden", in: Martin H. Möllers/Robert Chr. Van Ooyen: *Jahrbuch für Öffentliche Sicherheit 2016/2017*, Frankfurt on Main. 2017, p. 205.

Only a little after this a similar case sent reverberations through Great Britain: the murder of politician Helen Joanne ("Jo") Cox. Again, it was a murderous attack, with which the assailant wished to send a political message in a heated debate.[9] The murder was carried out only 1 week before the Brexit Referendum, whose advocates were massively stoking up fear of migration. When despatching a shot with his firearm, according to witness statements the 52-year-old Thomas Mair called out: "Britain first, keep Britain independent. Britain will always come first." Cox stood for *Remain* and advocated refugees' concerns, even committing herself for example for Syrian refugees.

Mair was born in Scotland in 1963 and was entirely socially isolated. Neighbours scarcely knew this notorious man of few words; he was a completely blank page to the police. His parents, father an industrial mechanic and mother a factory worker divorced shortly after his birth, whereupon he was raised by his grandparents.

Prior to his deed which was a complete surprise to officials, Mair had informed himself in great detail about his victim, as he generally collected meticulous information for his hobbies. He used the Internet and the local library for this, which is why we know that he was very interested in the Waffen SS, the Ku Klux Klan and serial killers. There were several treatises in his impressively well-stocked bookcase on the "Third Reich," amongst them a copy of *Ich kämpfe. Die Pflichten des Parteigenossen*—this troth or expression of loyalty was issued to members of the NSDAP in 1943. He was in particular fascinated with SS-Obergruppenführer Reinhard Heydrich, who directed the Wannsee Conference. He also had books denying the Holocaust in his bookcase. Evidently, he likewise studied the assassination attempts on Martin Luther King and John F. Kennedy.[10] He had also collected newspaper articles about Anders Behring Breivik and his terrorist activities.

Similar to Steffen, Mair had a relevant offensive past. He supported the neo-National Socialist faction National Alliance in the USA, which the author of the Turner Diaries William L. Pierce had started. He ordered extremist right-wing literature there, as well as operating instructions for weapons.[11] He subscribed to the *S. A. Patriot*: a South African magazine committed to apartheid. He sent a letter to the publisher Alan Harvey in 1988.

---

[9] Cf. for the case Paul Jackson: The Murder of Jo Cox MP: a Case Study in Lone Actor Terrorism, in: Alan Waring (ed.): The New Authoritarism, Vol. 2: A Risk Analysis of the European Alt-Right Phenomenon, Stuttgart 2019, pp. 149–169.

[10] Cited after Tom Burgis: Thomas Mair. The Making of a neo-Nazi Killer, in: Financial Times of 23 November 2016.

[11] Ian Cobain/Nazia Parveen/Matthew Taylor: "The slow-burning hatred that led Thomas Mair to murder Jo Cox", in: *The Guardian* of 23. November 2016, https://www.theguardian.com/uk-news/2016/nov/23/thomas-mair-slow-burning-hatred-led-to-jo-cox-murder.

In it Mair expressed his hope that "the white race would reign supreme [in future], both in Great Britain and in South Africa." However, he was also concerned, that "this would lead to a bloody race war."[12]

He appeared to have a very difficult relationship with his mother. More than this: Whilst he carried out gardening work for her, as she lived nearby, he nevertheless frequently googled the term "matricide" on the Internet. His mother's new husband was originally from the Caribbean island of Grenada, she obviously preferred his half-brother. This appears to be the sole reason for explaining his racial hatred from his real life.

Just like practically all lone wolves, the unemployed gardener who lived a withdrawn lifestyle never had a girlfriend. After his grandmother died, he lived the last few years before his deed completely alone. Mair too received repeated treatment for mental problems, in particular because of obsessive-compulsive disorders. And so, for example he experienced an obsessive compulsion to wash. One day prior to his deed he visited a drop-in centre for depression—and was given an appointment for the following day. Following his arrest, however, he was declared to be fully criminally liable.[13]

In spite of his activities and attitudes, Mair certainly never belonged to any extreme right-wing organisation, although there would have been plenty of opportunities for this in his local surrounding area of Birstall and Batley, close to Leeds. Many Muslims live in this area; this region is a stronghold for the right-wing extremist *British National Party*. He was merely spotted once at a demonstration by the English Defence League, at a meeting of Nationalists in London.[14] Clearly, he did not find any rigid affinity or any type of belonging there either. His access to right-wing extremist material normally took place through the post. Even if the deed in the end was carried out as if from nowhere and the actor lived and acted autonomously, Mair was still a long way removed from living beneath the radar in society. He had even tried to obtain help for himself.

A further case took place in Macerata in Italy on 3 February 2018. The 28-year-old Luca Traini shot at six African migrants there from Nigeria, Ghana, Gambia and Mali from his car. There is no doubt of the actor's motivation—on his arrest Traini had wrapped himself in an Italian flag and shouted „Viva l'Italia". In addition, the Italian flag tattooed on his neck alluded to this, the *Wolfsengel* or wolf trap is displayed above his right eyebrow and is a symbol admired by militant right-wing extremists, which amongst other things is supposed to demonstrate the ability to put up a fight. Wearing this symbol is

---

[12] Ibid.
[13] Ibid.
[14] Ibid.

a punishable offence in Germany, when used in connection with right-wing extremist symbols.[15]

The man left a votive candle behind at the scene of his attack with an image of the former fascist "Duce" Benito Mussolini. After his deed, he said that the triggering event for his act of terror had been the murder by a Nigerian asylum seeker, a drug dealer without valid registration documents, of an 18-year-old Italian woman. The crime against the young woman from Rome, who had escaped from a treatment centre for drug addicts, was bestial. Her corpse was found in two suitcases cut into small pieces only a few kilometres away from Traini's home. At the time of the deed, however, nothing had been known about the circumstances surrounding her death, and there was also speculation she had overdosed on drugs. Traini's decision to become a terrorist had clearly been made a long time before. He put on a camouflage uniform and embarked on his path.

Numerous pieces of National Socialist material were found in his apartment, amongst other things Hitler's „Mein Kampf" as well as a flag bearing a Celtic cross, which is considered a symbol of right-wing extremism. The clean-shaven Traini was pleased to have called himself *Lupo* ("Wolf") for some time, and by so doing to have demonstrated his dangerousness. He also took part in a large demonstration by the neo-fascist movement CasaPound in Rome.[16]

He had unsuccessfully stood as a candidate in the local elections in 2017 for the radical populist right-leaning Lega Nord, known for its agitating against migrants. He is also alleged to have had links to the neo-fascist Forza Nuova. His friends stated to investigators that his opinions had become significantly more radical following his election defeat. They tried to avoid the man who lived in the same house as his mother and grandmother.[17]

What we can say with certainty about Traini is that he was a social drop out. He kept his head above water with short-term jobs as a security guard in a supermarket or as a delivery driver, after he had lost his job as a bouncer, which was very important to him because of his racist and extreme right-wing views. He was even refused admittance to his favourite fitness club. His last

---

[15]The SS and Hitlerjugend (*Hitler Youth*) used the Wolfsengel or wolf trap during National Socialism as a symbol for some of their units.

[16]Cf. Südtirol News (2018): https://www.suedtirolnews.it/italien/ich-fahre-nach-macerata-um-ein-massaker-anzurichten.

[17]The Guardian.com (2018): Italy Shooting. Mein Kampf found in home of suspect, 4 February, https://www.theguardian.com/world/2018/feb/04/macerata-shooting-mein-kampf-found-in-home-of-suspect-italy-luca-traini.

relationship had failed.[18] In addition, he supposedly suffered from a bipolar disorder.[19]

He showed no remorse following the deed—on the contrary, he regretted that the victims had not died.[20] The deed became a political issue as it took place in the middle of the election campaign, just 1 month prior to the election. Allocating this as a right-wing extremist assassination attempt was played down to a great extent. The former Italian Prime Minister, Silvio Berlusconi regarded the deed as the act of a "mentally disturbed person [with no] political understanding." The Chairman of the party Lega Nord, Matteo Salvini, Italian Minister of the Interior since 1 June 2018, whilst convicting the man who had nevertheless been a candidate for his party in regional council elections and whom he had allowed himself to be photographed with, nevertheless drew his own conclusions: "It is a fact, that this immigration which has gotten out of control will cause anger and confrontations in society."[21] In this way, Salvini implicitly granted "locals", the "concerned citizens" the right to "defend" themselves against foreigners and in times of emergency and to bear arms.

Even if the deeds mentioned above were committed by lone wolves who were almost completely isolated from society, every third example is still connected to the polarising discourse on refugees and immigrants being conducted in many European countries, and above all which appears to radicalise social losers. The triggering event at least has a direct correlation to this, in concrete terms with the debate which commenced in autumn 2015. Frank Steffen and Thomas Mair had already turned away from society living for a long time in seclusion, seeing their last chance to set an example. Two resolute female politicians served as their targets, who had become involved in the refugee question on humanitarian grounds. Traini wished to become involved in politics himself and saw an opportunity in Lega Nord to do something against immigration. He perceived the murder of a young woman in Rome to be confirmation of his views. Black migrants should pay for the deed, which a Nigerian drug dealer was supposedly responsible for. These lone wolves' deeds were politically motivated and were an expression of their right-wing extremist orientation. In addition to this and by no means by way

---

[18] Cf. Südtirol News (2018): https://www.suedtirolnews.it/italien/ich-fahre-nach-macerata-um-ein-massaker-anzurichten.

[19] Cf. Notizie.it (2018): Luca Traini, perizia psichiatrica affidata a Massimo Picozzi, https://www.notizie.it/luca-traini-perizia-psichiatrica-affidata-a-massimo-picozzi/.

[20] Cf. The Local.it (2018): Italy's centre left warns of a return of fascism, 8 February, https://www.thelocal.it/20180208/support-macerata-shooter-luca-traini-return-fascism.

[21] Cited after Paul Schwenn: Gewalt schamlos ausgenutzt, in: Der Tagesspiegel of 6 February 2018, https://www.tagesspiegel.de/politik/terror-in-italien-gewalt-schamlos-ausgenutzt/20934210.html.

of contradiction, the people described above suffered from severe mental disorders. These did not take place in seclusion, however. All the actors were known to officials, therapists, employers or former friends.

3.2 Failures, Megalomaniacs and Dangerous: Franz Fuchs, John Ausonius, Anders Breivik, Brenton Tarrant

Alongside these first categories of lone wolves, who clearly did not have things easy throughout their lives, there are also lone wolves who initially appeared to be entirely positive assets to society. They were conspicuous during their life due to their special talents, be it their intelligence or a certain business acumen. Moreover, they possessed a tendency for megalomania and wished to impress certain people or to manipulate targeted individuals. This type of actor at least had a fixed place in society for a time, with entirely upwardly mobile prospects. Yet their wish to belong failed, both in their professional as well as their private lives, for different reasons. Usually, we were dealing with people, who often were not able to get their life "in order" on the basis of over-inflated ambitions, and over and above this were too proud to seek help on their own, or who blocked out anything else after the first failed attempts of this kind. Their search for a scapegoat then led to radicalisation. The subsequent terrorist activity often highlights abilities which were there in principle—for example by developing meticulously planned deeds or being operationally highly intelligent. People who have failed in their lives consider themselves to be part of a movement as a terrorist, which clearly is a completely fantasy. The actor also has great plans here and wishes to profess that he can achieve more than he actually can. The process acts as a stage for him, which he uses for tirades of swearing and provocative gestures.

One of the largest criminal cases in the history of the Alpine Republic and beyond took place in Austria during the 1990s. At that time, the phenomenon of a lone wolf with an extreme right-wing motivation entered public consciousness for the first time in Europe. A series of letter bomb and pipe bomb attacks (as well as anonymous letters) frightened and terrified people during the period from 1993 to 1997.[22] According to the letters of acknowledgement the Bavarian Liberation Army, the BLA [or *Bajuwarische Befreiungsarmee (BBA)*] was behind these. In reality, however, the lone wolf

---

[22] See for the whole case Paul Schliefsteiner, Paul (2018): Austria's Homegrown Lone Actor Terrorist: Franz Fuchs and the Letter Bomb Campaign of the 1990's, in: Journal for Intelligence, Propaganda and Security Studies, 12 (1), pp. 67–92.

Franz Fuchs committed these deeds. The letters of acknowledgement embellished with wide-ranging historical discourses led to the conclusion, German nationalists hostile to minorities and in particular with anti-slavic and anti-Turkish dispositions were at work.

One of these pamphlets contained the words "People are welcome in this country, who look like us, pray like us and talk like us." And in another place: "They all have no idea and believe that we fully accept stray Mediterranean people, Asians, Africans and heathens along with leather display cases from Slavs." Fuchs complained about his country's immigration policy, considered the "German-Austrian Nation" had been discriminated against and was threatened by "super alienation". His inflammatory leaflets were quoted widely in the media.[23]

These years were marked by feelings of uncertainty. Investigators and the public concentrated on militant Neo-National Socialists—right down to the arrests of two known persons of interest. There were also numerous phone calls to officials from copycats and freeloaders. An appeal went out on television in all three German-speaking countries to millions of members of the public on *Aktenzeichen XY* (cf. "Crimewatch"—BBC tv). Yet no hot trail could be found. Instead, it became more and more apparent, that the justiciary, the executive and politics were marking time, running on the spot. For a long time, the letters of justification, riddled with technical details of refined structures for bombs as well as with allusions to history, often from early mediaeval times puzzled droves of investigators and investigative journalists. Based on the well-informed content of the letters, the assumption was that the supposed terrorist organisation BBA must have contained at least one chemist, a mathematician, a historian and a Germanist amongst their number.[24] No one suspected Fuchs, the "Patriot" as he liked to describe himself, he was clearly never of any interest. Fuchs lived alone with no social contact and entirely without any links to relevant well-known organisations or people. The supposed Alliance of Austrian Patriots did not exist.

The victims of his murderous attacks included four Roma people for example or Vienna's former Mayor, Helmut Zilk, who committed himself for the concerns of foreigners. Along with this, various bombs were sent to people with immigrant backgrounds and therefore—in the perpetrator's opinion—were worthy of being hated: a country doctor originally from Syria, people

---

[23] *Profil (2013)*: „Franz Fuchs: Mythos und Realität", 19 November, https://www.profil.at/home/franz-fuchs-mythos-realitaet-369482.
[24] Cf. Joachim Riedl: „Heimat und Terror", in: *Die Zeit* vom 28. Juli 2011, https://www.zeit.de/2011/31/A-Manifest/komplettansicht.

assisting refugees or the TV presenter Arabella Kiesbauer.[25] 15 people were injured by his attacks, some seriously. A further 25 letter bombs were discovered in time.

The Austrian police remained helpless over a lengthy period in their search for the perpetrator, and they were not able to apprehend Fuchs until 1 October 1997 during a routine stop and search of motor cars. Shortly before this, it had circulated in the press that the search for perpetrators would now follow a computerised dragnet approach. The investigators "stress strategy" produced a positive result: In addition, the story had spread through the media, that a suspect had already been encircled and that the computerised dragnet approach introduced would lead to the perpetrator.[26] The increasingly paranoid Fuchs set off a pipe bomb whilst his car was being checked, because he believed he had been discovered.

It is worth noting that criminal proceedings against him concentrated heavily on his personality disorders, and the matter of his xenophobia was disregarded. Neither his motives nor his convictions which lay behind his deeds, nor the ideological surroundings in which he had developed them were mentioned during his trial. This was down to Fuchs himself, who continually interrupted the proceedings—obviously with the objective which he was able to achieve, of being excluded. For example, he shouted in a staccato voice "Zionist persecution of Germanic people, no thank you! First people and genocidal people, no thank you! Austrian fields for Austrian cows!"

Fuchs was highly intelligent and extremely gifted technically. He was diagnosed as having an IQ of 139.[27] Fuchs also wished to demonstrate this to the court along with his tirades, for example by accusing the bomb experts and expert witnesses of a lack of intelligence. The Austrian had no police record or criminal record, as he commenced his terrorist acts relatively late, aged 44.

Fuchs grew up in modest surroundings on his parents' farm in southern Styria in the village of Gralla near Leibnitz, close to the border with Slovenia. He quickly showed that he was highly intelligent and had been blessed with a number of gifts, in particular regarding natural sciences. When sitting his "A" levels he was amongst the group of pupils, who could provide evidence of understanding the theory of relativity.

---

[25] Cf. Karin Kneissl: Lebenslange Haft für Bombenbauer Franz Fuchs, in: Die Welt of 11 March 1999, https://www.welt.de/print-welt/article567912/Lebenslange-Haft-fuer-Oesterreichs-Bombenbauer-Franz-Fuchs.html.

[26] Cf. Wolfgang Zaunbauer: Der Anfang des Bombenterrors, in: Wiener Zeitung of 29 November 2013, https://www.wienerzeitung.at/nachrichten/oesterreich/politik/590867_Der-Anfang-des-Bombenterrors.html.

[27] Cf. Gisela Friedrichsen: „Nur irgendein Kasperl?", in: *Der Spiegel* of 22 February 1999, pp. 184–186.

The genius was obviously too much for his family surroundings—a father, who often had to work away from home as well as a strict mother. Some problems were evident at an early stage in spite of his intellectual potential: he spoke slowly in a country dialect, which also hampered communication with teaching staff. He discontinued his study of theoretical physics in Graz and in this way also laid rest to his dream of becoming an atomic physicist. Supposedly, he did not like student life; however, actually it was far sooner due to financial problems. Although Fuchs received a grant, the sum was however significantly less than he had calculated. In the end he worked for Daimler-Benz as an assistant engineer on the production line. He was supposed to have been accommodating and loyal towards his foreign colleagues, who at that time mainly came from Yugoslavia. After failed attempts at a modest promotion—he applied successfully to a former school friend for an office job and for a draughtsman's job—he was finally fired after 11 years in 1988. His boss at the time's opinion was: "His work was characterised by often far exceeding the degree of precision required in construction, leading to conflicts with clients."[28] This ate away at him, yet he was especially pedantic, willing and able to work, even after office hours and at weekends.

Fuchs, who has left his parent's home as a highly gifted wonder child, now arrived back home again completely socially isolated with neither a job nor a girlfriend. Even during his student days, there had been numerous signs of depression ranging as far as suicidal thoughts. And so, Fuchs had written to his parents in a letter dated August 1976, that his self-esteem was at zero. His father sent him for psychiatric treatment, and he was discharged after 2 months considered to have been cured. However, no precise diagnosis was made. In addition, throughout his entire life Fuchs never had a lengthy relationship with a woman. He hated himself and developed thoughts of enacting his revenge on mankind for his screwed-up life, which had once offered so many opportunities. The at one time so brilliant school pupil now wished to become just as brilliant a bomb maker. This can surely be attributed to be a cry for acknowledgement of his abilities.[29]

In the opinion of Reinhard Haller, Consultant in Psychiatry and Neurology as well as the expert witness for Franz Fuchs: "My assessment must also detail that Fuchs was a hypersensitive person, extremely easily offended and was a narcissistic person. When he received a student grant which was not as big as he had expected, he gave up his studies. When he fell in love with a young woman, who however knew nothing about this, he immediately interpreted this as rejection and developed an unbelievable hatred of

---

[28] Ibid., p. 186.
[29] Cf. ibid.

women. Whilst working for Daimler, he was of the opinion that a foreigner had snatched a certain job away from him. This resulted in an extreme hatred of foreigners, which then led to the murderous attacks."[30]

His history may have started a wide-ranging debate on the xenophobic climate, which the FPÖ (Freedom Party of Austria) initiated at that time under the leadership of Jörg Haider, with the anti-foreigners petition for a referendum and campaigns against the Slovenian minority. Yet this did not occur, also because Fuchs' deeds including his letters of acknowledgement and with regards to dangerous societal debates were never mentioned, which contributed to making a highly intelligent young man from a rural area into a brutal attacker and murderer.

The lone wolf must not correspond to the current cliché of an isolated, socially excluded loner per se, he may also exist in the form of a successful, smart person as an example from Sweden shows, who threw up numerous explainable and unexplainable references to Germany. This was the case of John Ausonius whom we have already mentioned; eloquent, at times wealthy and dandy-like in appearance and a "player", who was able to impress women. He shot a total of twelve people with a migratory background, without having any personal connection to them in the years 1991 and 1992. However, Ausonius disputes up until today that there was any connection.[31]

Ausonius was extradited to Germany for criminal proceedings at the end of 2016. The Swede who had turned 64 years of age in the interim was also sentenced to lifetime imprisonment here because of a murder almost 26 years before. The court considered it had been proven that on a visit to Frankfurt in 1992, he robbed a 68-year-old Jewess on the street in broad daylight and shot her dead with a bullet to the head. It is unclear whether he had an anti-Semitic motive or whether pure greed lay behind this. Frankfurt District Court decided it was the latter: He wanted to get a so-called Casio calculator back by these means, which he believed the cloakroom attendant had stolen from him. The judge did not consider him to be an "ideological actor".[32]

Ausonius was not a member of any organisation himself, however, made benevolent comments regarding the then ambitious populist right-wing party

---

[30] Reinhard Haller: „Und dieser heilen Welt werde ich es jetzt zeigen", in: Profile of 14 March 2016, (Interview), p. 59.
[31] Cf. Julia Jüttner: „Der Lasermann und der NSU", in: *Der Spiegel*, 12 November 2017, http://www.spiegel.de/spiegel/nahm-der-nsu-den-serientaeter-john-ausonius-zum-vorbild-a-1182707.html.
[32] Cf. Peter Maxwill: „Kaltblütig, zornig, gewaltbereit", in: *Spiegel online* of 21 February 2018, http://www.spiegel.de/panorama/justiz/frankfurt-lasermann-prozess-wie-die-richterin-das-urteil-begruendet-a-1194522.html.

"New Democracy".³³ Ausonius told the Swedish journalist Gellert Tamas, who was allowed to interview him in prison and published a book on the serial killer in 2002, that in his opinion the high level of immigration was presenting society with a problem. He wished to contribute to "the solution" with his shots.³⁴

In the early days nothing in Ausonius' life, who was born as Wolfgang Alexander John Zaugg, pointed towards the fact that he could develop into an extreme right-wing assassin with an ideology based on personal grievances. As the son of a Swiss father and a German mother, he attended a school for the elite and was considered smart. Then he left school without completing any type of leaving exams, apparently through apathy, and made a go of things as a dishwasher and as a cinema projectionist.

Ausonius actually had a lot of chances in life. But whoever takes a closer look, can detect a multitude of grievances, a development, "of how the nicest child turned into a murderer," as one journalist put it.³⁵ His father was a womaniser, his mother compensated for her frustration by beating her son. The youth, who stood out in Sweden with his dark hair and eyes, was teased and called a "Negro" and a "Black man" at school. His yearning for acceptance and acknowledgement (by society) started at a young age. Therefore, he also made himself stand out with his extremely smart appearance, for example turning up for lessons with a stylish narrow tie.

He finally passed his school leaving exams in his mid-20s. Going on to study engineering, however, he discontinued his studies. Then he had a job as a taxi driver and spent a number of months in prison following a fight in a bar. Isolating himself more and more, headaches and sleeplessness ate away at him. He noticed that something was not right with himself, went for treatment and was diagnosed with a borderline disorder, and in addition doctors noticed delusional disorders and mental disorders right up to schizophrenia. He was called up for military service without finishing treatment in 1981. He was trained to use sub-machine guns and bazookas there, and even received an award as the best shot in his company. At the same time, his aggression was increasing. When Ausonius appeared before a court on account of a brawl in

---

³³ Cf. for the case of Armin Pfahl-Traughber: „Das "Lone-Wolf"-Phänomen im Rechtsterrorismus in Deutschland und Schweden", in: Martin H. Möllers/Robert Chr. Van Ooyen: *Jahrbuch für Öffentliche Sicherheit 2016/2017*, Frankfurt/Main 2017, p. 202f.

³⁴ Cited after Øyvind Strømmen: „Der Soloterrorist als Kulturphänomen", in: Frank Decker/Bernd Henningsen/Kjetil Jakobsen (eds.): *Rechtspopulismus und Rechtsextremismus in Europa*, Baden-Baden 2015, p. 253.

³⁵ According to Sarah Kempf: „Wie das netteste Kind zum Mörder wurde", in: *Frankfurter Allgemeine Zeitung* of 11 December 2017, http://www.faz.net/aktuell/rhein-main/prozess-gegen-lasermann-john-ausonius-15334800.html.

1983, the psychiatric expert witness judged him to be "violent" and "clearly mentally ill." Another expert attested there were "paranoid traits". Yet he did not receive any treatment following his imprisonment.[36]

Outwardly, however, to begin with he appeared to have turned over a new leaf. Ausonius was a speculator on the market and achieved a considerable degree of affluence. His life of luxury entered an ecstatic phase: Addicted to gambling, he travelled to Las Vegas and to Germany in order to gamble in casinos. He owned a sports car and furnished his apartment with expensive English furniture. The upstart now appeared to be fully integrated into Swedish society: He changed his name first to John Stannermann, then to John Ausonius.

Yet supposed good luck does not always last forever: the market crash and the roulette table made a poor man out of him. He started robbing banks in the autumn of 1990, in order to be able to continue gambling. He was only ever able to win over women for short periods, which appeared to radicalise him in a crude manner. This man who had in the meantime turned 37, started a love affair with a 17-year-old schoolgirl in the summer of 1990 and even proposed marriage to her after the first night. When she said no, he immediately went and bought himself a gun with laser sights. Another relationship had likewise failed. He unloaded his pent-up frustration on a 27-year-old student from Eritrea, whom he shot.[37]

It is precisely this amalgam-like mixture of personal and political motives which turned Ausonius into a terrorist. He unloaded frustrations concerning his own insecurity and his own misfortune on immigrants, as he himself stated in an interview with the *Berliner Zeitung* in 2015: "During the 1980s, with my economic problems growing ever larger, a hatred of immigrants grew in me. I noticed this when I read reports about them in the newspaper or watched them on the television, and sometimes even when I came across them on the street. I can still remember one situation clearly: A foreigner was heading straight towards me on the street. And I thought, let's see whether he gets out of my way. No, he kept going. He was acting as if he was a king in his own country, I thought to myself back then, and I still remember this today."

Ausonius allowed further glimpses of his psyche at the request of the journalist Andreas Förster: "This also increased my dislike of immigrants. Of course, this has to do with my own problems and with the fact that I could not get my life together. I know this today and perhaps I even knew it then but preferred to suppress it. I was unhappy with myself and my life and

---

[36] Cf. Ibid.
[37] Ibid.

sought parties responsible for this. And so I thought back then: I must give up my studies, because I do not have any money and the state cannot help me, because it must pay up for immigrants of course."[38] In this way, Ausonius revealed a grievance ideology, which can be found in a similar form in almost all radical right-wing lone wolves. It also demonstrates that self-pity is a characteristic of lone wolves. This is clearly true for our next case, which described a new dimension of lone wolf terrorism, and provided firm evidence of how dangerous they can be.

Since 22 July 2011, we now know that lone wolf terrorism can be equally as dangerous as that of an organisation—with reference to the ideology propagated, the number of victims and the copycat effect. First Anders Behring Breivik exploded a car bomb in the government district of Oslo and just a few hours later, perfidiously disguised as a policeman, he carried out a massacre shooting young Social Democrats on the Island of Utøya, 30 km away from Oslo. To do this Breivik pretended to be helping out in an emergency, wishing to report on the terrorist attack in the Norwegian capital and therefore was able to easily travel across to the island from the mainland by ferry.

A total of 77 people died and over 200 were injured. The traditional conference of the youth wing of the Social Democrat Party had been taking place on the island that weekend. Breivik doped himself up with steroids for his bestial undertaking, but acted in a reflected manner, not in the typical arbitrary manner as with a killing spree or frenzy. Thus, he had even shot a few victims who were trying to escape in the water, and merely aimed at others without shooting. Amongst others, he spared a 14-year-old girl because according to his subsequent statement, he had not been "brainwashed" yet.

He had left a political message behind before his deeds, along with a sinister YouTube Video, even if it was crude—the wish for a Europe free from "Cultural Marxism and Islamism". This "manifesto", written in English to attract greater publicity, and covering more than 1,500 pages has been actively distributed since then.

Breivik carried out a meticulous and rational undertaking on this day, as he had been preparing for this terrorist act for years with his writings and his intensive preparations in a cool and calculated manner. We can assume there was a period of 9 years, and so almost an entire decade—starting from his financing to his research and writing phase right through to his concrete operational implementation. He even goes down as one of the most written about mass murderers in history because of his voluminous manifesto. In it,

---

[38]John Ausonius: „Ich sehe mich nicht als Mörder", Interview mit der *Berliner Zeitung*, 16 January 2015, https://www.berliner-zeitung.de/gespraech-mit-dem--laser-mann--john-ausonius--ich-sehe-mich-heute-nicht-als-einen-moerder--773144.

he envisages Europe as now coming to an end. This catastrophe was triggered by a "Marxist Muslim conspiracy," against which we must fight in a "cleansing civil war". He makes use of anti-jihadist conspiracy theories here, according to which Europe would become an Islamic-Arabic colony—"Eurabia".[39]

Breivik is not a well-read intellectual on this matter, but rather had unstructured and abstruse arguments.[40] His choice of victims was that much more considered, because he selected young Social Democrats, explicitly those with a migratory background. Breivik frequently referred to the British, anti-Muslim English Defence League (EDL) in his manifesto—he claimed to have been involved as one of the founder members of an offshoot, boasting about his network. Their founder Paul Ray in the meantime was living on Malta "in exile" and founded an anti-Muslim group there called *The Ancient Order of Templar Knights*. Breivik adopted this name for his own Knights Templar fantasies. Ray, who was in direct contact with him online stated, Breivik was a loner without any organisational superstructure. The secret meetings for a conspiracy Breivik talked about had never taken place. Even the court found no evidence of such "Knight Templar meetings".[41] As a consequence, Breivik was just as isolated as other lone wolves, however, he fantasised to himself about attracting groups of supporters and co-combatants.

In the meantime, Breivik is considered to be a hero and a role model by many, as we are able to read on the gaming platform Steam or in legacies other actors leave behind.[42]

His terrifying mass murder was the last stage of a long history of failure. He came into conflict with the police as a youth, as he was active as a graffiti sprayer in the hip-hop scene.[43] This was the reason his father, a diplomat, broke off all contact to him when he was 15 years of age. His parents divorced relatively early on. Anders remained with his mother who was unable to cope. His behaviour had already been conspicuous as a child, which is the reason he came under the auspices of a family counselling centre. A psychiatrist discovered that he had difficulties displaying empathy and recommended a care

---

[39] Cf. Spiegel 2011: Ein bisschen Reue, ein bisschen Ausrede, http://www.spiegel.de/politik/ausland/breiviks-vordenker-ein-bisschen-reue-ein-bisschen-ausrede-a-777315.html.

[40] Cf. Tore Wehling/Stefan Hansen: Breivik, Terrorist oder Amokläufer?, in: Joachim Krause/Stefan Hansen (eds.): Jahrbuch Terrorismus 2011/2012, Opladen 2012, p. 125 f.

[41] Cf. ibid.

[42] Cf. Florian Hartleb: „Einsamer-Wolf-Terrorismus" – Neue Dimension oder drastischer Einzelfall? Was lernen wir aus dem Fall „Breivik" in Norwegen?, in: Kriminalistik. Unabhängige Zeitschrift für die kriminalistische Wissenschaft und Praxis, 67 (2013) 1, pp. 25–35.

[43] Cf. Åsne Seierstad: Einer von uns. Die Geschichte des Massenmörders Anders Breivik, Zurich 2016, p. 23 f.

home. On learning of this, his natural father tried to get his son to move in with him. He then developed a love-hate relationship towards his mother whom he alleged had gotten involved with too many men, who would infect her with a Sexually Transmitted Disease. His strained attitude towards women also becomes apparent in his manifesto.

Even during his formative years, Breivik was concerned only with becoming rich and counting as one of life's winners. He was extremely vain, wore make-up and received cosmetic surgery for a nose job. He tried to belong and make friends, but always quickly came into conflict with others and then quickly walked away again disappointed. And thus, he joined the Progress Party in Norway (FrP) at 17 years of age—a populist right party, which moreover can be considered as moderate in a European context. Then he left this party again in 2006, probably out of disappointment, because he did not receive a place on the list for regional elections he had been working towards.[44] He also attempted to find acceptance amongst Freemasons, but this likewise remained an intermission. He also failed at school, left the commercial school early and without passing any leaving exams. He pursued his plans of becoming rich and famous in Liberia, where he unsuccessfully tried to get involved in smuggling blood diamonds ('*conflict diamonds*'). Even without a degree himself, he was then able to sell bogus university degree certificates very successfully from 2003 until 2006. In addition, he operated a mailbox company and sold software. He achieved a great deal of success in a short period and had assets of 470,000 Euros at his disposal. Yet once again the fraudster suffered defeat, losing everything again whilst speculating on the market and by making poor business decisions. He moved back in with his mother at the age of 27 and spent his days in his childhood bedroom in front of his computer.[45] His hatred of women grew in him, as became clear in his manifesto. He dreamed of days when men were men, women stayed at home, children were well-behaved, and there was no criminality nor Muslims and Western countries.[46]

At the same time Breivik started with his terrorist plans. He then founded an agricultural company, in order to rent a small farm in 2009, where he built the bomb for the explosion in Oslo on his own. He was also able to acquire the six tonnes of artificial fertiliser he required by means of this "company".

---

[44]Cf. ibid. pp. 91–113.
[45]Cf. ibid.
[46]See Mattias Gardell: Crusader Dreams: Oslo 22/7, Islamophobia, and the Quest for a Multicultral Europe, Jeffrey Kaplan/Heléne Lööw/Leena Malkki (eds.): Lone Wolf and Autonomous Cell Terrorism, London/New York 2015, pp. 128–155, here p. 139.

Following his failure, the Norwegian also appears to have totally isolated himself in his childhood bedroom, for long periods sacrificing himself to political ideologies and thoughts of megalomania. And thus, he gave his plagiarised manifesto the pretentious title *2083: A European Declaration of Independence*. The year in question refers to the Battle of Kahlenberg in 1683 which signalled the final defeat of the Ottoman Empire outside Vienna. Breivik chiefly compiled his manuscript by copying from other sources; amongst other things, we see there are multiple passages from the Unabomber Manifesto of American bomb maker Ted Kaczynski—without mentioning him—wherein he replaced the classifications "left wing" with "Cultural Marxist" as well as "blacks" with "Muslims". Breivik explained in court he had learned a lot from al-Qaeda. This organisation gave him the idea of wearing a policeman's uniform for the massacre on Utøya.

There is no doubt that the Internet played a central role in his radicalisation process. Breivik spent his time practically day and night on the Internet, devouring all possible ideologies and conspiracy theories. When doing, so he acted entirely ambivalently. And so, whilst registering for an Internet forum for neo-National Socialists, however at another point, he expressed his great distaste for National Socialism: "*If there is one figure that I hate, then that is Adolf Hitler*" he wrote and fantasised about time travel, so that he could kill him. Breivik clearly regarded Hitler as the reason why right-wing extremist thinking in Europe was frowned upon publicly after 1945, and in his opinion why left-leaning tendencies were able to spread.

He appeared at his trial in court using a right-wing greeting and readily explained, that his rhetoric and his behaviour in part too were characterised entirely by tactical considerations. He even wrote in the manifesto that any proximity to National Socialists would be damaging.

As one of the first lone wolves, Breivik used social media excessively, even when preparing his propaganda. In his YouTube video he played the part of a Teutonic Knight and a Knight Templar, with martial music and self-portraits. He was very clearly aware of the effect he had over the Internet. Apparently, he had even attempted to commission an online company to erase some of the negative reports which he expected following his mass murders. He purchased a few domain names such as *thenewknighthood.com* and *thenewknighthood.net* for propaganda purposes. As a consequence of the investigations, he additionally planned to send his manifesto to 8,109 radical right-wing activists by e-mail, whose e-mail addresses he had meticulously collected over many months with the help of Facebook accounts. However, he failed with this intention, as his spam filter merely permitted him to send 1,000 e-mails a day from a single account.

The terrorist Breivik has been associated with many labels[47]:

- Christian Fundamentalist (Self-portrayal or self-aggrandisement),
- Conservative revolutionary (Self-portrayal as a contradiction in itself),
- Mediaeval warrior or anti-modernistic terrorist (Self-stylising as a Knight Templar),
- The first anti-Islamic terrorist in Europe or representative of European anti-Islamic sentiment (because of his compatible hatred of Islam),
- Terrorist 2.0 (because of his affinity with the Internet, blogs and virtual war games),
- Cut and paste or Wikipedia Terrorist (because of multiple plagiarisms in his "manifesto" and the reference Wikipedia, in the words of Breivik, the most important source of inspiration),
- Right-wing populist (because of his brief membership of the youth arm of the Progress Party in Norway (*FrP*),
- Right-wing extremist (because of his views hostile to mankind and to democracy),
- Simply as a psychopath.

During the court case, an argument arose between an expert witness and experts about his mental condition. The first expert testimony reached the conclusion that he was suffering from „paranoid schizophrenia", and thus had acted under the influence of a psychosis. His manifesto was "banal, infantile and pathetically egocentric." A further expert report which the court affiliated themselves to, espoused a different opinion. Psychologists diagnosed "a dissocial personality disorder with narcissistic traits." Breivik had "neither been psychotic at the time of the assault nor was he presently." Therefore, he could be considered to be legally accountable and criminally responsible. The court finally adjudged that although Breivik had the "mental state of a fanatic," it was, however, "politically motivated". The court was of the opinion that "the accused did not have any obsessive thoughts in a clinical sense." Breivik was then also declared to be legally accountable in a unanimous judgement on 24 August 2012, following 10 weeks of legal proceedings and was sentenced accordingly to the maximum penalty of 21 years with subsequent preventative detention. Breivik confirmed the coldness and lack of feelings he was

---

[47] Cf. Florian Hartleb: „Einsamer-Wolf-Terrorismus" – Neue Dimension oder drastischer Einzelfall? Was lernen wir aus dem Fall „Breivik" in Norwegen?, in: Kriminalistik. Unabhängige Zeitschrift für die kriminalistische Wissenschaft und Praxis, 67 (2013) 1, pp. 25–35.

attributed as having during the trial. He only had tears in his eyes when the court played his YouTube video and by so doing awakened his narcissism.[48]

There is no question of Breivik's distinct narcissism. His manifesto oozes vainness, raving about his appearance and his charms; in real life however, he never had a steady girlfriend. It also contained an interview which he conducted with himself. He admits in it, that he had been self-centred in the past and had not done much for other people, but at the same time he makes the decline of society in moral regards responsible for this. However, it appears rational in his choice of emotions and arguments.[49]

In the proceedings in court, the psychiatric backgrounds also took up a lot of time regarding the dispute between the experts. The diagnoses reached the conclusion a form of megalomania existed in Breivik, but there were no obsessive thoughts involved. Autism or Asperger syndrome bears testimony to a lack of empathy towards others. Nevertheless, his ideas were an expression of a radical right-wing way of thinking, which he presented along with an over-inflated opinion of himself—as a Saviour or Commander.[50] In a letter from prison he proudly describes himself as the "worst ultranationalist terrorist since the Second World War," and signed it "with narcissistic and revolutionary grounds."[51] His psychiatric disorders which were undoubtedly present must recede into the background for the assessment of the case, as Breivik predominantly wished to send a political message. During the trial as well as in prison in the meantime, he rather presented a pitiful figure. His biographer Åsne Seierstad commented: "After his arrest, he complained about lukewarm coffee and a lack of skin moisturiser in prison and whined that he did not have PlayStation 4."[52]

An Australian named Brenton Tarrant can be considered a copycat actor of Breivik's, who murdered 51 people in Christchurch, New Zealand and injured dozens more. This applies for the justification and implementation of the barbaric act. Although he was active in a different part of the world, he clung to European discourse. What traces can be found in the right-wing terrorist's biography? Brenton Tarrant grew up in Grafton, a small town in the north-east of the Australian state of New South Wales. He wrote in his

---

[48] Cf. Åsne Seierstad: *Einer von uns. Die Geschichte des Massenmörders Anders Breivik*, Zurich 2016, pp. 433–456.
[49] Cf. Cecilia H. Leonhard et al. (2014): The Case of Anders Behring Breivik—Language of a Lone Terrorist, in: Behavioural Sciences and the Law, 32 (3), pp. 408–422.
[50] Cf. Åsne Seierstad: Einer von uns. Die Geschichte des Massenmörders Anders Breivik, Zurich 2016, pp. 433–456.
[51] Ibid., p. 528 f.
[52] Åsne Seierstad: The Anatomy of White Terror, in: New York Times, 19th March 2019 (Opinion), https://www.nytimes.com/2019/03/18/opinion/new-zealand-tarrant-white-supremacist-terror.html.

manifesto: "I am just a regular white man, from a regular family, who decided to take a stand to ensure a future for my people," it says. "My parents are of Scottish, Irish and English stock. I had a regular childhood, without any great issues."

His father Rodney, a dustbin man and enthusiastic sportsman (who competed in the Ironman several times), died in a tragic manner at exactly 49 years of age. According to statements from his grandmother, he committed suicide after contracting incurable cancer. Brenton was 19 years of age at the time and was clearly traumatised, as he and his sister actually discovered his father's corpse.[53] The father–son relationship was clearly an intimate one. The son shared his enthusiasm for athletics with him for example. A photograph from the early 1990s shows Brenton as a small child alongside his sister during a family holiday in Hawaii. His father was running in the Ironman there. His father had his arm around Brenton. His parents later divorced, during Brenton's early childhood. His mother worked as an English teacher in a high school. In her profile on social media, she stated she was against forms of violence. Brenton Tarrant worked as a personal trainer in a gym in Grafton from 2009 and 2011. His boss described him as a diligent trainer, and not conspicuous due to any aggression. He had also offered children training sessions free of charge. Former companions from his hometown described Tarrant, who spent the first 20 years of his life there, as introverted and withdrawn. Grafton itself is a "town of 18,600 inhabitants, without any large Muslim concentrations in the population or any conflicts arising from migration."[54] He obviously had no great ambitions regarding education or training for a career. He wrote in his manifesto: "I had little interest in education during my schooling, barely achieving a passing grade. I did not attend university as I had no interest in anything offered for studying at university."

By his own estimates, he made a fortune from Bitconnect, a cryptocurrency similar to Bitcoin. This could have been a one-off stroke of luck similar to Breivik and may have inspired delusions of grandeur.[55] Strange online comments also attest to this, which he wrote whilst still not having any fixed political direction. Thus, he wrote of himself in an entry in 2011: "I am a

---

[53] Washington Post (2019): 'Hiding in plain sight': In quiet New Zealand city, alleged gunman plotted carnage, 21 March, https://www.washingtonpost.com/world/asia_pacific/hiding-in-plain-sight-in-quiet-new-zealand-city-alleged-gunman-plotted-carnage/2019/03/21/1846de9e-4a7b-11e9-8cfc-2c5d0999c21e_story.html?utm_term=.1e22d94101c0.
[54] See The Guardian (2019): Grafton was known for jacaranda blossom, but mosque shootings have changed that, 16 March, https://www.theguardian.com/world/2019/mar/16/grafton-australia-christchurch-killer-home-town.
[55] See Newshub.co.nz (2019): Christchurch terror attack: Life of alleged killer Brenton Tarrant, 16 March, https://www.newshub.co.nz/home/new-zealand/2019/03/christchurch-terror-attack-life-of-alleged-killer-brenton-tarrant.html.

monster for strength of will. I only need a goal." In a further entry from the same year, after this he accordingly stated: "I direct fitness courses for more than 20 people every day, who look at me the whole time, ask me questions and copy my movements for 60 min. And I enjoy this. My self-confidence goes through the roof. I feel like the best person in the city." He named his favourite past-times at that stage as being video games and "hiring strippers".[56]

Tarrant then wished to explore the world at any rate—clearly also as a reaction to the death of his father and his circumstances. The former class clown withdrew into himself. He spent increasing periods of time on video games and various social media activities on the internet. At the same time, he yearned to be far away. In 2011, a few months after the demise of his father, he embarked on a journey right across the world, from Argentina via Israel and Iceland right across to Pakistan. He sought out remote travel goals. A photograph shows how Tarrant even spent time with a travel group in North Korea. The photograph was taken in September 2014, in front of the large monument in Samjiyŏn in North Korea. The 15 m high bronze statue of the founder of the state Kim Il-sung is a fixed point on any tour of North Korea. The Australian had travelled to North Korea with a Swedish tour operator, Korea Konsult. 25 people were in this group. The booking had been bizarre, an employee stated on record. The Australian who was 22 years of age at the time had given his profession as "retired". And when asked about this he replied: "I have enough money to retire, even permanently."[57] A certain delusion of grandeur can also be detected here. And questions can be asked of the purpose and aim of the journey: did he travel to totalitarian North Korea, because the Kim tyranny had defended the purity of the blood of their race so successfully? At least this is what right-wing radical forums state.

The root causes for Tarrant's radicalisation process clearly lie in his journeying, which he undertook as a classic backpacker, travelling alone without anyone else. There are a few signs here. Tarrant followed the "Crusader trail" and travelled to sites of mediaeval warlords from the Ottoman Wars. He travelled to Bulgaria, Romania and Hungary in the autumn of 2018. By the second half of 2016, Tarrant had already even travelled to Serbia, Montenegro, Bosnia–Herzegovina and Croatia. According to media reports,

---

[56] Cited after The Australian.com (2019), 'I'm a monster of willpower', 15 April, https://www.theaustralian.com.au/nation/nation/i-am-a-monster-of-willpower-i-just-need-a-goal/news-story/5023a018b8b40c20b153dbcbdfb1b90d.

[57] Die Presse.com (2019): Der seltsame Nordkorea-Trip eines Terroristen, 29 March, https://diepresse.com/home/ausland/aussenpolitik/5604143/Der-seltsame-NordkoreaTrip-eines-Terroristen.

he visited historical battlegrounds, where fights against Muslims took place. Accordingly, his weapons and magazines were adorned with names and logo, for example with Ernst Rüdiger von Starhemberg. He had been the leader defending the city of Vienna during the second Siege of Vienna in 1683. One logo even showed the word "Vienna" itself. Another inscription bore the name "Turkofagos". This is the name the Greek revolutionary Nikitas Stamatelopoulos (1784–1849) was known by during his battles in the Greek war of independence. It actually means "he who eats Turks".

There is a further reference point in his "manifesto". As he wrote himself, two events with serious repercussions occurred in 2017: the murder of Ebba Ackerlund in an Islamic terrorist attack in Stockholm and the French presidential elections. A 39-year-old asylum seeker Rakhmat Akilov from Uzbekistan killed five people in Stockholm under the pretext of "IS", including a girl. Tarrant used this case to stylise himself as a fighter against Islamic terrorism. He wrote in a pathetic tone in his manifesto: "I could no longer ignore the attacks. They were attacks on my people, attacks on my culture, attacks on my faith and attacks on my soul."

He names the French Presidential elections of 2017 as a further shock, and therefore as a clear political connotation. Tarrant was staying in France at that time. The confrontation was typical for modern times: "on one side the capitalist, egalitarian globalist and ex-investment banker without any national sensitivity" (he was alluding to Emmanuel Macron here), "on the other side the figure of the fearless citizen and Nationalist, who was speaking out against the deportation of illegal immigrants" (Marine Le Pen is meant here). Every French city and every French village was just swarming with "invaders". It is obvious that Tarrant obtained ideas here at least online from the Identitarian Movement. After all, he named his manifesto „Der große Austausch" [*The Great Replacement*] after the French author Renaud Camus.

Tarrant also donated money.[58] What is certain is that Tarrant considered himself to be part of the Identitarian Movement. His also making donations into the private account of their Austrian spokesman Martin Sellner provides evidence of this. 1,500 Euros were received by him on 5 January 2018. In May 2019 it was announced that Sellner maintained contact by e-mail with the subsequent mass murderer Brenton Tarrant from January until at least July 2018 and that they had invited one another to visit each other's respective countries. Sellner had invited Tarrant to Vienna for a face-to-face meeting and had offered to admit him to the Identitarians. Tarrant had spoken to Sellner

---

[58]The Guardian (2019): Grafton was known for jacaranda blossom, but mosque shootings have changed that, 16th March, https://www.theguardian.com/world/2019/mar/16/grafton-australia-christchurch-killer-home-town.

as an ally in an international network "It will be a long path to victory …" Sellner was advertising for his YouTube channel, which Tarrant praised as "fantastic". Tarrant booked a trip to Austria and a rental car for this, 1 day after Sellner's last e-mail in July 2018.[59]

The "case" of his interest in Pakistan on the other hand is peculiar. He travelled around this country in October 2018. In light of his anti-Muslim atrocities, one would expect that he busied himself with the religious war prevailing in this country, with the circumstance that militant Muslims were supposedly fighting against infidels and unbelievers. The state appeared to be overwhelmed. Tarrant on the other hand posted on Facebook: "Hello everyone my name is Brenton Tarrant and I am visiting Pakistan for the first time. Pakistan is an incredible place filled with the most earnest, kind-hearted and hospitable people in the world, and the beauty of Hunza and Nagar Valleys in autumn is unsurpassable. Hopefully in the near future the Pakistani government and Mr. Imran Khan will make the necessary changes to the visa program so as to encourage tourism and make it viable once more for the world to come and experience the beauty of Pakistan."[60]

The globetrotter moved to New Zealand in August 2017, to Dunedin, a city of 120,000 inhabitants, which is 360 km away from Christchurch, where he committed his fatal deeds. He rented a one-bedroom duplex apartment. Neighbours in Dunedin likewise described him as being quiet. He apparently did not make any political statements there. Instead of this, he was happy to talk about his trips around the world, when he did make any social contact. He did not have a job, lived alone and did not have any friends who visited him. The apartment itself was sparse—with no pictures, photos or posters. Instead of this, he spent his days planning his deeds. He practised at a gun club in the woods, a 45-min drive away from Dunedin. He obtained a gun permit in November 2017, a precondition for owning a firearm in New Zealand. He also bought himself a hunting rifle. In addition, he undertook weight training in the local gym, which he had joined.[61] He did not have a police record. At the start of the trial, he displayed a symbol of "white supremacy". He, who had never been in any army, conducted himself in

---

[59] Der Standard.at (2019), Nach E-Mail-Kontakt mit Sellner buchte Christchurch-Attentäter Mietauto in Österreich, 14th May, https://derstandard.at/2000103145053/Sellner-koennte-doch-mehr-mit-Christchurch-Attentaeter-zu-tun-gehabt?ref=rss.
[60] The Clover Chronicle (2019), Christchurch Shooter Reportedly Visited Pakistan Last Year, 17 March, https://cloverchronicle.com/2019/03/16/christchurch-shooter-reportedly-visited-pakistan-last-year-and-called-it-an-incredible-place-filled-with-the-most-earnest-kind-hearted-and-hospitable-people-in-the-world/.
[61] Nzherold.co.nz: Christchurch mosque shootings: Accused gunman Brenton Tarrant was a 'model tenant' in Dunedin, 18th March 2019, https://www.nzherald.co.nz/nz/news/article.cfm?c_id=1&objectid=12213826.

a martial demeanour and considered he was in a shooting war. During his deeds, he announced his fascination for religious conflicts in Europe and in the Balkans via livestream. The soundtrack he used on his trip to the mosques in Christchurch contains a song from radical Serbian Nationalists. They sang it during the War in Bosnia, which took place from 1992 to 1995. Amongst other things on his weapon, in Cyrillic lettering, he had written the names of historical Serbian and Montenegrin fighters and military personnel, which could only have been known by experts. This is also a parallel to Breivik, who similarly referred to the Balkan War in his manifesto time and again. He conducted an interview with himself in his manifesto, as Breivik had done. Like him, he was concerned with reaching a worldwide public—using an elaborate propaganda strategy. Tarrant posted a thread on 8chan in order to distribute his manifesto. In order to make his crime as prominent as possible, Tarrant filmed his deed using a helmet camera and transferred this live to the Internet. The video was 17 min long. Even though the video and Tarrant's Instagram profile were blocked by Facebook after a certain period of time, the video spread quickly by other means.

Tarrant considered himself an "Ethno-nationalist Eco-fascist," who did not belong to any group. In addition, he considered he had been selected, "to ensure the existence of our people and a future for white children." In his statement he considered the white populations of Australia and New Zealand to be European. He even pointed out proudly in his manifesto: "My parents are of Scottish, Irish and English stock." His comparing himself to Nelson Mandela also makes reference to his distinct narcissism. He likewise mentioned being released from prison after 27 years. Tarrant maintains that he was also once briefly in contact with Breivik. He received his "true inspiration" from the „Knight Justiciar Breivik". His farewell message to his like-minded followers read: "We will meet again in Valhalla." Like Breivik he was not an intellectual, but a person with a little knowledge gleaned from the Internet which he soaked up like a sponge. Tarrant does not appear to have been a true scatterbrain or idiot either. The meticulous planning tells us otherwise. At one point he argued he had selected certain firearms because he hoped to achieve a certain effect in the media in the United States and after this in the Rest of the World from them. He wished to further stir up the weapons debate in order to further intensify society's "social, cultural, political and racist divide."

His decision on a deed had been fixed two years prior to the attacks. The expert reports on him in the court case show to what extent mental disorders were evident or could be detected in Tarrant. His constant travelling could veil any possible conspicuous aspects. The statements in his manifesto—self-interviews, expecting a Nobel Peace Prize, a comparison to the South African civil rights campaigner Nelson Mandela, who later became president and a statesman honoured the world over—allow us to conclude he had similar symptoms to Breivik. Åsne Seierstad worked out numerous similarities here:[62]

- Not referring much to their respective homelands of Norway and Australia/New Zealand; focus on Europe (and the United States);
- Obsession with birth rates, accounts of Europe as growing weaker and older;
- Using symbols of the West for emphasising its nihilism and degeneracy
- Restoration of "traditional family values" (as Tarrant writes in his manifesto)
- Main agenda: crushing Muslim immigration;
- Manifesto as a "call to action";
- Self-interview using a Questions & Answers style as an indicator of narcissism.
- Mixing it with self-pity: Portraying themselves as "victims" with terms such as "invasion", "mass immigration" and "white genocide".

Personal frustrations enter into consideration. And thus, the traumatic experience with the drama surrounding the death of his father must be examined in more detail. The court case should start in May 2020. Similar to Breivik, Tarrant does not regret his deeds. The fanatic considers himself not guilty.

The type of assailant described in this section displays a particular tendency for narcissism. The actors would have been able to succeed in real life but lost the plot. A certain perfectionism was involved in planning the deed on the day. Franz Fuchs and John Ausonius remained undetected despite multiple deeds and atrocities. Both even played cat and mouse with the police. Their need for admiration ensured that the actors sought the widest possible effect on publicity. They clearly wished to change the spirit of society. Fuchs and Breivik both admitted in addition, that they had acted in the name of an organisation which did not exist. They wished for the largest possible effect in the media, Ausonius also spoke to journalists readily and freely.

---

[62] Åsne Seierstad: The Anatomy of White Terror, in: New York Times, 19 March 2019 (Opinion), https://www.nytimes.com/2019/03/18/opinion/new-zealand-tarrant-white-supremacist-terror.html.

3.3 Uprooted and Radical: Peter Mangs, Pavlo Lapshyn, David Sonboly

Right-wing radicals are normally connected to the fight against foreigners, dissidents and political opponents. This is why native people with nationalist mindsets come into question as actors. The following cases show that this estimation does not go far enough from time to time. Unsolved identity issues may be considered the key to explaining the unexplainable here. We know from Islamic terrorism, that alienation is precisely that which may decisively lead to radicalisation. Living between two worlds is not considered to be an enrichment by the individual, but as a burden or as the starting point for an inflammatory overidentification. Uprooted people laden with complexes yearn to be able to put down roots. They are driven by a special mercilessness, directed towards other uprooted people. Any feelings at all of consideration are alien to them. Ethnic minorities should be murdered especially treacherously.

The Swede Peter Mangs clearly became a racist and a threat to society, after living in the USA for a few years. Back in Sweden he committed a number of murders, which were not solved until years later. The court considered it proven, that Mangs then aged 31 had killed a 65-year-old male immigrant in his apartment on 13 June 2003. Likewise, he was found guilty of shooting at a 20-year-old Swedish woman on 10 October 2009. The grounds for the verdict informed us that this crime "bore the signs of an extreme lack of consideration and a complete lack of any compassion for other people." At the same time the court declared him "criminally liable and compos mentis," although he had been diagnosed as suffering from Asperger Syndrome.

As his parents had divorced at an early stage, Mangs grew up alone with his mother. He was very gifted musically and following high school he attended the jazz department of an adult education centre. He played in an Afro-Funk band, where his enthusiasm was sooner for the style of music than for the people behind it. Originally he had wanted to take up a study of the arts, as he was interested in philosophy and in Friedrich Nietzsche in particular. However, he was not able to realise his plans. We note here again that lone wolves suffer from the widest range of frustrating experiences, with their self-defined expectations left behind in tatters as a result.

Mangs then decided on an apprenticeship as a carpenter, in order to be able to build better musical instruments. He lived in the USA from 1996 to 1999 in order to give his career as a bass guitarist and instrument designer a boost. His father who had a nationalistic frame of mind also emigrated to the USA and became a member of the National Rifle Association (NRA) there. He taught his son how to handle weapons and introduced him to an environment of people knowledgeable about guns. Peter happened upon the Turner Diaries there, which obviously fascinated him. In his three years spent in Florida, he was unable to succeed as a musician, for example by recording an album. He turned his back on the "land of endless opportunities" in 1999 in order to train as a male nurse in Sweden.[63]

He found an apartment on the outskirts of Malmö. Apparently reintegrating into Swedish society was difficult for him, however. He developed a militant hatred of immigrants. He attracted attention in 2003, because he walked about the town centre wearing a military bulletproof vest. When darkness set in, he visited apartments and businesses where he suspected he could find migrants and intimidated them. In certain regards Mangs was a "serial terrorist" similar to John Ausonius, which is why a lot of parallels were drawn. Nevertheless, he never turned his back completely on a civic lifestyle, for example getting a job employed as a technical dental assistant. The police were finally able to trace him and arrest him in his apartment in November 2010, where they discovered numerous weapons. He was clearly planning further attacks.

The football star Zlatan Ibrahimović appears to have only narrowly escaped a violent assault. Mangs coincidentally spotted him parking his Ferrari illegally in Malmö. Inflamed with rage at this "Balkan behaviour" he quickly went and got a weapon. When he returned, however, Ibrahimović had already left.[64]

Mangs was never a member of any right-wing extremist organisation. However, he had subscriptions to several publications from the right-wing extremist spectrum and left xenophobic comments in Internet forums using a variety of usernames. Mangs considered himself to be a hero. He developed a regular schadenfreude or malicious delight around his terrifying and awful deeds and said in an interview: "It really does not take a lot. Look at the panic I caused, and I was just one individual person. A handful like that in the country, and the system collapses."[65]

A further peculiar reference case for this category is that of the 25-year-old Ukrainian Pavlo Lapshyn, himself an immigrant from the industrial city of Dnipro. Just after arriving as a seemingly ambitious postgraduate student at Coventry University in the West Midlands with a temporary employment visa at a software company in Great Britain, he mutated a blink of the eye he had

---

[63] Cf. Mattias Gardell: "Urban Terror: The Case of Lone Wolf Peter Mangs", in: *Terrorism and Political Violence*, 30 2018 (5), pp. 793–811.
[64] Cf. *The Guardian* (2015): https://www.theguardian.com/football/2015/may/11/swedish-gunman-nearly-shot-zlatan-ibrahimovic-bad-parkinguring.
[65] Cited according to ibid., p. 15.

merely felt into terrorism. After only 5 days on British soil, he murdered the 82-year-old Mohammed Saleem on 29 April 2013, whom he ambushed on his way back from a local mosque in Birmingham. A little later he detonated three homemade bombs in the vicinity of mosques. His last murderous assault would have certainly delivered hundreds of victims, if the faithful had not left an hour earlier because of Ramadan.[66]

Lapshyn occupied himself intensively with chemicals and bomb-making, as searches on his laptop later showed. He made no secret of his hatred for Muslims or his racism during court hearings. Moreover, he too never belonged to a criminal organisation, but was known to the Ukrainian authorities. Nevertheless, little is known about his former life in Ukraine, apart from the fact that he was the son of a high school teacher. Puzzles remain from this period.[67]

All the same his activities on social media must be assessed as indicators. Lapshyn read Russian texts on right-wing terrorists such as Timothy McVeigh and played a racist video game, which had been developed by American neo-Nationalists. He read the Turner Diaries enthusiastically and associated himself with the virtual realms of the network "Wotan Jugend – The Hammer of National Socialism".[68] Questioned about his motives, Lapshyn said he wished to intensify the "race war".[69]

Obvious it is significant for the radicalisation process, that people should feel uprooted and should already possess the potential for xenophobia, directed towards certain ethnic groups. By no means, must any assumption of a blitz or turbo radicalisation be made. The assailant had had too much relevant material for this.

An even more extreme case occurred in Germany. A young man with a background of migration, who was born and raised in Munich, whose parents had come to Germany as refugees, wished to become an "elite German", wishing to defend his fatherland. The teenager had never been in trouble with the police. His parents appeared to be integrated; his ambitious father ran a

---

[66] Cf. Matthew Goodwin: "'Lone wolves' such as Pavlo Lapshyn are part of a bigger threat" in: The Guardian, 23 October 2013, https://www.theguardian.com/commentisfree/2013/oct/23/pavlo-lapshyn-extremist-bomber-lone-wolves.

[67] Cf. Anton Shekhovtsov: "A transnational lone-wolf terrorist: the case of Pavlo Lapshyn", in: University College London, Research Blog, 21. November 2013, https://blogs.ucl.ac.uk/ssees/2013/11/21/a-transnational-lone-wolf-terrorist-the-case-of-pavlo-lapshyn/.

[68] Cf. The movement openly behaves as fascists and played a belligerent role in the conflict between Ukraine and Russia. Forbidden in Russia because of "activities hostile to the state", it is on the side of Ukraine.

[69] Cf. Matthew Goodwin: "'Lone wolves' such as Pavlo Lapshyn are part of a bigger threat" in: The Guardian, 23 October 2013, https://www.theguardian.com/commentisfree/2013/oct/23/pavlo-lapshyn-extremist-bomber-lone-wolves.

flourishing taxi business. His son, Ali Sonboly, was proud of his Persian roots and at the same time of having German nationality. But he did not wish to also show this outwardly: A few weeks prior to his murderous deed he insisted on only continuing to use his second given name, in order to not run the risk of being taken as an Arab. His father had already become aware that he was struggling with the name "Ali". The son was of the opinion, this concerned a "low" name for him. For example, he indicated a kebab shop, the name of which included "Ali" and had been unhappy about this.[70]

The father-son relationship was not entirely straightforward: Ali accused his hardworking father of driving the wrong car and of living in the wrong apartment and as a consequence had not achieved enough yet. He did not do very much together with his brother, four years his junior. His brother displayed blatantly aggressive behaviours, acting out his violent fantasies in games as well as at school on his friends. There were few activities together with his father too, but there were definitely several visits to Teheran, the last one in December 2015. At that time, they visited a sports hall in which a photograph was taken in the presence of his uncle who lived there, showing Ali firing a gun. The trainer in this Iranian sports centre praised him for his very good aim when firing the gun, which made the father and son proud to an equal extent.[71]

As a consequence of his strong desire to be considered as German, which is also clear from his changing his name, he developed a true hatred of other groups of immigrants, seeing himself as somewhat surrounded by "Kanak people" in the area of Munich he lived in. He changed his name from Ali to David on 6 May 2016—at a juncture when fine-tuning his plans for his murderous assault had long since commenced. We can only speculate, but it is clear that the assailant really wanted to be remembered in history books as David and not as Ali—in addition since he had made a firm decision to perpetrate the deed over a year previously.

Sonboly was accused by some of his fellow pupils of liking Adolf Hitler; however, there is no confirmation of this. He obviously provoked several of his fellow patients with his National Socialist symbols and phrases in the context of his admission to the psychiatric department of Harlach Hospital. And so, he is alleged to have repeatedly scrawled swastikas on his drawing pad and once gave a fellow patient a "Hitler salute" and to have shouted out "Sieg Heil". He also named himself "Running Amok Z" and wanted to

---

[70] Cf. Maik Baumgärtner/Martin Knobbe: „Rassistischer Terrorplan", in: *Der Spiegel*, No. 30, 2017, pp. 42–44.
[71] Cf. Britta Bannenberg: *Gutachten zum Fall von David S. für das Bayerische Landeskriminalamt*, Gießen, February 2018, p. 25.

be addressed in this way. According to witness statements, Sonboly was questioned as to whether he was a Nazi, which he is supposed to have answered in the negative. However, he stated to have found some of what Hitler achieved to be good. David S.' possible right-wing radical tendencies were also discussed in the context of treatment.[72]

With the benefit of hindsight, we can say that David Sonboly especially hated Turks, Albanians and Bosnians. He probably supported a pseudoscientific racist theory, which clearly still continues to play a role in young people originally from Iran. He searched the Internet for posts on Aryans. It may sound absurd at first appearance, but there are definitely connections and affinities from Iranians for National Socialism. The Iranian-American journalist Alex Shams, when casting a glance over David S. is able to detect here "an attempt by Iranians in the diaspora, to assimilate themselves, to stand out from other immigrants and to present themselves as associated as closely as possible with white Europeans. This attitude is really common in night-time chatroom forums, which are mainly used by young, male Iranian teenagers living in the diaspora, for example by David S."[73]

The journalist Charlotte Wiedemann, who published a book about the "new Iran", in addition recalled a connection between Iran under the Shah and National Socialism in the *Neue Zürcher Zeitung*. Influenced by nationalist thinking in Europe, Reza Shah Pahlavi dreamed up his Iran in the 1930s to be an ethnically homogenous Persian–Aryan nation. As a reward, Iranians were then excluded from the Nuremberg Race Laws by a decree from the "Third Reich" in 1936: as officially pure-blooded Aryans. Clearly many Iranians still follow this myth up until today and consider themselves to be in an especially close, even a blood relative's relationship to Germans. Moreover today's exaggerated Persian-ness strengthened the unholy alliance between Iran and National Socialism.[74]

On the anniversary, exactly 5 years after Breivik's attacks, the 18-year-old David Ali Sonboly set the City of Munich into uproar on 22 July 2016. Using the same weapon for his crime as Breivik, a Glock 17, he killed nine people before ending his own life.[75] What is conspicuous is: All his victims

---

[72] Cf. Bayerisches Innenministerium (2017): Antwort auf die Schriftliche Anfrage des Abgeordneten Florian Ritter (SPD-Fraktion im Landtag), Munich, July. Part I, p. 4

[73] Quoted according to Shahrzad Osterer: „Warum David S. Rassist war", in: Bayern 2 *Zündfunk* of 27 July 2017.

[74] Cf. Charlotte Wiedemann: „Das Selbstbild der Iraner. Achtet uns", in: *Neue Zürcher Zeitung* of 22 March 2017, https://www.nzz.ch/feuilleton/das-selbstbild-der-iraner-achtet-uns-ld.152699.

[75] Whether he really had planned his suicide as Bavarian officials accused him of, is questionable. A few days prior to his deed David S. had in any case even made an enquiry in person about available flights to Iran. Likewise it is dubious, whether he was really raised in an unremarkable home with

had an outwardly recognisable migratory background, six were young people aged between 14 and 17 years of age, two were young adults aged between 19 and 20. Three young people were of Turkish origin, in addition a 45-year-old Turkish woman was killed. Three other young people, a boy and two girls, were Kosovo Albanians. During his assault, Sonboly shouted loudly about his hatred of foreigners. Therefore, whilst shooting his last victim in the head, Dijamant Zabërgja who was originally from Kosovo, he shouted for example: "I am not a Kanak, I am German!"[76]

Precisely his choice of victims distinguishes right-wing terrorism. At the same time his political image of the world, an ideology of hatred, was not always logically constructed. Sonboly travelled to Istanbul as an adolescent and was fascinated by the city. And so, he told a chat partner during a WhatsApp Chat in April 2014, how nice the Turks are and how enchanting he found Istanbul to be. On the other hand, he used the Turkish flag in July 2017 and a panoramic image of Istanbul for a fake Facebook Account, in order to invite potential victims to the Olympia Shopping Centre and to increase the proportion of young people originally from Turkey at the location.

In real life Sonboly was isolated to the greatest extent. Like all lone wolves, he shut himself away to a great extent shortly before his deed. In the virtual world, he gave his phantasies of violence and hatred a free rein however and exchanged views with others. David S. concerned himself extensively with Breivik in his chats with an Afghani friend. He considered him to be a warning signal and a portent of a threatening mass immigration by Muslims to Europe, but also as a role model and as "a hero, who protected his nation." A further impressive piece of evidence: "David S. even chose the same time of day for his murderous act, early evening, in order to revere his idol Breivik."[77]

The suspicion that David Sonboly was impersonating Breivik, is not only evident, it positively imposes itself. The Bavarian Ministry of the Interior uttered their opinion on this: "According to a number of statements, David S. lauded the Norwegian assassin. The latter had been a type of role model for him. Whether this bears relevance to his murderous actions alone or also

---

his parents, as officials assumed. Nevertheless, his father's first reaction after the murders was that his business had now been ruined. In the *Bild newspaper* he subsequently portrayed himself as a victim.
[76] Cited after Andreas Förster: „Ein auffällig einsamer Wolf", in: *der Freitag* of 2017/41, https://www.freitag.de/autoren/der-freitag/ein-auffaellig-einsamer-wolf.
[77] Florian Sendtner: „Alles spricht für politischen Mord", in: *Bayerische Staatszeitung*, 13 October, 2017, p. 2.

towards the political attitudes of this assailant attributed as being a right-wing extremist and Islamophobic, remains open."[78] In response to a subsequent question they stated: "We can only assume, that David S. purposefully selected the date of the anniversary of Breivik's attack, our investigations did not deliver any concrete evidence for this."[79]

We can at least attribute one extreme right-wing ideology to Sonboly with certainty. According to chat protocols, he complained that "Munich was losing the steadfastness towards the cockroaches," and "everything was always determined by economic migrants, who call themselves refugees." He also left a "manifesto", which he had already written a year prior to his deed. *My revenge against those who have me on their conscience* is the title of the two-page exposition. The "tidal flood of refugees" was a thorn in his side, his Fatherland needed protecting. He circled the districts of Feldmoching-Hasenbergl and Milbertshofen on a map of the city, both districts with a proportion of around 50% of foreigners. In his writings he talks of a "virus", which had afflicted the "foreign subhumans" usually with "Turkish and Balkan roots."

With reference to the district of the city of Feldmoching-Hasenbergl, he wrote: "The foreign subhumans mainly with Turkish and Albanian roots rule through criminality and are responsible for destabilising this district of the city. They are of below-average IQ, are very aggressive and take absolutely no consideration of buildings, chemist's shops etc. The life expectancy for civilised people there is virtually zero."[80] Sonboly attached a second document to this text on the day of his deed. In the text he stored on his computer he wrote: "The bullying will pay for itself today. The harm that was done to me, what was done to me, will be returned." The name of the file is: "Now I will wipe out every German Turk no matter who.docx."[81] The State Prosecutor takes this point of reference to be the starting point, that we were dealing with spree killing by a victim of bullying. This false impression was clearly reinforced by a dialogue, which Sonboly delivers from an angry resident, who swore at him from his balcony of "Damned Turk". Sonboly shouted back: "I was bullied for seven years on account of arseholes like you. Now I will f**k all of you up!" Whoever knows the background, knows how this was meant.

---

[78] Bavarian Ministry of the Interior: Response to the written enquiry from the Delegate Katharina Schulze (Faction of Greens in Bavarian State Parliament): May 2017, p. 4.
[79] Ibid.
[80] Cited after Andreas Förster: „Ein auffällig einsamer Wolf", in: *der Freitag*, 2017/41, https://www.freitag.de/autoren/der-freitag/ein-auffaellig-einsamer-wolf.
[81] Cf. Jan Sternberg: Der Nazi aus dem Darknet, in: Dresdner Neue Nachrichten of 22 July 2017, http://www.dnn.de/Nachrichten/Politik/Der-Nazi-aus-dem-Darknet.

The assumption of an apolitical frenzied killing on grounds of bullying is a little lacking, in addition as there is very little evidence of this.

It is possible that actors were looking for scapegoats—in his case people with a migratory background. In general, he was annoyed by young women with "overly short skirts", although evidence proves that Sonboly, himself a Shiite Muslim, had a dislike of Islam. The liberal appearance of young people in McDonalds also disturbed him, which is why he did not invite his victims there entirely by coincidence.

In protocols of his chats with a clearly fictitious partner, Bastian, he wrote with regards to planning the deed he was preparing for, that supposedly different "Teams" were operating: "You will totally change Frankfurt and Offenbach. I wish the teams from Berlin and Stuttgart a lot of luck. I wish the teams from Berlin and Stuttgart a lot of luck." His partner Bastian responded to the suggestion of a vision of anti-Muslim acts of violence: "These two bombs going off [...] will even everything up. And I am doing this for my country, for Germany."

At another point he speaks of a "godlike fight" and of "Operation Munich cleansing".[82] To what extent this can be viewed as retribution for the bullying he suffered without any ideological background whatsoever, remains open.

David S. clearly related negative associations to the subsequent site of his assault, Munich's Olympic Shopping Centre (OEZ). The OEZ in München is considered to be a meeting point for people from immigrant families, who amongst other things come from Moosach—a part of the city with a high proportion of immigrants. Sonboly apparently spotted young people of Arab origins there, who were conspicuous against the older people there and amongst one another, which enraged him.

As compensation for his violent fantasies, the teenager who was addicted to computers made excessive use of computer games and violent games (such as Ego-Shooter, over 4,000 h of Counterstrike alone were on Steam), where he lived out his fantasies of the "superman". When doing so he used gaming names such as "Running Amok", "Dirty Bird and Shit Turkey" (in Cyrillic lettering), "Prophet 5 Godlike German", "Prophet of German Pride (AfD)" or "Executer GER".

He was also attending a psychotherapist because of his excessive gaming behaviour. His family was not allowed into his room, according to their own statements they knew nothing of his months of target practice in the cellar of the apartment building.

---

[82] Ibid.

He joined the "Anti-Refugee Club" on the online gaming platform Steam, which warned of a Muslim invasion of Europe and Germany and had 261 members at the time of his deed. The group apparently was formed as a reaction to New Year's Eve in Cologne in 2015/16. The group's description of themselves states: "Europe made the mistake, of allowing parasites in, who masquerade as 'Muslim refugees'. Chaos has reigned since the arrival of these migrants in Europe, and a large majority of Europeans are included in the 'Cucks',[83] and they have been brainwashed and manipulated in the media with sympathy for these parasites. If this mass invasion continues, then Europe as we know it will be destroyed. As we had to observe during the attacks on Paris in 2015, these immigrants can easily have the ability to become mass murderers and commit a massacre, which hundreds of innocent people fall victim to."[84]

The description of the contents also addresses the faked case of "Lisa", in which a Russian German girl was allegedly raped by a refugee in Germany, which subsequently turned out to be based on incorrect information. The contents fit the statements which David Sonboly for example uttered in a chat on 1 January 2016. He lamented, "if we think about it, we gave the terrorists a free ticket to travel to Germany."[85]

Numerous potential mass murderers were active in the Anti-Refugee Club, for example, the moderator of the group William Atchison or the Russian man, who moved to Poland and articulated his violent fantasies. In real life many of the statements uttered would have been punishable, for example, the holocaust denial rampant there and the link to adopting a hostile attitude towards refugees ("at that time you Germans also managed it"). There was one member of the group, who called himself „Gruppenführer SS" and there was a comment left under the heading "Fourth Reich, when."

In December 2017 Atchison then committed an assault himself on a school in New Mexico, finally taking his own life too. The 15-year-old David F. played a significant role in the network, which even adopted several accounts of David Sonboly's on Steam after the attack in Munich. David F. saw, that Atchison had been interested in people running amok. He asked him, whether he knew any other potential mass murderers in Germany, at

---

[83] Cucks, also Cuckold: This contemptuous expression refers to liberal men, who are themselves tricked by their wives.
[84] Original quote from the Steam platform's Anti-Refugee Club. The author has screenshots in his possession.
[85] Cited after Matthias Quent: *Hintergründe und Folgen des OEZ-Attentates, Gutachten für die Stadt München im Zuge einer Expertenanhörung*, Munich, October 2017, p. 31.

3 Offenders and Terrorism. Ideology, Motives, Objectives

which he referred him to the man in Munich.[86] The American, who had a large number of accounts and was the administrator for a variety of forums, also took care of Sonboly's admission into a virtual portrait gallery of right-wing assailants. This club continued to exist until September 2017, and thus long after the beacon in Munich.

Clearly, a murderous assault by David F. close to Ludwigsburg could only just be foiled in time. Amongst other things, police found a tactical response vest, evacuation plans for a high school, 350 rounds of small calibre ammunition, numerous knives and daggers, masking materials, notices and drawings with references to spree killings in his apartment. Apart from this, chemicals and objects for manufacturing explosive devices and pipe bombs were found in the cellar. Another potential spree killer was flushed out in Baden-Württemberg, likewise a youth, who attempted to build bombs along with David F.

The State Criminal Police Office in Stuttgart did not follow up the information from David F. to the man pulling the strings in the USA, Atchison, who put him in touch with Sonboly, nor did the Bavarian State Criminal Police Office as the leading authority in the investigation. The authorities did not consider David F. to be an accessory,[87] although expert witness Britta Bannenberg, employed by the Bavarian State Criminal Police Office (LKA) views this differently.[88] The investigators appear not to have caught up with the new reality yet. Nonetheless, David F. offered to distribute a possible manifesto for Sonboly ("I even told him specially, that he should send it to me because otherwise something like this will be delayed").[89]

They had obviously not even considered that such a network could exist secretly on Steam. With fatal consequences. The analysis of the environment and surroundings had a conservative regard for the real world, not extending progressively to virtual spaces and rooms, which were actually decisive. One could have quickly found out there what concerns comrades with right-wing mindsets: The 21-year-old Atchison had offensive neo-National Socialist tattoos on his body, believed in the superiority of the white race and appeared to

---

[86] Cf. Broadcast MDR ARD *Fakt* of 15 May 2018, report by Christian Bergmann, https://www.mdr.de/investigativ/video-197676_zc-f80c8d3a_zs-0fdb427d.html.

[87] Cf. Bavarian Minijstry of the Interior: Response to the written request from the Delegate Katharina Schulze (Faction of Greens in the State Parliament): May 2017; Broadcast ARD *Fakt* of 15 May 2018, reporter Christian Bergmann, https://www.mdr.de/investigativ/video-197676_zc-f80c8d3a_zs-0fdb427d.html.

[88] Cf. Britta Bannenberg: Expert report on the Case of David S. for the Bavarian State Criminal Police Office, Gießen, February 2018, p. 72.

[89] Screenshot of the discussion on Steam, which the author has to hand.

be enthusiastic towards Donald Trump.[90] And thus it is also incorrect here, to assess him as an apolitical spree killer (*'running amok'*).

During his preparations for the concrete deed, David S. displayed the new pattern for lone wolf terrorism, which simplifies the last step right down to implementation of the deed. Sonboly had, namely, acquired a pistol and large quantities of munitions on Darknet, where he paid with Bitcoin. At first, this party interested in a Glock appeared to run into a number of fraudsters. Finally, however, he found a right-wing extremist arms dealer, Philipp Körber.[91] Both met in person twice, for around 3 h each time in Marburg (a so-called "Real Life Meeting"). Sonboly cursed foreigners at both meetings. He told how he wished to enact his revenge on Turks, who had scratched his car and even told Körber, that he wished to blow away a couple of "Kanacks". The two of them were united by a right-wing extremist background as well as an affinity for terrorism.

Sonboly had no prior criminal convictions, was not a "person likely to threaten public safety" and in spite of years of mental treatment received continuous schooling—albeit with frequent changes. However, he did have the status of being an outsider or a loner, and according to statements from fellow pupils he was also bullied at school.[92] His hobbling gait from time to time was conspicuous, in addition he had a very Oriental appearance. A schoolfriend said, Ali wore "girls' clothes". In addition to this, his hobby was learning an extraordinary number of bus and train timetables off by heart and he also enjoyed reciting these.

However, there were also positive occasions; he was class spokesperson in Year 10, and also developed a special sense of ambition. He clearly also wanted to be the class clown. There were no longer any bullying events, which were only prevalent in one of the many different schools he attended. Shortly before carrying out his deed, he passed his driving test at the second attempt.

---

[90] *Daily Beast* (2017): "New Mexico School Shooter Had Secret Life on Pro-Trump White-Supremacy Sites", https://www.thedailybeast.com/new-mexico-school-shooter-had-secret-life-on-pro-trump-white-supremacy-sites.

[91] This commercial arms dealer, loser as well as militant right-wing extremist, who did not belong to any faction, but who also signed his posts in the forum with „Sieg Heil" was sentenced to seven years' imprisonment by Munich District Court because of culpable homicide in January 2018. It is the first time that an arms dealer on Darknet has not only been sentenced because of a weapon he sold, but also because of the deed this enabled. Cf. Martin Bernstein: „Amoklauf – oder Anschlag? (im Fall von David S.). Überblick über die wichtigsten Fragen", in: *Süddeutsche Zeitung*, 23/24 September 2017, p. 82.

[92] A fellow pupil stated in a witness statement, that he had bullied David S. He was charged because of an alleged assault on and physical injury to David S. in 2012. His parents then withdrew the charges, as the father told investigators under oath, after the aggressor's mother "invited us for a pizza, as if it were restitution. She wanted us to withdraw the charges, in order to prevent detrimental consequences for her son and the other children."

David Sonboly received inpatient medical treatment, suffered from anxiety attacks, phobias and depression. He had even been diagnosed as having autism as a small child.[93] He took antidepressants and was scared of the existence of a "virus" and a "matrix".

The accused also continuously expressed suicidal thoughts and made statements, allowing us to conclude aggression towards third parties, in particular against young people with south-east European migratory origins, who he held responsible for the bullying. All the therapists, however, negated his being a risk to himself or others. Clearly, David S. also experienced a form of exaggerated lovesickness. He got to know the girl M. at a martial arts course in 2013. In the records of the discussion he held with himself we find: "I will never be able to forget her."[94] He obviously also stalked her, she wanted nothing to do with him. He also attempted to approach her using fake accounts.

During his target practice in the basement of his apartment building[95] Sonboly worked himself up with xenophobic tirades, as a video shows. He cursed German-Turks as Salafists and cockroaches, shouting that the AfD (the parliamentary party 'Alternative for Germany') would eliminate them in Germany. The desire on the one hand to be regarded as a "true German", and the easy accessibility to radical ideas and people with similar mindsets on the other hand, still do not conclusively explain why a young person should decide to walk through Munich with a firearm and shoot people. However, the long process of radicalisation is easy to follow in this case. And so, he spent his time intensively on actors and victims of acts of violence, not only on the Internet, but also through actual personal visits. He travelled to Winnenden twice, in order to examine the site of the spree killing at that time by Tim K. in more detail. Ali Sonboly visited the grave of *Tuğçe Albayrak* who had Turkish origins in Offenbach on 25 May 2015. According to witness statements, the subsequent spree killer David S. made repeated disparaging statements about the female student and made fun of her death.[96] We can read of his hatred of Turks in his perfidious plan for 22 July 2016. Using a fake Facebook account, he pretended to be a Turkish girl from Hessen, in

---

[93] Infantile autism describes a form of autistic disorder, which typically manifests itself before the age of three and is especially prevalent in the fields "social interaction, communication and stereotype behavioural patterns." Cf. Kai Vogeley: *Anders sein. Autismus-Spektrum-Störungen im Erwachsenenalter*, Basel 2016, p. 119.

[94] Maik Baumgärtner/Martin Knobbe: Rassistischer Terrorplan, in: Der Spiegel, No. 30, 2017, pp. 42–44, here p. 42.

[95] According to testimonies, his parents and neighbours knew nothing about this.

[96] Cf. Bayerischer Rundfunk: David S. visited Tugce's grave prior to his deed, 19 July 2017, https://www.br.de/nachrichten/amoklauf-muenchen-tugce-100.html.

order to invite "friends" to the McDonalds Restaurant in the OEZ on the day of his attack.

The general assessment was soon fixed by the impression of messages from officials and the police. David S. "would fit the pattern of a conspicuous psychopathological loner, who had developed a bundle of motives of rage, hatred and thoughts of revenge, with no rational justification."[97] What was supposedly missing from his deed as a terrorist attack, was an ideological content. The Bavarian State Criminal Police Office made a clear judgment in its final report in March 2017 and firmly decided this had been a spree killing (*amok*): "Also, we may not assume that the deed was politically motivated."[98] This appraisal follows a popular psychological approach, which often negates a genuine interest in politics. All too often, instead of searching for political socialisation and radicalisation, the search is sooner for "personal needs".[99]

A lot is missed in this way. The Bavarian Intelligence Services Office issued a clear statement itself, which permits it to invoke itself against an allocation of an assailant running amok: "Sonboly's victims all had migratory backgrounds. And in this way his choice of victims appears to entirely match deeds perpetrated by right-wing extremists. The consequence of this was that few public opinions spoke of a murderous assault motivated by right-wing terrorism or xenophobia. In actual fact it is unlikely, that Sonboly's victims were purely coincidental victims: According to everything we know about him prior to this, although the victims were not known to Sonboly by any means at all and appeared to have been gathering at the site of the deed purely by coincidence. However, the actor appears to have selected victims according to visible facial characteristics. Contrary to most youthful actors running amok in spree killings, who in general take their revenge on fellow pupils, for example by returning to their former school, Sonboly took his 'revenge' on people who possibly visibly matched his personal, albeit generalised image of his enemies from the bullying he had suffered in the past."[100]

One may transcend these careful findings by the Intelligence Services: The actor very probably knew that some of his victims regularly met at McDonalds at about this time. He had observed this. All of his victims came from

---

[97] Cited after Solveig Bach: Kaum zu trennen. Was Amokläufe von Terror unterscheidet, in: n-tv.de of 25 July 2016, https://www.n-tv.de/panorama/Was-Amoklaeufe-von-Terror-unterscheidet-article18268756.html.

[98] Bavarian State Criminal Police Office: Ermittlungen zum Münchener Amoklauf abgeschlossen, Medieninformationen, Munich 2017, p. 2.

[99] Cf. John Horgan: The Psychology of Terrorism, London/New York 2014, p. 89.

[100] Bavarian Intelligence Services Office: Preliminary Initial Assessment, 7 December 2016, Munich.

immigrant families. The choice of victims is evidence of a prejudicial character and the political dimension of his deed.[101] Also the location which he chose in the end, has a symbolic effect at a second glance: "McDonaldisation" is considered as a symbol for cultural equalisation. Right-wing extremists on the other hand wish to stand for something culturally "of a higher value."

Why the intelligence services do not address the xenophobia and hatred towards certain ethnic groups, is not developed here. The evaluation has the effect of being badly put together, almost schizophrenic, wishing on the one hand to recognise a right-wing extremist point of view, on the other hand apolitical running amok and spree killing. Clearly, the deed was supposed to be depoliticised and therefore belittled, as it is not been established as a politically motivated criminal offence and does not appear in the intelligence service's report. A subsequent expert's report surfacing in May 2018 also speaks in favour of this, which the State Criminal Police Office entrusted the spree killing researcher Britta Bannenberg to cover. She does not detect a right-wing extremist in David S., it was established that he did not have any contact to right-wing actors and she considers his lovesickness as the trigger for his terrible deed—with a view to the girl he once got to know at a martial arts course.[102] And in this way Bannenberg still goes over and above the officials' opinion, who considered a case of bullying at school as decisive.

As a teenager David Ali Sonboly was by no means an apolitical person—quite the opposite. He spent his time on international political relationships and geostrategic considerations. It was soon clear to fellow pupils, that he always had radical solutions for political problems in the world, such as a war, for example. He was interested in politics and sympathised with the contents of the programme of the AfD Party. In a familial context he once said he had been to an AfD rally in Erfurt and wanted to vote for the AfD as soon as he was old enough to vote.

Whoever looks at all of Sonboly's statements together and in a political context will spot and will unavoidably recognise extremist thinking and an extremist philosophy. He acknowledges his pride whilst including the Persian Aryan chain of thought, of being an Aryan and a German. He chose himself for the purpose of saving his "Fatherland" of Munich, where he is supposed to have detected "super alienation". He was carrying out the assaults for his country, for Germany, he wrote in a chat.

---

[101] Cf. Matthias Quent: *Hintergründe und Folgen des OEZ-Attentates, Gutachten für die Stadt München im Zuge einer Expertenanhörung*, Munich, October 2017, pp. 6–8
[102] Cf. Britta Bannenberg: Expert's report on the Case of David S. for the Bavarian State Criminal Police Office, Gießen, February 2018.

Like Peter Mangs, David Sonboly also showed no compassion for his victims, perhaps also contingent on their autistic personality traits. The actors were never members of a right-wing extremist organisation or party; however, they had deep-seated hatred towards other groups. This is astonishing at first glance, as they had connections to different regions of the world. Mangs had gotten to know a multicultural society in the USA; Lapshyn had the opportunity to continue his development as a successful IT specialist in Great Britain. Sonboly considered Munich to be his fatherland, without denying his Iranian origins. The feeling of being uprooted, interlinked with an insidious radicalisation however, may clearly lead to people becoming criminal assailants.

3.4 Young and Fascist: David Copeland, Pekko Auvinen and Anton Petterson

Young people are often especially susceptible to extremist ideologies. They often appropriately become assailants and murderers through the opportunities in society today. Young fascists, in this regard, is one actor's profile for lone wolf actors. He succumbs to his violent fantasies, dreams of race war and proclaims himself the godlike judge of life and death. The enactment is a significant impetus; likewise, going down in the annals. This has not just been the case since Breivik.

David Copeland, who was 24 years of age at the time of his deed, transposed Great Britain into a state of uproar in April 1999. He carried out three nail bomb attacks in London within a matter of days. Three people lost their lives, numerous others were injured. This Briton had migrants, people with black skin and homosexuals in his sights. Accordingly, he committed the attacks in districts of the city inhabited by a lot of black people, in Brixton and in Brick Lane, where many Asian and Oriental people live. Over and above this, he planned an attack on a pub, which was predominantly frequented by homosexuals. The goal which he did not further realise was clearly an expression of his own frustration: Copeland, who had never had a girlfriend, feared he was homosexual himself. He visited prostitutes, where he dreamed of being a large, blond SS officer and of exercising power.

Copeland was raised working-class and had a difficult relationship with his parents, who divorced when he was 19. Psychiatrists determined he had an above-average IQ, but also noticed that he had remained well below his level of opportunities. He did not finish his training as an electrician. This also had to do with his own noticeable psychological problems, such as panic attacks for example, which he attended a doctor for. His consumption of alcohol and drugs characterised his life.[103] He compensated for his own psychological problems through his ideology. Copeland was a supporter of Combat 18 and allowed himself to be inspired by the Turner Diaries when proclaiming the race war. It would be misguided, to merely mention a psychiatric disorder here.

Copeland made no secret of his political views, as he set down on record during the police interviews following the attacks: "I am a National Socialist or Nazi, whatever you wish to call me. I believe in a master race; I believe in race and one's own country first, with the white race as dominant and a dominant Aryan race worldwide."[104] He was frank and free in mentioning not only that he wished to trigger a race war, but that he wished to go down in the annals as a lone wolf actor. Apparently no one had been informed about his plans.[105] During his arrest, investigators found National Socialist paraphernalia and propaganda in his apartment as well as a collection of newspaper cuttings with reports of the attacks. We also see here how important repercussions in the media were to the actor—a typical characteristic of terrorism.

Copeland had made contact with the right-wing scene. Thus, he joined the extreme right-wing British National Party; there is a photo showing him alongside the founder of the party John Tyndall. Later he affiliated himself to a neo-National Socialist organisation.[106] However, his inability to integrate himself evidently also raised its head there, which caused any form of attempts to latch on to fail in the medium-term. It is a decisive characteristic of lone wolves, that they try to make friends or find an affiliation but are not able to do so. Their personality is too narcissistic for them to integrate themselves into hierarchies and structures. Even the strength of the ideology itself is not sufficient for this. Frustrated, in the end they turn away from all groups, and become loners, who wish to strike out on their own.

Copeland did not have a police record. The question of his legal culpability sparked a violent debate between experts. A majority of psychiatrists detected paranoid schizophrenia, which would have reduced his legal culpability. The Public Prosecutor and also the jury did not, however, go along with this assessment. In the end, Copeland was sentenced to six counts of

---

[103] Cf. "The happy, loveable lad who grew up a hate-filled loner", in: *The Telegraph* of 1 July 2000, https://www.telegraph.co.uk/news/uknews/1345914/The-happy-loveable-lad-who-grew-up-a-hate-filled-loner.html.
[104] Cited after Ramón Spaaij: *Understanding Lone Wolf Terrorism. Global Patterns, Motivations and Prevention*, Heidelberg et al. 2012, p. 43.
[105] Cf. BBC news (2000): "Profile: Copeland the killer", http://news.bbc.co.uk/2/hi/uk_news/781755.stm.
[106] Ibid.

life imprisonment. The level of proceedings demonstrates the difficulty of adequately understanding the apparent mental and emotional disorders and the political motives of lone wolves. The culpability is usually attested, the philosophy is not explicitly punished.

Another especially young actor was the 18-year-old Finn Pekka-Eric Auvinen, who murdered eight people in a school and then killed himself on 7 November 2007. Prior to his deeds he uploaded a wealth of material to the Internet, including photos and videos of himself. He gave his document the title "Attack information". In it, he described his murderous deed as mass murder and political terrorism: "Although I chose a school as my goal, my motives are political and much deeper seated; therefore, I do not wish my attacks to be described as a school shooting."[107]

So-called "School Shootings" have become a mass phenomenon since the middle of the 1990s, from the United States via the Western world right through to countries such as Brazil, Argentina or Turkey. We are usually dealing with people running amok here, in which young people or young adults commit acts of excessive violence and attacks on schools, which they attend or once attended, seeking revenge for injustices supposedly suffered. Well over 100 of such types of acts of violence have been committed worldwide, wherein some stand out especially. Right-wing extremist motives usually only have a secondary importance with this form of individual violence, personal sensitivities dominate. National Socialism stands, if at all, rather for a code which includes generally violent fantasies and a revulsion of mankind.

Auvinen must, however, sooner be allocated as a right-wing radical actor than as someone running amok. The following underlying social Darwinist justification can also be found in his letter of acknowledgement: "I am a cynical existentialist, anti-humanist humanist, realistic idealist and a godlike atheist. I am prepared to fight and to die for my goals. I (…) will eliminate everyone, who proves themselves to be worthless, as a disgrace to the human race and as drop outs through natural selection (…) It is time, to allow Natural Selection and the Survival of the Fittest to take effect again."[108]

The contents of his manifesto clearly show that the actor was well-versed in philosophy and political ideology. Many people from his surrounding area confirmed his great passion for politics, describing him as a searcher. As early as eleven years of age he was interested in politics in general, ever increasingly he turned himself towards the more radical phenomena: first of all, to the

---

[107] Pekka-Eric Auvinen: Attack information, 2007, http://oddculture.com/the-pekka-eric-auvinen-manifesto/ (called up on 20 April 2018).

[108] Cited after Britta Bannenberg: *Amok. Ursachen erkennen – Warnsignale verstehen – Katastrophen verhindern*, Gütersloh 2010, p. 55.

Communist Party of Finland, then to the North Korean political system and finally to National Socialism. During the course of 2007, he started hatching his murderous plan and latching on to the ideology.

He wrote in his diary, that he wanted to leave something behind against the humaneness of the world with one single act. He continued writing his manifesto throughout his last 6 months. Auvinen studied a great deal of right-wing terrorists and school shooters, as a homemade video clarified. This underpins the assertion that lone wolves search for role models, even in order to elevate themselves and to set themselves on the same level as "successful" actors. In this case, they are always concerned with the effect in public: He also published his messages in English, in order to achieve a greater range.[109]

The Swede Anton Lundin Pettersson similarly chose a school as the site for his deed. He appeared at the school wearing a Second World War helmet and a black cloak on 22 October 2015, which was supposed to remind people of the figure "Darth Vader" from "Star Wars" films. The pupils at first took him to be a figure of fun, however, the 21-year-old then stabbed a 12-year-old pupil to death, then the classroom assistant Lavin Eskander—with both of them coming from a migratory background. Further pupils and teachers were injured. The school is situated in a district with a lot of migrants living in it. The actor who was described as being reserved had visited right-wing extremist groups on social media, which venerate Adolf Hitler and the Third Reich. This also becomes apparent from his YouTube page. He was not a member of any organisation at all; however, he backed a petition from the populist right Swedish Democrats to initiate a referendum on immigration.

He considered himself to be part of the movement against migrants. He put likes under various posts on Facebook for contributions to debates by the party chairman of the populist right Swedish Democrats, Jimmie Åkesson and under videos of the YouTuber "Angry foreigner", a blogger hostile to immigration. A native Bosnian was concealed behind the pseudonym, who moved to Sweden when he was five years of age. Evidently, Petterson psyched himself up with the video "Nazi Generator 2015", which has German marching music as a backing track and calls for "gas chambers".[110] His deed proved to be a puzzle to the general public. Frustration with his school can be ruled out.

---

[109] Cf. Leena Malkki: "Political Elements in Post-Columbine School Shootings in Europe and North America", in: Jeffrey Kaplan/Heléne Lööw/Leena Malkki (eds.): *Lone Wolf and Autonomous Cell Terrorism*, London/New York 2015, pp. 185–210, here p. 198 f.; Atte Oksanen/Johanna Nurmi/Miika Vuori/Pekka Räsänen, Pekka: Jokela: "The Social Roots of a School Shooting Tragedy in Finland", in: Nils Böckler/Thorsten Seeger/Peter Sitzer/Wilhelm Heitmeyer (eds.): School *Shootings: International Research, Case Studies and Concepts for Prevention*, New York 2013, pp. 189–215.

[110] *The Local.se*: "Who was Sweden's school sword killer", 23 October 2015, https://www.thelocal.se/20151023/who-was-swedens-far-right-school-killer-in-trollhattan.

In the end, the Swedish police described his deed as a "carefully organised, racist hate crime by a young man who methodically selected his victims."[111] Easy access to appropriate material, precisely through the internet and mutual instigation in the context of the dangerous current societal debate on "super alienation" may easily have had devastating consequences.

Copeland and Auvinen considered themselves to be godlike, measuring themselves by undertaking a social Darwinist selection according to their gusto. They justified their deeds with the conditions in society. On the cusp of becoming adults, the actors mentioned sought stability in fascist ideology. Auvinen in particular appeared reflective and had great philosophical depth. His excess of violence was planned with the greatest precision possible. Strong images of the enemy were quite obviously needed to unleash his violence, on the basis of resistant ideologies such as racism, which suppress the humanness of victims.[112]

Auvinen and Pettersson could also be considered to have run amok in killing sprees. They selected their school as the setting for their massacre, planned their own suicides, which is typical for such events. However, they had a political message, as Auvinen expressly stated. They experienced their political radicalisation in virtual spaces. Pettersson expressly targeted people with migratory backgrounds. In this comparison, they are comparable with other lone wolves with right-wing extremist motives such as Breivik or Sonboly.

3.5 Significance of Observing Individuals for the Overall Picture

"What type of people are these, who could do such a thing?", the observer often asks himself for attacks by lone wolves. We have now seen the development of a few of them and must say that these are very different people, but who do display a number of significant commonalities. Almost all of the actors had a disturbed relationship to their own sexuality or to the opposite sex, feeling as though they had been rejected. Many were social failures. Relevant literature, in particular the Turner Diaries, was found in almost all their homes. In many cases, the actors attempted to go for treatment and to receive

---

[111] Cited after Matthias Quent: *Hintergründe und Folgen des OEZ-Attentates. Gutachten für die Stadt München im Zuge einer Expertenanhörung*, Munichen, October 2017, p. 20.

[112] Cf. Vincenz Leuschner: „"School-Shootings" und "Lone Wolf Terrorism" als soziale Phänomene", in: *Berliner Journal für Soziologie*, 23 (2013) 1, p. 40.

therapy. Certainly, mental health issues are an important factor when we are trying to determine the types of actor.[113]

All the actors acted mercilessly and ruthlessly. Their crimes show this, which ranged from knife attacks right through to bomb-making. All the attacks were planned over a lengthy period, some even for years. By no means spontaneous actions can be inserted into the overall picture of terrorism, in which victims are merely regarded as nothing more than a number. Right-wing extremism predominantly targets people with migratory backgrounds by proxy. We are able to observe this victim profile with all of the actors. Political objectives were present in all cases, and were almost always distinct, even when they were not always assessed as such.

Whoever is concerned with right-wing extremist terrorists, will see the manner of appearance of the extremes and attitudes, which are simply not prepared to compromise.[114] As the people described proceed along the lines of "One against all", in the spirit of Hannah Arendt, they act out an "Extreme form of violence".[115] Extremist thinking often has already been formulated during their adolescence. Factors for this are foolishness, a spirit of adventure, lack of drive, a lack of tolerance, problems with their own ego after discovering their sexuality, a lack of perspective and lack of enthusiasm and then even constructing a parallel world through excessive use of the computer. Usually, the phase of a lack of orientation is of limited duration.

In Franz Fuchs, Frank Steffen and Thomas Mair however we are also able to observe that a lack of perspective during middle age may promote extremism. This type of lack of objective is not related to age. Depression and destructive intentions against whatever is held as being responsible for the personal plight. With David Copeland, Peter Mangs, Anders Breivik or Brenton Tarrant an ideologically based extremism was evident, which may be considered to be the most demanding form. Ideology fulfils the role of a quasi-religion, slavish obedience towards dogmatic ideas taking the place of personal responsibility. What is more, a rigid philosophy of life is a description of one's own emotional state, in a gloomy actual mood, riddled with destructive scenarios and conspiracy theories. The individual imagines he is part of a real or fictitious movement, with the objective of attacking other ethnic groupings or representatives of the democratic state or even of destroying them.

---

[113] Cf. Paul Gill/Emily Corner: There and Back Again: The Study of Mental Disorder and Terrorist Involvement, in: American Psychologist, 72 (2017), pp. 231–241.
[114] Cf. Barbara Zehnpfennig: „Extremes Denken", in: Uwe Backes/Alexander Gallus/Eckhard Jesse (eds.): *Jahrbuch Extremismus & Demokratie*, 25th year, 2013, pp. 40–44.
[115] Cf. Hannah Arendt: *On Violence,* Orlando et al. 1970.

Evidently very different causes may be responsible for an extreme right-wing mindset being able to emerge and come into being:

> - *Characteristics relating to personality*: Bullying, failure at school or at work, emotional disintegration for example because of one's upbringing, social phobias, autism and depression
> - *Social Characteristics*: Right-wing extremism as an offering granting a sense of meaning; disintegration processes for people; participatory effect in virtual environments and chatrooms; the wish to "imitate" previous frenzied killings or terrorist actions
> - *Political characteristics*: processes of change through immigration, offerings from extremist right-wing organisations, for example parties; dissatisfaction with the programmes of established parties; the attractiveness of blogs and chats in the spirit of "human captivation" and a cultivation of conspiracy theories

All actors "isolated themselves" at the latest during the concrete planning phase. The schizoid personality disorder applies to all types of actor here. According to the general classification scheme, this is distinguished by a withdrawal from affective, social and other contacts with excessive preferences for phantasy, solitary occupations and an inwards-facing restraint. Only a limited ability exists to express feelings and to experience friendship.[116] Persons concerned lack empathy, the ability to put themselves in someone else's position, to understand their socially opposite number's attitudes and arguments. They are narcissists, with reference to everything and they think they are the originator for everything which is going on around them. Criticism is perceived as being a personal attack. Nothing happens detached from their own person. The tendency is for actors to sooner have an inclination towards hidden instead of open narcissism. The first form is characterised by an inner emptiness and feelings of futility, the latter by a rebellious attitude, paired with impatience. Both forms nevertheless are closely connected to loneliness.[117]

A wealth of personality disorders was able to be determined in all of these people, which can be inserted into the current common dimensional model.[118] The same is also true for other lone wolf terrorists, for example, the "Unabomber" Theodore Kaczynski. Psychiatrists uncovered paranoid

---

[116]Cf. Helmut Remschmidt/Martin Schmidt/Fritz Poustka (Hrsg.): *Multiaxiales Klassifikationsschema für psychische Störungen des Kindes- und Jugendalters nach ICD-10 of the WHO*, Bern 2012, p. 251.
[117]Cf. Hans-Werner Bierhoff/Michael Jürgen Herner: *Narzissmus – die Wiederkehr*, Bern 2011, p. 152.
[118]Cf. based on Peter Fiedler/Sabine C. Herpertz: *Persönlichkeitsstörungen*, Weinheim/Basel 2016, p. 30.

schizophrenia during his trial. The terrorist believed he was defined by modern technologies. He had personal fantasies of being a woman (which is why he once considered a sex change). He attributed the blame for these phantasies to his parents.[119]

The personal style of the individual deviates, some characteristics can be especially attributed to certain people. In part these were also diagnosed by medical professionals:

Personal style	Personality disorders
Conscientious, careful	Compulsive (Mair, Fuchs)
Ambitious, self-assured, considers himself (egotistical)	Narcissistic (Ausonius, Breivik, Sonboly, Tarrant)
Watchful, considered	Paranoid (Steffen, Ausonius, Breivik, Copeland)
Emotional	Lacking in empathy (Breivik)
Volatile, spontaneous	Borderline (Ausonius, Traini)
Adventure-loving, risk seeker	Antisocial (Mair, Fuchs)
Reticent, shy, loner	Strong schizoid characteristics (Mair, Steffen, Fuchs)
Reflective, sensitive	Oversensitive, extremely touchy and very vulnerable (Fuchs, Sonboly, Auvinen)
Critical, hesitant	Passive-aggressive (Mair, Steffen, Ausonius, Sonboly)
Self-critical, careful, an avoider	Not self-assured (Fuchs, Steffen, Auvinen, Pettersson)
Convincing, equipped with a sales talent ("a player"), vain	Manipulative, traits of a megalomaniac, fanatical, a grumbler, know-all, "bluffer" (Ausonius, Breivik, Tarrant)

Even if neo-Nazis are often perceived publicly as being unintelligent thugs, none of the lone wolves described here were "stupid" or simple-minded, all were of average, from time to time even above-average intelligence. The conclusion that "entirely normal people became mass murderers"[120] would however be inappropriate. Their life histories are too peculiar for this. It is simply the case, that they were all "homegrown", which means they were socialised in our societies, were born and grew up in Western countries. This sets them apart them from many Islamic fighters.

---

[119] Ramón Spaaij: *Understanding Lone Wolf Terrorism. Global Patterns, Motivations and Prevention*, Heidelberg et al. 2012, p. 51.
[120] Cf. Harald Welzer: *Täter. Wie aus ganz normalen Menschen Massenmörder werden*, Frankfurt/Main 2005.

There were alarm bells in each man's biography. The people even deviated from the norm from time to time as early as whilst small children, for example after being diagnosed with autism. For example, this is true for Breivik and Sonboly. Frank Steffen came from an antisocial family and was raised by foster parents. A negative self-image developed in childhood and during adolescence, with Copeland for example. He assessed his self as incompetent. The actors in general come from a conspicuous family home. All of them had a disturbed image of women and were unable to become involved in a relationship. Hatred resulted from this from time to time. In the personal domain, many starting points can be found in each of the actors for grievances and a non-existent ability to empathise: the often broken family home, the lack of any ability to form social relationships or a relationship with a partner, a lack of job perspectives and illnesses which are diagnosed such as autism, depression or obsessive-compulsive disorders. The psychiatrist Norbert Nedopil consistently observes that terrorist single actors lack a social resonance in their biography over a lengthy period, with setbacks and grievances, right through to autistic delimitation.[121] They are socially isolated, a finding, the extent of which can, for example, be measured using questionnaires. Social Isolation is then indicated by the following factors, which refer less to objective contents, but to subjective experiences, which of course apply to many actors[122]:

- unmarried, no sexual intercourse
- little contact to children
- little contact to family members
- contact with friends less than once a month
- no participation in neighbourhood communities, religious communities or voluntary activities for example in clubs or associations

Whoever reduces their deeds to the psychological aspects, however, is not going far enough. Mental illness does not cause lone wolf terrorism. The following calculation was made for the USA: The USA had 308 million inhabitants in 2010, with an estimated 60 million suffering from mental illness. Only three were lone wolf terrorists. The chance of getting hit by lightning is estimated as being 1 in 700,000. The chance of a mentally ill person committing lone wolf terrorist acts is somewhere in the vicinity of 1 in 20 million.[123]

---

[121] Norbert Nedopil: „Gekränkte Eitelkeiten. Terroristische Einzelkämpfer", in: *Forensische Psychiatrie, Kriminologie*, 8 (2014) 4, pp. 246–253.
[122] Cf. Manfred Spitzer: Einsamkeit. Die unerkannte Krankheit, Munich 2018, p. 28f.
[123] Cf. Mark S. Hamm/Ramón Spaaij: The Age of Lone Wolf Terrorism, New York 2017, p. 54 f.

There is even another dimension as an important explanatory factor: the ideology of hatred, which not only motivates, but in the end also has a triggering effect for the deed. The actors engage themselves in self-psychology with the backgrounds of people running amok (*spree killers*) and terrorists. There is an "autodidactic element of lone wolf terrorism."[124] The expert textbook „*Amok im Kopf. Warum Schüler töten*" by the American psychologist Peter Langman was found in David Sonboly's room, which is considered to be a scientific reference work for this phenomenon.

Socially excluded people wish to exclude others themselves, not only denigrating people out of racist motives, but murdering them in cold blood or treacherously. The actor is not a patient, sitting in the treatment room, but someone who has assumed the right to kill out of political motivation. Whoever declares him to simply be mentally ill, is not taking his deed seriously.[125] Nonetheless, the tenet holds for them as for other terrorists that they "carried out their campaigns of terror with clear objectives, tenacity and commitment [...] traits, which are entirely atypical for psychopaths."[126] They act without scruples, fearlessly and focussed. Their targets are multidimensional. Thus, they direct their terrible murderous attacks not only against a broad public, but also against like-minded people, possible copycat actors. They are concerned about attention and their posthumous reputation. Thus, David Sonboly stated in a chat 7 months before his deed (a discussion was held concerning terrorists and Breivik): "If we look more closely, we will see that these people were simply running amok (for *spree killings*). They were not doing this because of IS. They were simply seeking attention [...] However, it is certainly also the fear of the terrorists. Everything has its reason for the respective persons. The most they will gain from this is attention."[127] We can clearly detect here what the actors think beyond mere acts of violence and random acts.

Actors wish to create a new consciousness for political subjects with their deeds, implementing an aggressively cleansing policy, excluding migrants and protecting native people. There are National Socialist beliefs in the structural support framework of their philosophy of life, teachings of the supposed superiority of the white race and above all a systematic denigration of ethnic minorities. Narcissistic patterns have their equivalent in this way. Numerous

---

[124] Ramón Spaaij: *Understanding Lone Wolf Terrorism. Global Patterns, Motivations and Prevention*, Heidelberg amongst others 2012, p. 99 f.
[125] Cf. Klaus Theweleit: *Das Lachen der Täter: Breivik u.a. Psychogramm der Tötungslust*, St. Pölten amongst others 2015, p. 13.
[126] Peter Waldmann: *Terrorismus, Provokation der Macht*, Munich 1998, p. 153.
[127] Cited after Britta Bannenberg: *Gutachten zum Fall von David S. für das Bayerische Landeskriminalamt*, Gießen, February 2018, p. 8.

actors have for example been inspired by the Turner Diaries and the desire to trigger a race war.

The "personal, individualised grievance ideology" characterises lone wolf terrorism: Personal frustrations and grievances produce a deadly cocktail when mixed together with political attitudes and a right-wing extremist ideas structure encapsulates, including conspiracy theories. Precisely the polarising subject of migration in Europe motivates the single actor, to allow their hatred free rein on other ethnic groups and to set an example as a warning. Whether in Austria, Great Britain, Sweden or Germany—in the countries where assailants struck home, where actors let fly in rage, in order to set an example, specially kindled by migrants. Therefore, it would be incorrect here, to disregard the societal context, especially as one general development can be regarded as a recruitment pool: in many places an era of narcissism is called into life. Psychologists recognise not only a rapid increase in depressive illnesses, but also of narcissistic personality disorders.[128]

It becomes apparent to us: Actors underwent a lengthy process of radicalisation; this does not set in overnight. In their own realities, actors are of course acting with self-regulation and consciously with an eye on the consequences. For years and years, they developed a political "image of the enemy," which they are attempting to fight against using terrorist means. A single actor such as Thomas Mair clearly dreamed for a long time of such a step, a Breivik planned his deeds for almost a decade. With actors such as Breivik, Auvinen and Sonboly the toolbox is opened especially wide in virtual rooms and spaces, from instructions on radicalisation through to realisation. Many actors were inspired by the Turner Diaries, which served as the screenplay for a "race war".

Many single actors pretended to be part of a fictitious movement.[129] A few of them had once tried to join an organisation; a few did not even try it at all. To a Copeland, Breivik or Traini, their membership of a radical tight-wing party did not seem to be sufficient for achieving their goals. Ausonius and Sonboly left things at mere professions of sympathy, without becoming members themselves. Nor was one Franz Fuchs a member of the FPÖ (*Freedom Party of Austria*), although it represented his central goals. On account

---

[128] Cf. Hermann Lang: *Der gehemmte Rebell. Struktur, Psychodynamik und Therapie von Menschen mit Zwangsstörungen*, Stuttgart 2015, p. 37.

[129] There are also other examples of this. The mysterious organisation FNAR ("Front National Anti Radar" oder „Fraction Nationaliste Armée Révolutionnaire") caused a stir in France between 2007 and 2008 with their bombings and sometimes curious, sometimes political right-wing demands. Their battle was against the "repression" of car drivers by radar traps and immigration. According to investigations by the French antiterrorist commission, the group only had one lone member, their founder Frédéric Rabiller. And only one victim: Rabiller himself, who lost a hand whilst working with explosives. The actor must be considered as being shy and isolated.

of their personalities, constructive involvement in firmly sealed units is in any case problematic.

The virtual room or space strengthens actors today, above all. Isolated in reality, they find people here who share the same interests, *Counterstrike*, *Matrix*, *Natural Born Killers* or the music of bands such as *Marilyn Manson* have been proven to be favourites for some of them. The fascination for such games which is especially widespread in youth cultures, films and groups take on the significance of a "cultural script". Staging such acts of violence can be understood by such means.[130] A subculturally motivated violent fantasy appears to be very typical. Over and above this they find role models, people of a similar mindset, and see how terror may be justified ideologically and operationalised.

The list of single actors given is by no means complete, also due to the fact that deeds may be foiled. Thus, there is a real and present potential for danger. And precisely for this reason, it would not be productive to downplay the radical right-wing thought process of actors and potential actors. We may also establish by means of the deeds, that a large terrorist cooperation between right-wing radicals seems rather improbable at the moment.

The examples of Peter Mangs and Anders Breivik illustrate this particularly well. They were both on trial at around the same time. The Swedish expert Mattias Gardell spoke to both of them in prison. He disregarded any differences, as letters sent and statements to one another showed us.[131] Mangs told him during discussions he considered the NSU's method to be the right one, and so of strategically remaining unobserved for as long as possible and carrying out a large number of acts. Breivik also considered the NSU as a fellow campaigner, however, criticised their means and their objectives. In a letter to Mangs, he accused him of selecting the wrong victims. The Swede also had to target local people. It would have been wrong, to attribute non-whites with blame for the demise of the Western world. Those really responsible are the "enemies within". Mangs accused Breivik of not having acted with a long-term view. One single spectacular event could cause a lot of commotion; however, equally it could also lead to his arrest and his death. Mangs was jubilant that he had managed to remain active in hiding for years. This aspect shows how closely individual terrorists relate to one another, but also, how disjointed and divided they are from one another. And also, for this reason, it is only relatively seldom that a violent response is staged by the government

---

[130] Cf. Vincenz Leuschner: "School-Shootings" und "Lone Wolf Terrorism" als soziale Phänomene, in: Berliner Journal für Soziologie, 23 (2013) 1, pp. 27–49, here p. 31.
[131] Cf. Mattias Gardell: „Urban Terror: The Case of Lone Wolf Peter Mangs", in: *Terrorism and Political Violence*, 30 2018 (5), pp. 793–811.

and carried out—for example with a declaration under martial law of a "war on terror". The actors are also not able to achieve by these means, that ethnic minorities will avoid these countries. Their plan to instil fear does not succeed. The deeds were also in vain and senseless from this point of view. Their poisonous ideology missed its target of spreading amongst the population and becoming worthy of receiving approval.

Virtual spaces and rooms are, however, suitable for cooperation, which (from time to time) may be encrypted and anonymised. The case of David Sonboly demonstrates this. He had his own Club on the gaming platform Steam with 261 members, who had explicitly turned their backs on the refugee policy in Germany, providing a link which was able to replace traditional forms of organisation. The cases "Breivik" and "Tarrant" clarify further: Each terrorist, whether socially isolated or not, always represents a broader movement, even without a mandate. The extensive manifesto, which Breivik published hours before his deed, arose from an ecosystem of right-wing extremist blogs, websites and publicity.[132] The same is true for Tarrant.

It is conspicuous, how greatly actors correlate to one another. Breivik admired Ausonius and Mangs. He had described the latter at the start of his trial as a role model for his deeds and as "perhaps Scandinavia's greatest resistance fighter" prior to 22 July 2011.[133] Jens Stoltenberg comments on precisely this aspect. He was Norway's Prime Minister at the time of Breivik's attacks and he travelled to Christchurch in August 2019, as NATO Secretary General. Stoltenberg spoke of a global challenge extending beyond national borders and said: "These attacks are committed by lone wolves, but they are connected at the same time, because they use each other for inspiration—and they refer to one another in the various manifestos."[134]

A Breivik dreams of being a role model for copycat actors—as with Lapshyn and David Sonboly, who admired him. Mair was also enthusiastic about Breivik, collecting newspaper cuttings about his case. The actors unite the wish here, of being displayed in a virtual portrait gallery and of self-aggrandisement. Brenton Tarrant apparently had one eye directed very precisely towards other single actors with extreme right-wing attitudes. He testifies in his manifesto not only to his admiration for Breivik, but also called out to "all those, who stood up against ethnic and cultural genocide". He mentions the Italian Luca Traini here, similarly the Swede Anton Lundin

---

[132] Cf. Jason Burke: "The myth of the "lone wolf"-terrorist", in: *The Guardian* of 30 March 2017, https://www.theguardian.com/news/2017/mar/30/myth-lone-wolf-terrorist.

[133] die tageszeitung „taz" (2012): „Breiviks Vorbild", 14 May, http://www.taz.de/!5093988/.

[134] Otago Daily Times (2019), Christchurch mosque massacre: Prime Minister Jacinda Ardern speaks to nation following shootings, 5 August, https://www.odt.co.nz/news/national/call-united-effort-stop-lone-wolf-attacks.

Pettersson. He was able to develop his cunning virtually via "lone wolves". The Internet is evidently a help here, to acquire the "superficial".

Frank Steffen deposited an article on Breivik and his pamphlets on Islam on his browser as a bookmark, which had appeared in the daily newspaper *Die Welt*. Lone Wolf terrorists act in a manner to advance the ideological convictions of an extremist movement; however, typically they never have had direct contact to the organisation they identify themselves with.

In the mind of the actors, real organisations quickly become fictitious ones: The Bavarian Liberation Army, the Knight Templars and others are merely figments of fantasy. The tissue of lies quickly has its cover blown; the facade is shattered and collapses like a house of cards. In the criminal proceedings against Franz Fuchs, Peter Mangs, John Ausonius, Anders Breivik and Frank Steffen the lie of self-aggrandisement quickly became clear, paired with tirades of swearing and aggression, which rebounded back from the wall of the state under the rule of law. The Norwegian tangled himself up in contradictions during criminal proceedings and in so doing lost his way, descending with a weak voice and defiant self-opinionated manner into the banal. The Knight Templar shrank during public proceedings back to his normal size.[135]

However, there were also links to parties which show, how dangerously far the thinking of lone wolves has already advanced in society. Breivik and Traini were members of a populist right party, and even wished to actively access events as elected holders of mandates—at a local level, where politics actually is most tangible in itself. However, they failed, with the result that they turned away and radicalised themselves. The Party appeared too harmless and unsuitable for them to achieve their goals. Following Breivik's hideous deed, the European Member of Parliament for Lega Nord, Mario Borghezio, found words of praise for him. He told an Italian radio station: "Some of the ideas he expressed—if we remove the violence—are good. Some of them are splendid."[136] After being symbolically excluded from the party for several months, he is still a sitting Member of the European Parliament today and repeatedly attracts attention to himself due to his racist comments against blacks. His party is still part of the Italian government.

None of the actors showed any remorse, the wish to stage their deed and their provocation for it was too large to do so. Nonetheless, political objectives have hitherto never been achieved through these deeds. After Breivik's deeds,

---

[135] Cf. Sebastian Balzer: „Der Musterprozess", in: *Frankfurter Allgemeine Zeitung* of 14 July 2012, p. 40.
[136] BBC news (2011): "Italy MEP backs ideas of Norway killer Breivik", https://www.bbc.com/news/world-europe-14315108.

the mantra in Norway ran "more openness, more democracy"—the opposite of what he had wished to achieve.

New Zealand's Prime Minister Jacinda Ardern made it clear in an address to the nation immediately after the attacks in Christchurch that the country would not allow itself to be intimidated: "we represent diversity, kindness, compassion, a home for those who share our values, refuge for those who need it. And those values, I can assure you, will not, and cannot, be shaken by this attack."[137] In this way she expressed herself similarly, to how the Norwegian Prime Minister of the day Jens Stoltenberg had done following Breivik's attacks, calling for increased sincerity as a direct response. The statements for example of a person such as US President Donald Trump on the other hand are in contrast to this.

References

1. Arendt, H. (1970). *On violence.* Orlando et al.
2. Bierhoff, H.-W., & Herner, M. J. (2011). *Narzissmus – die Wiederkehr.* Bern.
3. Bannenberg, B. (2010). *Amok. Ursachen erkennen – Warnsignale verstehen – Katastrophen verhindern.* Gütersloh.
4. Fiedler, P., & Herpertz, S. C. (2016). *Persönlichkeitsstörungen.* Weinheim/Basel.
5. Gardell, M. (2015). Crusader Dreams: Oslo 22/7, Islamophobia, and the quest for a multi-cultural Europe. In J. Kaplan, H. Lööw, & L. Malkki (Eds.), *Lone wolf and autonomous cell terrorism* (pp. 128–155). London/New York.
6. Gardell, M. (2018). Urban terror: The case of lone wolf Peter Mangs. *Terrorism and Political Violence, 30*(5), 793–811.
7. Gill, P., & Conner, E. (2017). There and back again: The study of mental disorder and terrorist involvement. *American Psychologist, 72,* 231–241.
8. Hamm, M. S., & Spaaij, R. (2017). *The age of lone wolf terrorism.* New York.
9. Hartleb, F. (2013). „Einsamer-Wolf-Terrorismus" – Neue Dimension oder drastischer Einzelfall? Was lernen wir aus dem Fall „Breivik" in Norwegen? *Kriminalistik. Unabhängige Zeitschrift für die kriminalistische Wissenschaft und Praxis, 67*(1), 25–35.
10. Horgan, J. (2014). *The psychology of terrorism.* London/New York.
11. Hudson, R. (2018). *Who becomes a terrorist and why?* Washington D.C.
12. Jackson, P. (2019). The murder of Jo Cox MP: A case study in lone actor terrorism. In A. Waring (Ed.), *The new authoritarianism, Vol. 2: A risk analysis of the European Alt-Right phenomenon* (pp. 149–169). Stuttgart.

---

[137] Nzherald.co.nzm (2019), Christchurch mosque massacre: Prime Minister Jacinda Ardern speaks to nation following shootings, 15th March, https://www.nzherald.co.nz/nz/news/article.cfm?c_id=1& objectid=12213187.

13. Lang, H. (2015). *Der gehemmte Rebell. Struktur, Psychodynamik und Therapie von Menschen mit Zwangsstörungen.* Stuttgart.
14. Leonhard, C. H., et al. (2014). The case of Anders Behring Breivik—Language of a lone terrorist. *Behavioral Sciences & the Law, 32*(3), 408–422.
15. Leuschner, V. (2013). "School-Shootings" und "Lone Wolf Terrorism" als soziale Phänomene. *Berliner Journal für Soziologie, 23*(1), 27–49.
16. Malkki, L. (2015). Political elements in post-Columbine school shootings in Europe and North America. In J. Kaplan, H. Lööw, & L. Malkki (Eds.), *Lone wolf and autonomous cell terrorism* (pp. 185–210). London/New York.
17. Mareš, M., & Stojar, R. (2016). Extreme right perpetrators. In M. Fredholm (Ed.), *Understanding lone actor terrorism. Past experience, future outlook, and response strategies* (pp. 66–86). London/New York.
18. Martin, G. (2013). *Understanding terrorism: Challenges, perspectives and issues.* Los Angeles.
19. Nedopil, N. (2014). Gekränkte Eitelkeiten. Terroristische Einzelkämpfer. *Forensische Psychiatrie, Kriminologie, 8*(4), 246–253.
20. Oksanen, A., Nurmi, J., Vuori, M., Räsänen, P., & Jokela, P. (2013). The social roots of a school shooting tragedy in Finland. In N. Böckler, T. Seeger, P. Sitzer, & W. Heitmeyer (Eds.), *School shootings: International research, case studies and concepts for prevention* (pp. 189–215). New York.
21. Pfahl-Traughber, A. (2017). „Das "Lone-Wolf"-Phänomen im Rechtsterrorismus in Deutschland und Schweden". In M. H. Möllers & R. Chr. Van Ooyen (Eds.), *Jahrbuch für Öffentliche Sicherheit 2016/2017* (pp. 199–213). Frankfurt on Main.
22. Pinker, S. (2011). *Gewalt. Eine neue Geschichte der Menschheit.* Frankfurt/Main.
23. Remschmidt, H., Schmidt, M., & Poustka, F. (Hrsg.). (2012). *Multiaxiales Klassifikationsschema für psychische Störungen des Kindes- und Jugendalters nach ICD-10 of the WHO.* Bern.
24. Schliefsteiner, P. (2018). Austria's homegrown lone actor terrorist: Franz Fuchs and the letter bomb campaign of the 1990's. *Journal for Intelligence, Propaganda and Security Studies, 12*(1), 67–92.
25. Seierstad, Å. (2016). *Einer von uns. Die Geschichte des Massenmörders Anders Breivik.* Zurich.
26. Simon, J. D. (2016). *Lone wolf terrorism. understanding the growing threat.* New York.
27. Spaaij, R. (2012). *Understanding lone wolf terrorism. Global patterns, motivations and prevention.* Heidelberg et al.
28. Spitzer, M. (2018). *Einsamkeit. Die unerkannte Krankheit.* Munich.
29. Strømmen, Ø. (2015). Der Soloterrorist als Kulturphänomen. In F. Decker, B. Henningsen, & K. Jakobsen (Eds.), *Rechtspopulismus und Rechtsextremismus in Europa* (pp. 245–254). Baden-Baden.
30. Theweleit, K. (2015). *Das Lachen der Täter: Breivik u.a. Psychogramm der Tötungslust.* St. Pölten et al.

31. Vogeley, K. (2016). *Anders sein. Autismus-Spektrum-Störungen im Erwachsenenalter*. Basel.
32. Waldmann, P. (1998). *Terrorismus, Provokation der Macht*. Munich.
33. Wehling, T., & Hansen, S. (2012). Breivik, Terrorist oder Amokläufer? In J. Krause & S. Hansen (Eds.), *Jahrbuch Terrorismus 2011/2012* (pp. 121–148). Opladen.
34. Welzer, H. (2005). *Täter. Wie aus ganz normalen Menschen Massenmörder werden*. Frankfurt/Main.
35. Zehnpfennig, B. (2013). Extremes Denken. In U. Backes, A. Gallus, E. Jesse (Eds.), *Jahrbuch Extremismus & Demokratie* (Vol. 25, pp. 40–44).

4

Radicalisation in Our Midst and in Virtual Rooms and Spaces

4.1 Terror as a Portrayal of Developments in Society

Terrorism reflects the mood in society in an extreme form, how the present mood in society is and any possible difficulties. In other words: The renegotiation of national identity is taking place in changing historical circumstances across the globe: "European countries in particular are facing tremendous change as they struggle to construct a new European identity, define their own national identities, and learn to incorporate millions of immigrants from predominantly Muslim societies in their national cultures. How and whether previously rather homogenous societies will come to terms with their new and increasingly multicultural communities will play a large part in determining the extent to which the inequalities and resentments experienced by alienated youth – as evidenced in (…) home-grown terrorism – can be reversed."[1]

Whoever concerns himself with extremists' biographies, cannot separate radicalisation from the conditions in society and from disintegration processes in democracies. A portrait of Michael Kühnen, who was Germany's most feared "neo-Nazi" during the 1980s, summed this up perfectly[2]: "A

---

[1] Cynthia Miller-Idriss: Blood and Culture. Youth, Right-Wing Extremism and National Belonging in Contemporary Germany, Durham/London 2009, here p. 179.

[2] Dishonourably discharged as a Lieutenant from the German army in 1977, Kühnen ever increasingly radicalised himself. And thus, the self-confessed National Socialist organised a march through the city centre of Hamburg wearing donkey masks in 1978 with the slogan: "As a donkey I still believe, that Jews were gassed in German concentration camps." The man who irradiated an intellectual nature quickly attracted the attention of the media, however he received embittered criticism in this milieu after professing he was a homosexual in 1986. Kühnen died of Aids in 1991.

© Springer Nature Switzerland AG 2020
F. Hartleb, *Lone Wolves*,
https://doi.org/10.1007/978-3-030-36153-2_4

sensible and refined consideration of Michael Kühnen [...] which did not apologetically repeat clichés and exclusions would need to ask, [...] which institutional exclusion mechanisms can be applied to these political biographies, give shape to their contours and, straighten them out". They would need to even out the relationship between free will and independent decisions in a person who has been shattered in an extraordinary manner on the one hand, and the power of the political, societal and social forces working on him on the other hand. [...] No-one is born a, fascist' or an, extremist' and nobody relegates themselves entirely out of free will to the political and societal shadows and backwaters."[3] Lone wolf terrorists too are "children of their time," for example reflecting xenophobia in our society.

The term lone wolf constantly resonates with the actor's isolation from society. Loneliness in itself is often interpreted as being a sickly, socially conditioned isolation, and is considered as not being normal. Lonely people are considered as disrupting to the peace and order of society, as they do not direct their actions towards society and by so doing deviate from existing norms and standards. However, loneliness does not automatically mean isolation. People may be objectively isolated, without feeling lonely. This pattern is also evident in the new virtual, parallel world. From time to time, being alone is the target or the vision here, for example for drop outs who long for a life à la Robinson Crusoe, far removed from civilisation.

Loneliness on the other side of this romantic transfiguration, however, is often surrounded by doubt and deep inner sadness. In relation to the "analogue" life, it can be divided into three forms[4]:

- *temporary loneliness*: by the minute, or the hour; a feeling which passes, for example melancholy
- *situational loneliness*: following events such as the death of a close relative, losing one's job, health problems
- *chronic loneliness*: with no definite event occurring; the feeling of not being able to trust anyone; possible causes: social phobias, failures at work or in one's private life, traumatic experiences during childhood

It is precisely this chronic loneliness which triggers aggression, especially as people can escape into a parallel, virtual world nowadays. Loneliness may be a symptom of people with depression, schizophrenia or delusional disorders,

---

[3]Hans-Gerd Jaschke: „Biographisches Porträt: Michael Kühnen", in: Uwe Backes/Eckhard Jesse (eds.): *Jahrbuch Extremismus & Demokratie*, 4 (1992), p. 168.
[4]Cf. Caroline Bohn: *Einsamkeit im Spiegel der sozialwissenschaftlichen Forschung*, Dortmund 2006, pp. 21–27.

which becomes especially noticeable in youth and in old age. Mental illnesses and loneliness mutually reinforce one another. The characteristics include a small social network, little social contact and a subjective feeling of being left alone. Whoever has a somewhat depressive nature, suffers from delusions of persecution or paranoia, or from some other obsession, does not want to be in contact with people, shuts others out of his life, considering them to be a nuisance or a threat. "Healthy" people in turn (thankfully) turn away from them, as they do not really know how to get along with these strange, stubborn or even aggressive (strange) personalities.[5]

Loneliness plays a major role in terrorism. Terrorism also includes dropping out of social life, and even if simply to not being conspicuous, to not "give oneself away."

Irrespective of this: Planning a terrorist deed requires a particular focus with a view to operationalisation, but also in a communicative sphere. In the end, the murder should serve a higher, political sense, which sensualizes an image of revulsion of society. In spite of loneliness and withdrawal, the reference to the surroundings may not be given up or disregarded: Individual terrorists soak up the mood of society like a sponge and to this extent is a reflection of developments in society. They move around in the murky circles of the following influential factors:

- Networking and internationalisation of radical right-wing forces
- Opening virtual rooms and spaces with elements of violent fantasies and ideologies of hatred
- Susceptibility to conspiracy theories on the path of "the search for absolute truth"

This is especially true for the debate surrounding supposed Islamification, which has disenfranchised parts of the population from the political system for the long-term. At present we are experiencing a radicalisation, paraphrased in social networks as "words instead of deeds" and which manifests itself for example in attacks on refugee hostels and homes for refugees. We are not only concerned with organised structures here, but with citizens with no organised background from the centre of society, who had not even been in trouble with the police prior to this. Right-wing terrorist acts against refugees and people with migratory backgrounds can no longer be ignored, in view of this

---

[5]Cf. Manfred Spitzer: Einsamkeit. Die unerkannte Krankheit, Munich 2018, p. 154 f.

massive expansion of new violence. Racist motivated deeds and attacks so-to-speak suspend society's condemnation of right-wing extremism. Studies on Germany during the course of the "refugee influx" have proven this.

A status report published in April 2016 by the Federal Criminal Police Office confirms the image of "new single actors," who are an entirely blank page for officials. Therefore in 2015, of 551 people suspected of terrorist acts, merely one quarter had prior criminal convictions because of acts based on right-wing motivations, only three people from this milieu were attributed the status "relevant person" by the State Intelligence Services Offices.[6] It is hard to design a European comparison,[7] as entirely different categories exist for *hate crimes*. For example, propaganda crimes in Germany such as the use of the swastika are included, which do not exist at all in other countries. In addition, some EU States only report acts of violence sporadically.[8]

Numerous scenarios of doom and gloom have been developed for Europe, focussing on an "Islamification of Europe" and which fantasise about the "suicide of Europe". Immigration is considered to be a project concocted by an elite with our enemies' interests at heart, directed against the interests of the European races. Young men, in particular, are evidently susceptible to being taken for a ride by the pied piper in this heated conflict situation and of following right-wing ideologies. They usually live in one of the metropolises and view foreigners as scapegoats for their own situation, which they perceive to be unsatisfactory. They scarcely inform themselves via traditional media any longer.

Right-wing terrorist potentials arose above all as a consequence of 11 September 2001. The new ideological mixture which was developed for example by the anti-Islamic English Defence League (EDL), can follow various patterns:

- The activists consider themselves to be Christian Crusaders (*Saint George's Cross symbol*) in the battle against the danger of Islam and as a reaction to the propaganda against the Western world by Islamic Fundamentalists.
- They consider themselves in the first instance to be a cultural, and less of a racist defence movement for their own identity, conjuring up a cultural battle ("*clash of civilizations*").[9]

---

[6] Cf. Lena Kampf: „Viele Straftaten gegen Asylunterkünfte", in: *Tagesschau.de*, 27 April 2016.
[7] Various data is recorded here, for example by the European Human Rights Agency, alongside reports from the Office for Democratic Institutions und Human Rights of the OSCE (*German: OSZE*).
[8] Cf. Uwe Backes: „Rechtsextremistische Gewalt in Europa", in: Gerhard Hirscher/Eckhard Jesse (eds.): *Extremismus in Deutschland*, Baden-Baden 2013, p. 44.
[9] Cf. Uwe Backes: „Rechtsextremistische Gewalt in Europa", in: Gerhard Hirscher/Eckhard Jesse (eds.): *Extremismus in Deutschland*, Baden-Baden 2013, p. 55.

The Norwegian terrorist Breivik made frequent references in his manifesto to the EDL—stating he was involved in a Norwegian chapter as one of the founder members, extolling the virtues of his own network to the British network. In court, he contested any contact with EDL had existed. EDL came into being in 2009 in a London suburb where there were frequent conflicts between the majority of the population and a Muslim minority, including militant-Islamic factions. The League, financed by an Islamophobic millionaire, recruited its members from football hooligans and supporters of the British right-wing parties British National Party (BNP) and the United Kingdom Independence Party (UKIP). The EDL has no formal membership and is highly active in virtual arenas. The EDL was shown to have an active membership of at least 25,000 persons in the UK, with groups also popular to a similar extent in Scandinavia.[10] It's founder Paul Ray is supposedly a religiously motivated skinhead, now living on Malta "in exile", where he leads an anti-Muslim group called the The Ancient Order of the Templar Knights. Breivik adopted this name for his own Crusader fantasies. Ray, who was in direct contact with Breivik online, however stated, Breivik had been a single actor without an organisational superstructure. The conspiratorial secret meetings Breivik alluded to did not take place. Nor could the court uncover any evidence of "Crusader meetings" with Breivik. Joining onto existing movements, without these movements knowing anything about it, appears to be typical for lone wolves.

4.2   Internationalisation of the Radical Right

From words to weapons: If a minority of people in the movement in 1968 developed into violent left-wing terrorists, the situation has changed somewhat half a century later. The far-right forces in various parliaments received a massive influx, a link to the new threat from right-wing terrorists at least merits discussion. Is there a revolution with reversed, diametrically opposed indications? What has been established: The present Zeitgeist in Western democracies is leaning to "the right", xenophobic attitudes are on the increase, with the patterns in many countries being similar. A restauration of authoritarian rule threatens as election results in countries such as France, Austria, Hungary or Poland show rather clearly. A few years ago, such a development would have been considered unthinkable.

---

[10] See Jamie Bartlett/Mark Littler: Inside the EDL: Populist Politics in a Digital Age, Demos Think Tank, London 2011.

Donald Trump, who was elected 45th President of the USA in November 2016, clearly demonstrates the global and European trend towards the return to authoritarian powers. Trump, the populist agitator, acts according to a so-called "reverse psychology", as we know it from the era of fascism: He approaches his public with precisely the opposite intention to that which an analyst approaches a person needing treatment with. The demagogue seizes on individual insecurities, neurotic anxieties and reinforces them with the targeted aim of not allowing the patient to become politically mature, in order to create a secure bond.[11] During his campaigning, he merely uttered tirades of swearing in all directions. Mexicans described the candidate in short as the "rapist". Even as President, the billionaire property dealer (the "Deal maker") makes out Islamic terrorism to be guilty as an automatic reflex, connected to the need for Law and Order—even when white Americans are involved from time to time, who have changed and commit violent acts out of extreme right-wing motivations. He even contrived a terrorist attack in Sweden during his election campaign.[12]

In addition to this, making things more difficult: Deep divisions have arisen during the refugee crisis. Europe with open borders is different from an isolationist Europe. Within the last ten years, Europe has recently experienced a revival of militant right-wing extremist groups, networks and incidents, as the expert Daniel Koehler points out. He also highlights that the dynamics of such militant far-right activity remains poorly understood, as a result of the focus in recent years on religion-based extremism.[13]

Europeans' anxieties regarding uncontrolled migration appear to have increased immensely. These extend to three points, as the author Julia Ebner sets out: First of all the anxiety, for example that young Arab men will block one's own perspectives, taking away women, jobs and housing, secondly, that areas of towns and cities and whole societies will be become Islamised, and that there is a threat of terrorist attacks by radical Islamists everywhere.

Election battles increasingly revolve around the subject of migration, whilst public scepticism towards the ability of elected politicians to come to terms with migration has greatly increased. This has caused the public to become more open and amenable to extreme right-wing slogans, which find approval

---

[11] Cf. Helmut Dubiel: „Das Gespenst des Populismus", in: Helmut Dubiel (ed.): *Populismus und Aufklärung*, Frankfurt on Main 1986, p. 42.

[12] *Focus.de* of 19 February 2017, „Donald Trump erfindet Terror" https://www.focus.de/politik/videos/us-praesident-donald-trump-erfindet-terroranschlag-in-schweden_id_6670387.html.

[13] Cf. Daniel Koehler: Right-Wing Extremism and Terrorism in Europe: Current Developments and Issues for the Future, in: Prism, 6 (2016) 2, pp. 84–104.

in this environment, where anxiety and worry dominate, and people perceive themselves to be victims.[14]

A cross-border "international right" has formed, which 50 years later is fighting against the achievements of the movement of "68, basically forming a counter-movement. Societal laissez-faire, emancipation and feminism (so-called "Gender Ideology"), tolerance and a multicultural society are considered anathema and, *foreign*" to them.

"Globalised right-wing extremism" has been considered a contradiction in itself for a long time. Parties and social movements seemed to be too strongly fixated on their own national identity. And therefore, Franz Schönhuber proclaimed, once Party Chairman of the "Republicans" (*in Germany*) and the defining force of the "extremist right" during the 1990s: "The only thing which many right-wing parties in Europe have in common, is that which divides them. Contrary to left-wing parties, which wish to overcome the historical burdens via new and common orders in society and have prescribed for internationalism themselves, parties on the right consider maintaining the essence of the people and the sovereignty of national territory to be to the fore. Europe's radical right collaborated so little with one another, that we could not describe them as independent political actors. This is what has fundamentally changed in the beautiful, new world of globalisation."

The new, popular approaches can be summarised by three points. The patterns are similar in the different countries throughout Europe:

- *Anti-establishment*
  - The government withholds the truth from their own populace
  - The ruling parties "up there" deceive and defraud the people, putting money into their own pockets
  - It is now time to provide active resistance to the present policies and politicians

- *Hostile Towards Democracy*
  - The established parties plunder the state and talk problems to death
  - It has become time again now, to put the power in the hands of a strong (ring) leader
  - There is no freedom of the press or media, a "press of lies" sets the tone

---

[14]Cf. Julia Ebner: The Rage. The Vicious Circle of Islamist and Far-Right Extremism, London 2017.

- *Right-Wing Extremism*
    - It is time again, to not only place the needs of one's own nation in the foreground (*Patriotism*), but also to place them before everything else (*Chauvinism*)
    - Foreigners merely exploit our social welfare system, and are usually criminals
    - Europe is subverted by "Islamic" migration
    - Problems occur, for example if any Muslims or Romany people stay in my area or a home for refugees is built nearby
    - Refugees are merely "benefits cheats" and should remain in their own countries.

There is a considerable overlap between the opinions presented here, which are those of parties or people who call themselves democratic, and the reasons lone wolves find for their deeds.

The capacity to adopt right-wing extremist thinking in the middle of society was displayed by successes in elections in Europe and the USA. "Trumpization" can now be considered as being a successful political and campaigning style.[15] Without needing to conspire to an equally pessimistic culture as the „Untergang des Abendlandes" (*"Decline of the West"*) in the spirit of Oswald Spengler,[16] we can nevertheless see that a brutalization of the political style impacts those in close proximity and that authoritarian patterns become more dominant—at the expense of tolerance and respect. And thus, the terrorist in El Paso, Patrick Crusius, adopted US President Donald Trump's rhetoric in his manifesto "The Inconvenient Truth". He has often derided highly regarded media outlets such as the *New York Times* and *Washington Post* as "fake news", even labelling reporters as "enemies of the people." He stated in a tweet in October 2018: "A very big part of the anger we see in our society today is caused by the purposely false and inaccurate reporting of mainstream media that I refer to as Fake News. It has gotten so bad and hateful that it is beyond description. Mainstream Media must clean up its act, FAST!".[17] He means basically, as pointed out in other tweets, that negative articles concerning him are "fake". The consequences of such statements are dramatic in the sense that they undermine the credibility (also in the sense

---

[15] Cf. Florian Hartleb: Die Stunde der Populisten. Wie sich unsere Politik trumpetisiert und was wir dagegen tun können, Schwalbach im Taunus 2017.

[16] Cf. Oswald Spengler: The decline of the West, Oxford 2007 (original 1918).

[17] Edition.cnn.com: Trump blames media for anger after attacks, 25 October 2018, https://edition.cnn.com/2018/10/25/politics/trump-blames-media-for-anger-after-attacks/index.html.

of authentic, credible, well-researched and authorised news) from the quality Western press, as part of the institutional system. The terrorist Crusius writes word for word: "I know that the media will probably call me a white supremacist anyway and blame Trump's rhetoric. The media is infamous for fake news. Their reaction to this attack will likely just confirm that."

4.3 Virtual Worlds

It's true, global networking via the Internet and the fixation on a Western lifestyle connected with this contributed significantly to a spread of democracy in the twenty-first century. Opaque activities by secret services which are not transparent also take place in the Western world, for example the monitoring and spying affair regarding the NSA uncovered in 2013, however, also testifying that mistrust has not disappeared, and that it is difficult to place protecting one's private sphere under the microscope in the course of the technological revolution. The data scandal concerning the US corporate giant Facebook has left its mark on the digital era. The question arises, of to what extent such corporate conglomerates' interests in profit, coupled with a destructive motivation of some users undermine traditional values such as privacy or respect for a culture of dialogue.

Can virtual communities really succeed in becoming involved in real politics? The communications scientist Otfried Jansen disputed this in 1998. He was of the opinion that existing social structures form the basis of technically underpinned forms.[18] The question arises 20 years later of whether this conclusion is still contemporary. Nevertheless, a digital-technological quantum leap occurred including an entirely new form of interaction. And it is precisely subcultural right-wing extremism notorious for being hostile to organisations which finds new opportunities to latch onto this. Many far-right groups were early adopters of the Internet. For example, the world's largest white supremacist website Stormfront was established in 1996.[19]

The American philosopher and legal scholar Cass Sunstein warned at an early stage, as early as 2002, of the dangers of a "Cyber-Balkanization" of public spaces, this means a political public which favours a structure defined by extremism. In a media system dominated by the Internet, small groups

---

[18] Cf. Otfried Jarren: „Internet – neue Chancen für die politische Kommunikation", in: *Aus Politik und Zeitgeschichte*, B 40 (1998), pp. 13–21.

[19] Cf. Stephen Albrecht/Maik Fielitz/Nick Thurston: Introduction, in: Maik Fielitz/Nick Thurston (eds.): Post-Digital Cultures of the Far Right. Online Actions and Offline Consequences in Europe and the US, Bielefeld 2019, pp. 7–22, here p. 8.

with shared ideas could shield themselves from arguments and facts which are contrary to their own opinions much more easily than in the traditional public spaces directed towards the mass media.

In contrast to traditional mass media, one can choose freely with new media, by whom one is informed and with whom one wishes to conduct a dialogue. In such types of isolated groups, the extreme versions of each commonly held view, which was the basis for forming a group, will look for support. Sunstein talks in this regard of "echo chambers". Arguments are not followed by counter-arguments, but by a reverberation effect which amplifies itself.[20]

The reduced contact thresholds on the Net favour weak ties being set up and maintained, which can be activated if necessary. Nevertheless, new opportunities present themselves. Virtual communities are not *unreal*, they simply follow different patterns of interaction than physical, real communities.

The fanaticism of potential terrorists finds a surface to be projected onto with the opportunity for 24-7 communication and interaction—and all from the comfort of the home. In addition: White supremacist groups were able to thrive due to the increasing ubiquity of online communication. One event which occurred in August 2017 in Charlottesville, North Carolina for example was organised by a broad coalition of white supremacists, many of them were highly active online. The violent gathering led to the death of a 32-year-old woman and 19 people being injured after one person, James Alex Fields drove his car into a group of counterdemonstrators. Communication regarding the event was carried out on social media platforms, but certain sites were also key conduits for divulging information, such as 8chan, the white nationalist message board Daily Stormer and altright.com.[21]

The murderous assailant in Christchurch had thought of broadcasting his crude ideas, for example on 8chan. This concerns an Internet discussion forum, an image board, where all users can post pictures and texts anonymously without registering. 8chan is a breakaway from the well-known 4chan, after this had become too harmless for the most extreme users. There is even talk of "gamification of terror," as one blog portal puts it: "What we see here is evidence of the only real innovation 8chan has brought to global terrorism: The gamification of mass violence. We see this not just in the references to "high scores", but in the very way the Christchurch shooting was

---

[20] Cf. Cass R. Sunstein: *Republic.com 2.0*, Princeton 2002.
[21] See Joan Donovan/Becca Lewis/Brian Friedberg: Parallel Ports. Sociotechnical Change from the Alt-Right to Alt-Tech, in: Maik Fielitz/Nick Thurston (eds.): Post-Digital Cultures of the Far Right. Online Actions and Offline Consequences in Europe and the US, Bielefeld 2019, pp. 49–65.

carried out. Brenton Tarrant live streamed his massacre from a helmet cam in a way that made the shooting look almost exactly like a First Person Shooter video game."[22]

These platforms such as 8chan may be considered to be Internet meme factories, which on first appearance appear to be harmless and a joke, which could be considered to be "lulz", as we call it online. Memes are really ideas, which propagate themselves analogous to genes. They not only provide identification, but also provocation as well as propaganda. Approximately 8,000 people watched the video of Christchurch live on Facebook. There were already 1.5 million versions of this before the platform started deleting it. The manifesto of the „Der Große Austausch" (*The Great Replacement*) is taken in the same cynical tone as posts on 4 and 8chan. Even in the foreground of the deed, memes call for a lone actor "to mow down Breivik". And in this way Breivik was thus delegitimised. The essence of these troll-forums is a mixture of offensive humour, transgressing limits and often also misanthropy, very individual codes and practices have evolved from this. We do not need to go so far here to talk about "troll terrorists".[23]

Following the massacre in El Paso, Texas, which took place in August 2019, and was announced once again on 8chan, Fredrick Brennan, the founder of 8Chan announced that the image board should be removed from the Internet. This very recent occurrence appeared to be the straw that broke the camel's back for CloudFlare Chief Matthew Price: His company, an IT services provider, which globally protects millions on dubious websites from time to time against overload attacks, announced it had ended its cooperation with 8Chan. 8Chan was "a cesspool of hatred," Price wrote by way of justification. "They have proven themselves to be outside the law, and this lawlessness has led to many tragic fatalities."[24]

Nevertheless, this can only be taken as one single drop onto a hot stone: The attack in Christchurch continues to be glorified in "dark corners" of the Internet. The spread of video material could not be stemmed completely, and it was even reworked into an Ego-Shooter video game instead. Original scenes from the video of the deed appear in one game, whose players similarly are inside a mosque and indiscriminately shoot at praying Muslims. So-called

---

[22] Robert Evans: The El Paso Shooting and the Gamification of Terror, in: The Bellingcat Podcast, 4 August 2019, https://www.bellingcat.com/news/americas/2019/08/04/the-el-paso-shooting-and-the-gamification-of-terror/.

[23] According to the prominent German columnist Sascha Lobo: Der Troll-Terrorist, in: Spiegel online of 17 March 2019, http://www.spiegel.de/netzwelt/web/christchurch-wie-der-troll-terrorist-sein-attentat-im-netz-bewarb-a-1258272.html.

[24] Matthew Price on the CloudFlare-Blog, Terminating Service for 8Chan, 5th August 2019, https://new.blog.cloudflare.com/terminating-service-for-8chan/.

memes also circulate alongside the video game, that is reworked images of the assailant, presenting him as a saint ("St. Tarrant"), as well as calls to follow his example.[25]

And it is true: The most popular gaming platform Steam continues to grow and grow. According to the latest figures, 33 million users use it, and around 14 million of these at any one time. Steam does not need any shops to register = sales, and only requires a small number of employees. The platform's profit is appropriately high, due to low costs of production, etc. It is in the realms of billions. Whilst it is judged to be controversial, whether (excessive) use of violent computer games leads to aggression and aggressive outbursts, the vast majority should consist of harmless users. Yet Steam predominantly represents sales of so-called killer games. Counter-Strike is one of their classic games, which in the meantime has progressed to the version Counter-Strike Source. Players meet up there as one of two parties in a network game (usually via the Internet) against an opposing team, in order to fulfil a certain order. This may be to defuse a bomb, for example. In this game, the order (*or commission*) of one party (the terrorists) would be to explode the bomb and to guarantee that it detonates, and that of the other party (Special Weapons and Tactics Unit or SWAT), would be to defuse the bomb. The player has the choice of a large selection of weapons in order to achieve this goal, and by using them the opponents may be rendered "non-harmful". The development moves quickly on, apparently disinhibited as well as unchecked. The games become ever more eccentric and glorify violence. Many real-world events are worked up by the PC gaming culture by visual means. Millions of people anonymously exchange ideas on certain subjects in image-based forums such as 4Chan and 8Chan as parts of an ecosystems. The Italian lone wolf Luca Traini for example was represented as "God of Race War", as an allusion to the computer game "God of War".

Lone wolves' practice with their violent fantasies, which they live out in their video games. Breivik was acting on the island of Utøya like one of the heroes in a violent game or as he saw himself, as a gladiator (one of the favourite films on Breivik's Facebook page). A discussion on spiritual arson by the Internet, blogs and violent games is therefore overdue, and must be held. Steam advertised the game *Active-Shooter* in May 2018, which simulates a school massacre. The player is transposed into the role of a member of a Special Weapons and Tactics Unit team, which is looking for a shooter in a school. This is how the perspective of a gunman shooting wildly in all

---

[25] Jamie Tarabay: As New Zealand Fights Online Hate, the Internet's Darkest Corners Resist, in: New York Times, 5th July 2019, https://www.nytimes.com/2019/07/05/world/asia/new-zealand-internet.html.

directions is first absorbed. The advertising clip ends with images of corpses lying on the ground. The number of civilians killed is counted in this way.[26]

This is also controversial because it did not become public knowledge until March 2018, that there are user groups in Steam 173, which frankly and freely laud school shootings.[27] Following immense protests, the realistic simulations have now evidently been withdrawn. Nevertheless, this need not mean very much. *Hatred*, another simulation of mass murders on innocent civilians, was first removed and was then installed again.[28] Therefore considerable doubt exists as to whether the gaming industry wishes to or is able to complete a volte face (*about turn*) in spite of the numerous school shootings. Commercial interests are put before troublesome ethical debates, which would actually be required precisely in the USA in view of the numerous incidents. One could even assume that the glorification of school shootings which takes place in the "Community" in any case, is used to drive profit margins up.

Black sheep frolic on Steam, who apparently form semi-public, extreme forums unchecked, send voice and text messages and communicate and share violent fantasies, remaining below the radar of security officers. In the meantime, we can no longer speak of one frenzied man running amok, as people of a like mind meet here and purposely network with one another.

In the meantime, the *Huffington Post* has detected a large problem for Steam, in its National Socialist contents. It becomes clear here: Not only violent games are the actual problem, but the social platforms, on which Communities such as "Kill the Jews" or "neo-Nazi Fascist Party" could be found as public or private groups in 2017. The newspaper was able to identify thousands of accounts and user groups, in which individual people profess to be National Socialists, school shooters or racists.

It is precisely the frequent and popular use of satire which should disguise their true intentions, wipe away the boundaries between tasteless fun and bitter seriousness until they are no longer recognisable. The drastic sounding conclusion: Relevant NS symbols have been "normalised".[29] The same is true

---

[26] *N-tv.de (2018)*: „Amokläufer oder Polizist? Schulmassaker-Spiel löst Empörung aus", 31 May, https://www.n-tv.de/panorama/Schulmassaker-Spiel-loest-Empoerung-aus-article20456765.html.

[27] *The Center for Investigation Report (2018)*: "The Hate Report: Gaming app has 173 groups that glorify school shooters", 2 March, https://www.revealnews.org/blog/hate-report-gaming-app-has-173-groups-that-glorify-school-shooters/.

[28] *Forbes.com (2018)*: "Valve Was Right To Remove 'Active Shooter' From Steam, But It's Not Enough", 30 May, https://www.forbes.com/sites/erikkain/2018/05/30/valve-was-right-to-remove-active-shooter-from-steam-but-its-not-enough/#37950b082e28.

[29] Cf. Andy Campell: "Steam, Your Kids' Favorite Video Game App, Has A Big Nazi Problem", in: *Huffington Post* of 8 March 2018, https://www.huffingtonpost.com/entry/steam-video-games-nazis_us_5aa006cae4b0e9381c146438.

for anti-Islamic blogs, which came into being as a direct or indirect reaction following 11 September 2001, and the spread of Islamic terrorism. Bloggers started exchanging information on texts critical of Islam in online forums such as "Politically Incorrect" in Germany or "EuropeNews" in Denmark and became active. They shared media reports, which were supposed to serve as evidence of a supposed Islamification: for example, an article on operators of public kitchens, which in "misunderstood" consideration for Muslims, had removed pork from the menu.[30] However, the hidden parallel worlds became worse than the public blogs a long time ago, in which groups communicate in their own language similarly to how they do on Steam or who run operational businesses or handle transactions on the Darknet, such as for example weapons sales and purchases. Calling the existence of these forums harmless or not even attempting to fight them at all with evidence of legal problems, will only further heighten the problem of lone wolves.

4.4 Boom Time for Conspiracy Theories

There is supposedly a plan behind everything that happens, and nothing takes place as a pure coincidence. At present, conspiracy theories are undergoing a renaissance and are spreading wildly via the Internet and are being received by broad sections of society. The extent of this new phenomenon may also not be forgotten in connection with the radicalisation of lone wolves.

Conspiracy theories not only concern the Internet. Customary publishers such as Kopp Verlag in Germany also serve the market, receiving a considerable impulse and reaching a considerable number of members of the public.[31] Anti-Semitic clichés, with their long tradition, play a role in this right up until today and are at the centre of the discussion on conspiracy theories. These are expressed in the main, as follows:

- Jewish capital financing controls the world. This view is based on forged "Records of the Wise Men of Zion",[32] and is supposedly personified by super-rich people such as Bill Gates, Warren Buffet or George Soros;
- General criticism of capitalism and globalisation (financial elite; globally dominant Jewish power-brokers on the East Coast of the USA in banks

---

[30] Cf. Oliver Wäckerlig: „Von Online-Blogs zu Anti-Islam-Parteien", in: *Medien Dienst Integration*, 29 April 2016, https://mediendienst-integration.de/artikel/gastkommentar-oliver-waeckerlig-islamfeindliche-netzwerke-und-rechtspopulismus-in-europa.html.
[31] Ibid., pp. 195–197.
[32] Cf. Michael Butter: „Nichts ist, wie es scheint". Über Verschwörungstheorien, Berlin 2018, p. 166 f.

and stockbrokers on Wall Street; interest slavery, which once served as a byword in the NSDAP's programme);
- Link to a hatred of Israel (mixed in with philo-Semitism);
- Changing significance of the Holocaust (denial, belittlement and relativization).

The anti-Semitic tradition has continued up until today and is also significant in terrorism. For example, it played a role in the murderous events in Oklahoma City in 1995. There is talk of a so-called "Zionist Occupation Government" (ZOG) in extreme right-wing circles in the USA, with which the government in Washington D.C. is what is really meant.

The Turner Diaries are the decisive source, which we already discussed in this book. Numerous abbreviations, overtones and encodings circulate on the Internet—from time to time with a clear reference to the National Socialist image of "rich, avaricious Jews with large paws". "USrael" means that the "true rulers" of the USA are Jews. "NWO" (New World Order) refers to the anti-Jewish (phony) "Records of the wise men of Zion."[33]

These are boom times for conspiracy theories in the virtual era, they are easy to locate on the net—from 11 September 2001 as independent stage management by the USA right up until the current refugee crisis of today. And so, the latter is no coincidence, but is part of the plan realised in the deed, carried out by enemies.[34]

Why are these experiencing such a boom, why are real or imaginary groups such as Jews, Freemasons, the Illuminati Order or Aliens being declared the evil of the world? How is it that far more people than merely the easily convinced and the uneducated follow such ideas? Different reasons can be listed for this:

- Compensation for the dwindling understanding of causal relationships in times of globalisation
- Ease of appointing scapegoats, also precisely as compensation for one's own lack of direction
- Wish to maintain and persist with a supposedly or allegedly threatened order
- The opportunity to raise oneself up out of the masses and by so doing to experience a new identity

---

[33] Cf. Sascha Lobo: Die vielen Formen des Netz-Antisemitismus, in: Spiegel online of 13 December 2017, http://www.spiegel.de/netzwelt/web/antisemitismus-im-netz-wie-judenhass-digital-verbreitet-wird-a-1183052.html.
[34] According to the arguments for example of the Hungarian Prime Minister Viktor Orbán.

Such conspiracy theories from time to time are skilfully controlled and are a part of targeted disinformation campaigns, for example by the Kremlin, whose efficiency was evident during the course of the Ukraine War and Annexation of Crimea, but also during the challenge from the refugee influx. Special trolls, stations and news agencies ensure this, such as Russia Today and Sputnik, which can be received in many countries.

Europe's right-wing radicals and Vladimir Putin's Russia formed an alliance a long time ago. By so doing, the former act in this way as "useful idiots". In the controversial referendum on Crimea in March 2014, Moscow relied on election monitors from the French Front National,[35] the Belgian Vlaams Belang, the Hungarian Jobbik-Partei, Italian Lega Nord and Austria's FPÖ. These delegations confirmed their democratic character true to their instructions. A rigid network has long since been formed of these, which also includes politicians from Germany's AfD. And therefore, contributions on conspiracy theories from relevant platforms are also shared in social media by Europe's right.

An especially crass example: Russian state television reported, that a 13-year-old Russian-German girl from Berlin had been raped by Arab refugees at the end of January 2016. The German authorities wished to hush this up, according to the harsh allegation. Lisa had lied about this, as the police later determined. Hundreds of Russian-Germans believed the propaganda from a parallel media world and demonstrated in different towns throughout Germany. And so, we see how easily one part of the population allowed itself to be taken in by manipulative reporting.[36] In general such a strategy from countries such as Russia appears to be a perfidious means of radicalising people and by so doing of weakening the West.

4.5   Reich Citizens [Reichsbürger]—Merely "Paper Terrorists?"

Whole groups congregate around conspiracy theories. This is demonstrated for example by the Citizens of the Reich movement, which even researchers of extremism were not aware of up until a short time ago and did not surface in any discussions on extremism. This milieu ready to act out violence of so-called Citizens of the Reich [*Reichsbürger*] in the meantime has amassed more than 18,000 followers in the Federal Republic of Germany—a rapidly

---

[35] In the meantime, this party has been renamed "Rassemblement National".
[36] Cf. Markus Ackeret: „Die Stunde der Manipulatoren", in: *Neue Zürcher Zeitung* of 6 August 2016, http://www.nzz.ch/international/europa/cyber-bedrohungen-die-stunde-der-manipulatoren-ld.109391.

4 Radicalisation in Our Midst and in Virtual Rooms and Spaces 139

growing number.³⁷ They form their own kingdoms or states. And in this way they are unified in their crude image that the Federal Republic of Germany is not a state recognised by a law of the people, but merely a company "BRD Ltd" or "BRD plc". The German Reich (*Empire*) still exists for them, the German State is an enemy to them, which one must flatly refuse to obey— with attention to the legal order as well as to paying taxes or penalty notices.

The phenomenon of Reich Citizens (*Reichsbürger*) is by no means peripheral and cannot be neglected as a collection of madmen, sectarians and notorious troublemakers. This became clear on 19 October 2016, when the movement finally appeared on the radar of the state apparatus and security agencies.³⁸ This is the day Wolfgang Plan shot at police officers he ambushed in the Bavarian town of Georgensgmünd. A police officer lost his life as the victim of this dastardly deed by the passionate hunter and sporting marksman, and former owner of a martial arts school, a further officer was seriously injured. Cases of use of violence against authorities appear to be piling up, which now also draws the public side into the equation.

The German state has been taking a closer look at this movement since the beginning of 2017.³⁹ It is not only court officials who have learned of the high propensity to use violence in this milieu. At first glance, Reich Citizens (*Reichsbürger*) appear harmless and quirky, whenever they design their own Personal Identity papers, driving licenses and motorway signs. Offices and officials are overwhelmed with untold submissions and voluminous written documents, really "bombarded". The word "paper terrorism" is already doing the rounds here.⁴⁰

Intelligence officers fear, that these could originate from the ranks of these single actors motivated to be right-wing terrorists.⁴¹ Still the danger extends far beyond this: some parts of this scene are evidently prepared to defend

---

³⁷Cf. Bundesamt für Verfassungsschutz: Aktuelle Zahlen der Reichsbürger und Selbstverwalter, Berlin, March 2018, https://www.verfassungsschutz.de/de/aktuelles/zur-sache/zs-2018-003-reichsbuerger-selbstverwalter-aktuelle-zahlen.

³⁸Cf. Andreas Speit: „Reichsbürger – eine facettenreiche, gefährliche Bewegung", in: Andreas Speit (ed.): *Reichsbürger. Die unterschätzte Gefahr*, Berlin 2017, p. 8.

³⁹Cf. „Bundesregierung wusste bis Anfang 2017 nichts über "Reichsbürger"", in: *Süddeutsche Zeitung* of 20 February 2017, http://www.sueddeutsche.de/politik/kleine-anfrage-der-gruenen-bundesregierung-wusste-bis-anfang-nichts-ueber-reichsbuerger-1.3385865.

⁴⁰A Reich's Citizen (*Reichsbürger*) for example demanded more than 203 million Euros from a table of fees via an "affidavit" (a term from the Middle Ages for sworn testimony under oath) from the District Council Offices in Passau in June 2018, as a 63 page catalogue of demands outlines. The money should have been paid out as silver ingots. Cf. Stefan Brandl: „Echt irre: Reichsbürger fordert von Vize-Landrat über 203 Mio Euro!", in: Passauer Woche of 27 June 2018, p. 7.

⁴¹Cf. Zeit online, 20 April 2016, „Ein Volk, viele Reiche, noch mehr Führer", https://www.zeit.de/politik/deutschland/2016-04/reichsbuerger-verfassungsschutz-radikalisierung-einzeltaeter/komplettansicht.

their ideology in the spirit of self-defence through the use of violence. Reich Citizens (*Reichsbürger*), who have now achieved notoriety in Germany, also exist in other countries, being especially prevalent in Austria. The intelligence services treat them as "deniers of the state" and likewise indicates a growth in this scene. Contrary to the case in Germany, until now there have not been escalations of violence, for example towards police officers.

The so-called Federation of States of Austria (*Staatenbund Österreich*) is worthy of a special mention, established in November 2015 and which operates using terminology from the "One People's Public Trust" (OPPT) which originated in the USA. According to them, the Republic of Austria is merely one company—the Austria, which they purport to represent, as opposed to an "untouchable, sovereign and absolute object under international law".

This confederation is led by Monika Unger, a farmer from Styria, who classed herself as President for Life. In her speeches, which sometimes attracted hundreds of people, she perceived it to be a conspiracy of the powerful against "little people". On the other hand, sums in billions exist in an account held in trust, which "the Vatican, the City of London and Washington D.C. withhold from every single person."[42] Unger linked her webpage to texts which deny the Holocaust.

The Austrian state denier scene is swarming with citizens who have dropped out and idealists, conspiracy theorists, but also anti-Semites and Putin-lovers. Twenty deniers of the state, including Unger, were arrested for participating in an association hostile to the state in April 2017.[43] Some 40 Reich Citizens also disrupted a trial in Aarau in Switzerland for a traffic violation, and questioned the legitimacy of the judge. One activist in particular created an uproar: Daniel Model, an eloquent economist with a PhD and wealthy co-owner of a family business in the packaging sector.[44]

Deniers of the state have also been active in the USA, and indeed very heterogeneously. They base themselves on the concept of the free man. One prominent denier of the state is called Winston Shrout. He propagates his theories on lecture tours and on the Internet, of why the state has no authority over people. According to his own admissions, he did not pay any tax for 20 years. He was called before the court in 2017 and was found guilty.[45]

---

[42] Cf. Hinnerk Berlekamp: „Der Reichsbürger, ein internationales Phänomen", in: Andreas Speit (ed.): Reichsbürger. Die unterschätzte Gefahr, Berlin 2017, pp. 181–183.

[43] Cf. „Staatenbund der Staatsverweigerer", in: Die Zeit of 25 April 2017, https://www.zeit.de/politik/2017-04/staatsverweigerer-oesterreich-staatsleugner-gesetz-verbot.

[44] Ibid., pp. 187–190.

[45] See Hinnerk Berlekamp: Die Reichsbürger, ein internationales Phänomen, in Andreas Speit (ed.): Reichsbürger. Die unterschätzte Gefahr, Berlin 2017, pp. 192–194.

A new phenomenon has shown its face. Ideologically charged fanaticism, firm rejection of the state, the constitutional order and its representatives in politics and administration and the high degree of readiness for violence move some of the Reich Citizens closer to right-wing terrorism. The motive corresponds to a defensive attitude, which may entirely take on the traits of a communicative message—a definite natural characteristic of terrorism.

It is probable that single actors, who acknowledge themselves as Reich Citizens, not only attack police officers, but look down somewhat on ethnic minorities and refugees too.[46] Of course, every Reich Citizen is by no means a potential terrorist. But the danger grows of people from the Reich Citizens Movement becoming single actors. Not only homeland security officers have feared for a long time that at some time or other a person like Anders Behring Breivik would emerge from the crowd.[47]

4.6 Identitarians and the Christchurch Terrorist

Another movement considers it is being subjected to allegations of having at least taken mental and spiritual steps for the terrorist in Christchurch: the Identitarians (IB). Founded in the South of France in 2003, the movement is active above all in Germany and Austria. The book by the French author Renaud Camus functions as their "bible:" "The Große Austausch" (or *"The Great Displacement"*), which after appearing in 2011 quickly took care of the spread of the idea of a change of population. His book finds great resonance in the community, even if it is not read.[48] The assailant in Christchurch named his manifesto after it. Proponents of the Great Replacement theory believe that mass migration and demographic shifts will not necessarily end all life on the planet, but rather the meaningful civilisation which has been created by white Europeans. They often paint Muslim communities as implicit in these plans because of the perception that they innately wish

---

[46] And thus it was announced in April 2017, that a right-wing extremist group was planning attacks on asylum-seekers and Jews across Germany. The ringleader was evidently an avowed Reich Citizen (*Reichsbürger*) from Baden-Württemberg. N-tv.de 2017, „Reichsbürger plante Anschläge", 25 January 2017, https://www.n-tv.de/politik/Reichsbuerger-plante-Anschlaege-article19640627.html.

[47] Cf. Zeit Online, 20 April 2016, „Ein Volk, viele Reiche, noch mehr Führer", https://www.zeit.de/politik/deutschland/2016-04/reichsbuerger-verfassungsschutz-radikalisierung-einzeltaeter/komplettansicht.

[48] Camus' book with the title of the same name has not been translated into English up until now. It is also concerned with the placing the exchange of population on an epoch-based level. Camus sees significance such as with the Great Plague here (die *Große Pest, La Grande Guerre* (or the First World War) or the *Great Depression*). Camus' case is the expression of a dilemma: It shows that thoughts can be made independently of their authors. Others continued his "fight with purely intellectual means" with weapons.

to destroy Western civilisation. Proponents of the Great Replacement theory frequently overlay it with anti-Semitic theories, blaming "globalist Jewish elites" for mass migration (in this context the wording of a shadowy global elite is used, named as "illuminati").[49] An example here is the Jewish philanthropic investor George Soros—who was the target for a campaign Hungarian Prime Minister Viktor Orbán endorsed.[50] Orbán described refugees as "Muslim invaders".[51] Similarly, "Eurabia" was promoted in the early 2000s by the British author Gisèle Littman, who argued that Western countries are slowly being brought under Islamic rule. She published many books under her pseudonyms Bat Ye'or (Hebrew: "Daughter of the Nile") and Yahudiya Masriya. The Norwegian terrorist Anders Breivik published strong references to the Eurabia Islamisation concept.[52]

The number of activists at around 800 people (in July 2018) is comparatively small there. Nevertheless, a spiritual feeding ground had come into being, which in the meantime has caused German intelligence officers to consider the movement to lean towards "right-wing extreme". In the official reasoning in July 2019 we are told: "IBD's (*Identitarian Movement Germany's*) positions are incompatible with Basic German Law. IBD, in the end, aims to exclude individuals of non-European extraction from democratic participation and to discriminate against them in a way which violates their human dignity. From IBD's point of view, individuals who do not share similar ethnic qualifications will never be part of a common culture."[53]

Supporters associated with the Identitarians number many tens of thousands. Symbolic actions allowed a political myth to arise. The IB carried out

---

[49] See Jacob Davey/Julia Ebner: "The Great Replacement". The Violent Consequences of Mainstream Extremism, Institute for strategic dialogue, London 2019, pp. 10 and 12, https://www.isdglobal.org/wp-content/uploads/2019/07/The-Great-Replacement-The-Violent-Consequences-of-Mainstreamed-Extremism-by-ISD.pdf.

[50] The Hungarian Prime Minister, once a Liberal and ironically when a student he had held a grant from the Soros Foundation, led a crusade against George Soros, who was born in Budapest. This led to the fact that in the meantime, the Central European University he had founded as well as the Open Society Foundation had to leave the country. Soros is considered to be enemy Number One of the state, who is made responsible for wanting to "Tempt millions of refugees to come to Hungary".

[51] This was quoted during an interview with the German tabloid newspaper "Bild". Bild.de on 7 January "You want the migrants, not us!", https://www.bild.de/politik/ausland/viktor-orban/orban-interview-54403736.bild.html.

[52] See Liz Fekete: The Muslim conspiracy theory and the Oslo massacre, Race & Class, 53 (2011) 3, pp. 30–47.

[53] The domestic intelligence service of the Federal Republic of Germany (BfV): Press release, 11 July 2019, https://www.verfassungsschutz.de/en/public-relations/press/pr-20190711-bfv-classifies-ibd-as-a-movement-which-beyond-doubt-pursues-right-wing-extremist-efforts.

a few actions with effects on publicity: For example, they disrupted the theatrical performance „Die Schutzbefohlenen" by the Austrian Nobel Prize winner Elfriede Jelinek in April 2016, which refugees were also acting in. However, there were also repeated setbacks. And thus, Facebook and Instagram blocked the IB's pages in Germany and Austria in May 2018. Shortly before this Génération Identitaire was "blocked" in France.[54]

We are able to discuss a link to violent right-wing extremism. After all, the Christchurch terrorist Brenton Tarrant donated the not inconsiderable sum of 1,500 Euros to the private account of the Austrian speaker of this movement, Martin Sellner, in January. The sum went into his private account. Following the attack, the domestic intelligence services and the office for counteracting terrorism in Austria (*Bundesamt für Verfassungsschutz und Terrorismusbekämpfung (BVT)*) searched Sellner's home in March 2019, and opened investigations because of suspected involvement in a violent terrorist attack organisation. The following was reported: A number of e-mails had been exchanged. Sellner once offered him to go for a coffee or a beer, if the murderous assailant was ever in Vienna.[55] Tarrant travelled twice to Austria himself, in the context of his trips around Europe. It also came to light that the Australian had also donated a total of around 2,000 Euros to French Identitarians in four tranches in September 2017.[56] Sellner had also written a German version of the dedication to Renaud Camus' „Der große Austausch" (*The Great Exchange*).[57] The Frenchman is considered the central reference figure for Identitarians. Here too, there is a direct link to the murderous assailant from Christchurch: The latter named his 74-page manifesto after the title of this book, with appropriate symbolism.

Sellner was refused the right of entry into Britain to travel to London on 9 March 2018. It had been his intention to make a speech at Speakers' Corner on "Freedom of Expression in Europe."[58] The British Home Office justified their decision, in that Sellner's organisation "actively provoked racial hatred

---

[54] Cf. Andreas Speit: APO on rechts? Vorwort, in: Ders. (ed.): Das Netzwerk der Identitären. Ideologie und Aktionen der Neuen Rechten, Berlin 2018, pp. 9–16, here pp. 11–15.
[55] Die Presse.com, Identitäre: Sellner wollte mit Christchurch-Attentäter „auf ein Bier gehen", 15 May 2019, https://diepresse.com/home/innenpolitik/5628349/Identitaere_Sellner-wollte-mit-ChristchurchAttentaeter-auf-ein.
[56] taz.de (die tageszeitung), Noch mehr Spenden an Identitäre, 3 April 2019, https://taz.de/Christchurch-Attentaeter/!5585652/.
[57] Renaud Camus: Revolte gegen den Großen Austausch, Schnellroda 2016.
[58] Any person is actually permitted to make a speech on any arbitrary subject in London's Hyde Park without prior registration or notification. The basis for this is a Parliamentary ruling from the 19th century.

and worked against the cohesion of society."[59] The Public Prosecutor in Graz had even started proceedings before this because of "sedition", forming criminal association and of a statutory offence (similar to the German "incitement of the masses") against the IB. It went so far as to search apartments, business premises and local association meeting places at the end of April 2018, predominantly in Graz. The leadership around Sellner was also affected by this.[60] An Austrian intelligence services' report on the Identitarians had noted as early as 2016: "At present, the Identitarian movement is attempting to develop an active mass movement throughout Europe from the confused and muddy reservoir of ideas from the new right intellectual pioneers. They have not succeeded in doing this hitherto. However, the Identitarians are concerned with a renewed attempt to create a network of modernised right-wing extremists, as a continuation of the New Right discussed above and to occupy public spaces and territory with anti-Islamic and xenophobic actions."[61]

There was possibly also a connection to Estonia. The Christchurch terrorist had travelled thence from Austria in December 2018. One week after the attack on two mosques in the city of Christchurch, New Zealand, in which 50 people were killed, according to reports in Estonian media, an event was held including a lecture programme on the subject of "Australian Culture" in the university city of Tartu in the regional offices of the „Blaues Erwachen" ("Blue Awakening"). According to the list of participants on Facebook, the Chairman Ruuben Kaalep was also present there.[62] The event was announced on the same Facebook page on which the alleged Australian terrorist also supposedly made posts. The printed matter "Foundations of Culture in Australia" (1936) by P. R. Stephensen, one of the co-founders of the fascist party "Australia First Movement" was at the centre of this lecture event, as the Facebook invitation also proves. Stephensen set out his anti-Semitic and fascist way of thinking in his publication. Tarrant who was born in Australia is supposed to have spent around one week in the Baltic states at the start of December, following his stay in Austria.[63]

---

[59] Cf. Tobias Wolf, Großbritannien weist Lutz Bachmann an der Grenze ab, in: Sächsische Zeitung of 18 March 2018, under: https://www.sz-online.de/nachrichten/grossbritannien-weist-lutz-bachmann-an-der-grenze-ab-3900220.html (16 April 2018).

[60] Colette M. Schmidt, Staatsanwaltschaft führt Hausdurchsuchungen bei Identitären durch, in: Der Standard, 27 April 2018.

[61] Bundesministerium für Inneres [*Austrian Federal Ministry of the Interior*] (ed.), Staatsschutzbericht 2016, Vienna 2017, p. 44.

[62] See "Blue Awakening", Event on 22 March, https://www.facebook.com/events/645447295891644/ (called up on 2 July 2019).

[63] Die Presse.com, Hatten estnische Rechtsextreme Kontakt mit Neuseeland-Attentäter?, 2 April 2019, https://diepresse.com/home/ausland/welt/5605973/Hatten-estnische-Rechtsextreme-Kontakt-mit-NeuseelandAttentaeter (called up on 2 July 2019).

Kaalep, who entered the Estonian Parliament at the age of 25 in the course of national elections in 2019, has a list of neo-National Socialist activities. Kaalep's links with Paul Hickman can serve as proof, the British founder member of the National Action neo-Nazi group, which has been recognised as a terrorist group by British authorities and placed on the same list as ISIS and al-Qaeda as well as an approving quote about US white supremacist Richard Spencer, who had himself quoted Kaalep.[64] In his manifesto, Anders Breivik quoted Spencer numerous times, also due to the fact that Spencer runs a "jihadi watch" website.[65] Kaalep described himself on his twitter account as a Finno-Ugrian Supremacist and showed his solidarity with Sellner, when the latter was refused entry to Britain, to travel to London.[66] He also attracted attention as an Internet troll.

Whilst being sworn in as a Member of Parliament, he used the same symbol as Tarrant, the clear and interpretable OK gesture, and also used it later in a joint selfie during a visit to Marine Le Pen. However, when Le Pen discovered Kaalep's background, she immediately distanced herself from him. Kaalep was compelled to withdraw the selfie. Le Pen was also concerned, standing in the 2019 European Parliament elections, with not unleashing a new debate on fascism.[67] What is certain, is that lone wolves join onto existing movements, even if they are not directly a fixed component of them. The fluid and international structures appear to have been created just for lone actors, who search for movements on the Internet, which campaign against supposed superalienation. They wish to find a pretext so to speak for themselves and to give themselves the aura of working for higher objectives.

---

[64] ERR news (national Estonian broadcasting): Ruuben Kaalep has a long history of neo-Nazi activity, 3 April 2019, https://news.err.ee/926367/weekly-ekre-mp-ruuben-kaalep-has-long-history-of-neo-nazi-activity.

[65] See also Jeffrey D. Simon: *Lone Wolf Terrorism. Understanding The Growing Threat*, New York 2016, p. 52.

[66] Twitter account of Ruuben Kaalep: https://twitter.com/ruubenkaalep?lang=de (called up on 2 July 2019).

[67] New York Times (2019): Marine Le Pen Denies Making White Power Gesture in Selfie, New York Times, 16 May, https://www.nytimes.com/2019/05/16/world/europe/marine-le-pen-selfie-gesture.html (called up on 2 July 2019).

4.7 Consequences

The circumstances in society contribute towards susceptible people being more easily radicalised. And what is more: The cases, especially of "Breivik" and "Tarrant" in particular also demonstrate "the importance of seeing the terrorism of loners as embedded in, and motivated by, the rhetoric of larger movements."[68] In the virtual world, people with a similar mindset can find one another beyond national boundaries, for example in their own forums on apparently innocent gaming platforms. The general "pressure from the right" in society and the fear of foreigners and of an "Islamification" accompanied by hysteria may be the final nudge to permit an enraged citizen to become a ticking time bomb. The Reich Citizens (*Reichsbürger*) movement demonstrates typically for this ideal, how evidently harmless "nutters" (*madmen*) can become a danger to public safety—through individuals who go one step further than simply harassing officials with written correspondence. This is the climate of society in which lone wolves prosper well.

Lone wolf terrorism is the product of self-radicalisation of an individual, which is triggered by personal grievances and political and ideological motives in a mixture which must be evaluated in each case. The difference between lone wolf terrorism and somebody running amok (*killing spree or frenzy*) is political motivation of the former and systematic planning. Personal experiences are perceived as being unjust and may mark the point of departure for self-radicalisation. This, however, does not take place overnight, but is a process of maturing, in which short-term, medium-term and even long-term developments congregate. Thus, identification of the actor with radical movements plays just as great a role as the influence through extremist teaching. Politically motivated implementation of acts of violence may be decided upon as an individual decision or following interaction with a group. However, a certain separation from the real world always arises (Fig. 4.1).[69]

---

[68] See Lars Erik Berntzen/Sveinung Sandberg: The Collective Nature of Lone Wolf Terrorism: Anders Behring Breivik and the Anti-Islamic Social Movement, in: Terrorism and Political Violence, 26 (2014) 5, p. 760. 759–779, here 760.

[69] Cf. Farhad Khosrokhavar: Radikalisierung, Bonn 2016, here pp. 38 and 45 f.

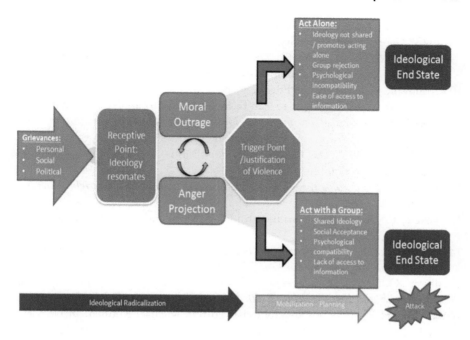

Fig. 4.1 A model for radicalisation and mobilisation of lone wolves, based on Connor/Flynn 2015: 19 (On the basis of Jeffrey Connor/Carol Rollie Flynn: Report: Lone Wolf Terrorism, Georgetown University, Washington D. C. 2015, p. 19, http://georgetownsecuritystudiesreview.org/wp-content/uploads/2015/08/NCITF-Final-Paper.pdf.)

References

1. Albrecht, S., Fielitz, M., & Thurston, N. (2019). Introduction. In M. Fielitz & N. Thurston (Eds.), *Post-digital cultures of the far right. Online actions and offline consequences in Europe and the US* (pp. 7–22). Bielefeld.
2. Backes, U. (2013). Rechtsextremistische Gewalt in Europa. In G. Hirscher & E. Jesse (Eds.), *Extremismus in Deutschland* (pp. 43–62). Baden-Baden.
3. Bartlett, J., & Littler, M. (2011). *Inside the EDL: Populist politics in a digital age*. Demos Think Tank, London.
4. Berlekamp, H. (2017). Die Reichsbürger, ein internationales Phänomen. In A. Speit (Ed.), *Reichsbürger. Die unterschätzte Gefahr* (pp. 192–194). Berlin.
5. Berntzen, L. E., & Sandberg, S. (2014). The collective nature of lone wolf terrorism: Anders Behring Breivik and the anti-Islamic social movement. *Terrorism and Political Violence, 26*(5), 759–779.
6. Bohn, C. (2006). *Einsamkeit im Spiegel der sozialwissenschaftlichen Forschung*. Dortmund.
7. Butter, M. (2018). *Nichts ist, wie es scheint. Über Verschwörungstheorien*. Berlin.

8. Connor, J., & Flynn, C. R. (2005). *Report: Lone wolf terrorism*. Washington D.C.: Georgetown University.
9. Davey, J., & Ebner, J. (2019). *The great replacement. The violent consequences of mainstream extremism*. London: Institute for Strategic Dialogue.
10. Donovan, J., Lewis, B., & Friedberg, B., (2019). Parallel ports. Sociotechnical change from the Alt-Right to Alt-Tech. In M. Fielitz & N. Thurston (Eds.), *Post-digital cultures of the far right. Online actions and offline consequences in Europe and the US* (pp. 49–65). Bielefeld.
11. Dubiel, H. (1986). Das Gespenst des Populismus. In Ditto. (Ed.), *Populismus und Aufklärung*. Frankfurt/Main.
12. Ebner, J. (2017). *The rage. The vicious circle of Islamist and far-right extremism*. London.
13. Fekete, L. (2011). The Muslim conspiracy theory and the Oslo massacre. *Race & Class, 53*(3), 30–47.
14. Hartleb, F. (2017). *Die Stunde der Populisten. Wie sich unsere Politik trumpetisiert und was wir dagegen tun können*. Schwalbach im Taunus.
15. Jarren, O. (1998). Internet – neue Chancen für die politische Kommunikation. *Aus Politik und Zeitgeschichte, B 40*, 13–21.
16. Jaschke, H.-G. (1992). Biographisches Porträt: Michael Kühnen. In U. Backes & E. Jesse (Eds.), *Jahrbuch Extremismus & Demokratie* (Vol. 4, pp. 167–180).
17. Koehler, D. (2016). Right-wing extremism and terrorism in Europe: Current developments and issues for the future. *Prism, 6*(2), 84–104.
18. Khosrokhavar, F. (2016). *Radikalisierung*. Bonn.
19. Miller-Idriss, C. (2009). *Blood and culture. Youth, right-wing extremism and national belonging in contemporary Germany*. Durham/London.
20. Simon, J. D. (2016). *Lone wolf terrorism. Understanding the growing threat*. New York.
21. Speit, A. (2017). Reichsbürger – eine facettenreiche, gefährliche Bewegung. In A. Speit (Ed.), *Reichsbürger. Die unterschätzte Gefahr*. Berlin.
22. Speit, A. (2018). APO on rechts? Vorwort. In Ders. (Ed.), *Das Netzwerk der Identitären. Ideologie und Aktionen der Neuen Rechten* (pp. 9–16). Berlin.
23. Spengler, O. (2007, original 1918). *The decline of the West*. Oxford.
24. Spitzer, M. (2008). *Einsamkeit. Die unerkannte Krankheit*. Munich.
25. Sunstein, C. R. (2002). *Republic.com 2.0*. Princeton.

5

Counter-Strategies and Prevention

There are two opposing strategies for monitoring and containing terrorism. Terrorism may exist according to the *conservative strategy* purely because the state is too liberal, and society is too open and tolerant. Accordingly, rigid law and order measures under the narrative of the "fight against terrorism" would be in order, which should give the state some powers of self-assertion again. According to the *liberal strategy*, liberal democracy as such is not the reason for the terror, but misuse of the freedoms this makes possible. Therefore, we assume that ideological terrorism in any case does not garner any support here, which is why we need not immediately assume an existential danger for the State and Society. The State should not overreact at all, and cut back the freedoms of the great majority, in order to take up (useless) measures against a few extremists.

Actually, it is self-explanatory that we cannot defend freedom by placing restrictions on it. The absurd consequences this causes became clear at the latest with the ban on face covering on French beaches or the ban on covering the full face in Austria. Repression by the state will not solve the problem. Much rather, we are concerned with introducing preventative as well as sustainable measures. It is, however, in the nature of the matter, that results cannot be achieved immediately. This is true for both strategies. The difference is simply that the conservative strategy unveils measures which all citizens will become aware of at once but are seldom able to suppress the criminal acts they are aimed at in the long-term. Thus, the rigorous approach by President Rodrigo Duterte of the Philippines against narcotics dealers and drug-taking, which affected the lives of thousands of people has not yet led to his islands becoming completely free of drugs. Inhabitants of Hamburg will still be able to recall the interjection by Minister for the Interior Ronald Schill as a result of the mayoral election in 2001. The populist, who was named "Judge Ruthless" by the media and grandiosely promised in an offhand manner he would successfully cut criminality in half with his party (19.4%) and would banish widespread drug dealing from Hamburg's main train station. In the end, he was merely a symbolic figure in politics.

Measures as part of a liberal strategy on the other hand remain invisible to most citizens, as they follow the need to reach such people who are actually at risk of descending into extremism. Prevention cannot be facilitated overnight, but nevertheless is immensely important, requiring support from the state, and what is more for the long-term. Offers of assistance with a low threshold should not form the primary mainstay of opportunities for criminal prosecutors to prevent terrorism. Such offerings can of course only exist, once we admit the problem exists.

The new technical possibilities which actors have at their disposal in the digital era, in addition, have significantly changed investigative practices: Whenever police and the Public Prosecutor's office search the apartment of an accused person, they are commissioned with seizing written documents, along with objects relating to criminal deeds such as weapons. In earlier times, actors communicated using landline devices or conspired and remained elusive by using telephone boxes. This now lies in the past: Actors have long since discovered Cloud computing as their preferred means of communication. Anonymisation and encoding are increasingly becoming standard communication tools for the most serious criminals.[1] Law enforcement agencies, whose officers are not fully cognisant with such modern methods of communication, are useless. This is also a reason why I refer to the case of Sonboly to such a great extent below, as he is of course an example of the latest developments within Lone Wolf terrorism, with his strong affinity for communicating via the Internet, which up until now has not been worked through and analysed.

Access to material which baits peoples and races was never easier than it is today, in particular for the young too. In most cases, a look at the comments under any random article or video will suffice. A few clicks further will open up a relevant forum with a bright panopticum of misanthropic images, inflammatory remarks, encoded bywords and pseudoscientific analyses, which would never be permitted to appear like this in German media.

---

[1] Cf. the assessment of the President of the Federal Criminal Police Office even years ago, see Jörg Ziercke: „Freiheit und Sicherheit im digitalen Zeitalter", in: Bundeszentrale für politische Bildung, 22 October 2010, http://www.bpb.de/internationales/europa/europa-kontrovers/38187/standpunkt-joerg-ziercke?p=all.

The brutalisation of open discourse is a characteristic of our era, and the rhetoric leads directly to murderous assailants such as David Sonboly. Nevertheless, it appears that it scarcely disturbs anyone in our society to a large extent, that people can evidently express themselves in such a manner, and how easy access to this written material is. The persistent stubbornness, with which the Bavarian State Government up until recently was concerned with keeping Adolf Hitler's *Mein Kampf* under wraps, on the other hand has had a really laughable effect.

Prevention must also always begin wherever it can achieve success relatively easily. Protecting young people should be a special concern for our society, in particular. This is why I go into the case of Sonboly so extensively. It elucidates, how lone wolf terrorists act in today's society and therefore provides us insights into the best strategies for prevention. That these also incorporate preventing mistakes on the part of officialdom, is a sorry, yet important aspect of the debate.

5.1 Rethinking Required by Security Officials

Security officials in Germany at least are a long way removed from accepting the category of lone wolf terrorism into their own jargon and terminology. Intelligence services reject this in principle, which also applies to their readiness to discuss this and their accessibility for argumentation. The cases of Breivik, Steffen and Sonboly have evidently not changed this. And thus, their newsletter stated in 2017: "The violent deeds (of single actors) are generally directed towards 'soft' targets and are committed in part using freely accessible objects for perpetrating violent acts, such as an axe or a kitchen knife. We have increasingly conducted research on this subject in recent years,[2] in order to obtain a better understanding of the single actor phenomenon and to work against glorification of 'lone wolves'."

The case of "Sonboly," however, clearly shows that nothing has changed up until now. This type of actor is still not being acknowledged. These circumstances are alarming to the extent that communication and interaction processes have been carried out in the virtual arena for a long time. For it is precisely in this sphere that "untold publicity material", and the opportunity, for example, to find "friends" on these platforms exist. However, no

---

[2]Bundesamt für Verfassungsschutz (Domestic intelligence service of the Federal Republic of Germany): Einzeltäter – weder einsamer Wolf noch isoliert, Newsletter, June 2017, https://www.verfassungsschutz.de/de/oeffentlichkeitsarbeit/newsletter/newsletter-archive/bfv-newsletter-archiv/bfv-newsletter-2017-02-archiv/bfv-newsletter-2017-02-thema-08.

regard is given to this state of affairs. It still remains vague, what their research actually covers and whether prior assessments up until now should not be adjusted—and the fault lying with rapidly changing developments. Perhaps we could also reconsider the customary pattern in criminal law, which still fundamentally excludes terrorism by single actors. As a consequence, proceedings against terrorists are considered to be apolitical criminal cases. An example: "On the morning after Jo Cox's murder, there was a heated debate (…): endless e-mail chains discussed the wording of a press release to condemn the incident. 'Let's call this terrorism', some advocated. 'No, let's go for terrorist-inspired', others argued."[3]

There is an absence of clear legislation and laws to proceed against single actors from the radical right. Up until now there simply has not been any statute, with which a (murderous) assailant could be sentenced as such. When analysing assailants, we observed that violent assassins with extreme right-wing attitudes are no longer merely young, drunken and spontaneously violent, raised in broken homes. Nevertheless, extreme right-wing attitudes and violent assaults in Germany by and large are interpreted as being problems of young people or young adults from broken homes and disrupted families as well as well as those with a low level of education. This "pathologicalising approach" continues to be in great demand for explaining individual motives. It appears appropriate to re-think our approach towards right-wing extremist murderers and assailants and our accentuation of a group process, a social community. Anything else is merely superfluous window dressing and will not prevent terrorist attacks.

Other countries view the risk level differently, not just the USA, which recognises the central threat to the here and now. The fight against terrorism reached a new repressive dimension immediately after 11 September 2001, with the Patriot Act in the USA. The investigating authorities were empowered by this to exchange data between each other to a great extent, and to carry out extensive monitoring as well as checks on the civilian population. The regulation recognised as "Lone Wolf" permits special monitoring of individual people, who are not allocated to any particular terrorist association. And in addition, the CIA was also empowered for example, which previously had only been authorised to operate abroad (*overseas*).[4]

---

[3] Julia Ebner: The Rage. The Vicious Circle of Islamist and Far-Right Extremism, London 2017, p. 113.
[4] Cf. Elizabeth B. Bazan: Intelligence Reform and Terrorism Prevention Act of 2004: "Lone Wolf" Amendment to the Foreign Intelligence Surveillance Act, Report for Congress, Washington D.C. 2004, https://fas.org/irp/crs/RS22011.pdf.

Scotland Yard also warned as early as November 2009 of an increase in right-wing extremism and terrorism, carried out specifically by "lone wolves". It was clear that this new concept of being less organised was on the increase.[5]

The secret service in the Netherlands, AIVD commented in 2012: "AIVD has become aware of the fact, lone wolves both plan and execute violent transactions independently and as conspirators, but seldom carry these out in complete isolation; however, AIVD considers radicalisation to be a social phenomenon. This also applies for the majority of lone wolves. When following up such events we frequently see that lone wolves scarcely had any contact to people of a similar mindset in real life – but maintained active contact with people on the Internet. It is precisely these contacts and discourses which made a significant contribution towards radicalising them and inspired them to act out in violence."[6]

And thus, it has been appropriate to rethink the customary maxims used for these acts and deeds for a long time. If the current pattern continues, of merely regarding terrorism as appearing in group form, there will not be any further development in preventing it or cracking down on it. The British expert on extremism and terrorism Matthew Goodwin passed harsh judgement in the course of the case of Pavlo Lapshyn in 2013: "Security officials have spent at least 50 years creating new law enforcement instruments – under the assumption that terrorism is centred on a cell-based system with a command chain. But destruction of the group dynamic, the infiltration of organisations and dissolution of weak bonds in the command chain suddenly appear superfluous in the battle against isolated individuals, who have perhaps never even met a 'fellow believer'."[7]

The political controversy over an appropriate response to terrorism frequently serves to profile people (for example politicians, who wish to create a reputation for themselves as unyielding enforcers of *Law and Order*), parties and officials. In principle this is legitimate, reactions must be taken against dangerous situations. However, we cannot usually reckon on swift successes. It is far sooner the case, that a certain inability or to put it less dramatically, a powerlessness to uncover right-wing terrorists governs things. The NSU was able to carry out murders the length and breadth of Germany undetected for years, although intelligence services were acting in the same spheres as they

---

[5] The Telegraph (2009): "Warning of threat from right wing 'lone wolf' terrorists", https://www.telegraph.co.uk/news/uknews/5940740/Warning-of-threat-from-right-wing-lone-wolf-terrorists.html.
[6] AIVD, General Intelligence and Security Service in the Netherlands: Jihadism on the Web. A Breeding Ground for Jihad in the Modern Age, Amsterdam 2012, p. 20f.
[7] Matthew Goodwin: ""Lone wolves" such as Pavlo Lapshyn are part of a bigger threat", in: The Guardian, 23 October 2013, https://www.theguardian.com/commentisfree/2013/oct/23/pavlo-lapshyn-extremist-bomber-lone-wolves.

were, and the actors also had a network backing them up. The case of Franz Fuchs clearly shows that this problem occurs with lone wolves in particular, as does the case of Peter Mangs from Sweden, however, too. Both were able to remain incognito and undetected for years.

The political debate follows a cyclical pattern, as it is comprised similarly to terrorism with a direct relationship to events. The call soon went out in Germany to provide security agencies with additional authorisations and competencies.[8] This is also evident in the general concern, that the NSU was able to act as a right-wing terrorist group in this form for years without being discovered. Whether this forms the basis for effective prevention may be the subject of some doubt after the Sonboly case. Daring to allow additional democracy, more openness and tolerance would be contrary to the reaction to Breivik's right-wing terrorism in Norway. Up until now, there have not been any copycats in this country.

Unlike the situation in Germany. The investigative authorities were renowned for their exemplary work,[9] whilst people with a similar mindset to Sonboly continued to operate in a virtual anti-refugee club—with deadly consequences. Although dozens of professional investigators and detectives were at work, the assumption was made that the forum Steam was a harmless platform for violent video games. It is equally incomprehensible, that the authorities knew Sonboly had his e-mail account with the American corporate giant yahoo.com, although the German officials, however, neglected to commence requesting information from the USA. Far right violence was ignored and trivialised in the case of "David Sonboly". The intelligence services reports kept quiet, and no charges were brought against politically motivated criminality.

The political statement could also have turned out accordingly. A warning of right-wing terrorism could have been given, to watch out for lone wolves. This did not ensue. It did not take place. EUROPOL, the European Union's police department which records trends in right-wing terrorism each year, could also have taken up the case of David Sonboly. In the report for the year 2016, we learn far right extremist activities were increasingly directed by small groups or by individuals. David Sonboly is not mentioned in it.[10]

---

[8]Cf. Patrick Gensing: Terror von Rechts. Die Nazi-Morde und das Versagen der Politik, Berlin 2012, p. 224f.
[9]For example in the expert discussion with the author, Cf. München.de - Das offizielle Stadtportal (2017): „Gutachten zum Münchener Amoklauf präsentiert", https://www.muenchen.de/aktuell/2017-10/gutachten-zum-amoklauf-oez-vorgestellt.html.
[10]EUROPOL (2017): EU Terrorism and Trend Report 2017, The Hague, pp. 45–47, https://www.europol.europa.eu/activities-services/main-reports/eu-terrorism-situation-and-trend-report-te-sat-2017.

The image of many officials, which views militant far right extremism as sustaining itself solely from the fruits of the skinhead and comradeship scenes, and not able to occur on apparently harmless gaming platforms, has long since become outdated. A subculture increasingly thrives in the niches of these boards, distinguished by militant and racist hatred, highly interactive and in addition to this, networked internationally. However, this new type of actor has not yet reached every corner of officialdom. In brief: The image and understanding from the 1980s or the 1990s still prevails. The statement from the Bavarian Minister of the Interior Joachim Herrmann which we have already mentioned proves this, according to which David Sonboly was not a far right extremist, as no documents relating to membership of a relevant party or organisation could be unearthed.

In crass contradiction to this announcement, the instruction and continuous training of police and Justice Department officials take into consideration that anyone can become a right-wing extremist, without being a member of an official party or organisation. Similarly, as with other phenomena such as with Islamic Fundamentalism, we are concerned here with an extremely dynamic field. Officials and the media would both also find problems with the assessment that David Sonboly's parents once came to Germany as refugees (which the Bavarian Minister of the Interior Joachim Herrmann emphasised constantly, in order to substantiate the theory of someone running amok). According to the motto: How can someone who has a migratory background himself in turn become a right-wing extremist?

5.2 Virtual Platform as a Source of Danger

The virtual proprietary rights of Twitter, Facebook and Co., include the right to exclude individual users, whether temporarily or permanently. Every user accepts this, the minute they set up their account. According to its own admissions, Facebook finally took more decisive steps against extremist posts under pressure from the authorities. The European Union finally demanded that Facebook and their competitors must remove such contents more swiftly.

Facebook uses automated software in order to detect this kind of post. In addition, the company published a definition of the term "terrorism" for the first time, which however excludes single actors and refers to groups. Prior to this it is not known, according to which criteria posts could be attributed as being extremist. An official opinion on this was issued in April 2018: "Albeit that the challenges of online terrorism are not new, it has still achieved significant growth, as digital platforms now occupy a central position in our lives.

We can detect a significance in Facebook, in that people are certain why we use technology as well as our counterterrorism team for ensuring this."[11]

The claim and the reality, however, diverge widely. The founder of Facebook, Mark Zuckerberg makes public relations assurances for his own company ad absurdum. He spoke out in an interview in July 2018 against blocking Facebook posts denying the holocaust. As a Jew himself he finds it deeply offensive if people doubt the holocaust ever took place: "But in the end I do not believe that our platform should remove things, because I believe there are things other people are mistaken about. I do not believe they are mistaken on purpose."[12]

The Christchurch Call directly targets "eliminating extremist terrorism and violent online extremism".[13] But a troubling sign can be seen in the United States' refusal to add its name to the list. Officials in the Trump administration told the *Washington Post* that doing so would pose "constitutional concerns." A White House statement explained that, whilst it stood "with the international community in condemning terrorist and violent extremist content online," the United States was "not currently in a position to join the endorsement." Close examination and a close reading the Christchurch Call does not support the White House's position. The document avoids any mention of government-mandated codes of speech. It emphasises that any action must abide by "human rights and fundamental freedoms."[14] The significance of the American position should not be underestimated, for not only is their voice very important, they are also host to many of the most powerful social media and gaming platforms in the world. The other problem with the Christchurch Call is that it is unclear how success will be measured, and what should happen next with the overall initiative.[15]

---

[11] Facebook: "Hard Questions: How Effective Is Technology in Keeping Terrorists off Facebook?", April 2018 (author's own translation), https://newsroom.fb.com/news/2018/04/keeping-terrorists-off-facebook/.
[12] Mark Zuckerberg: "The Recode Interview. Everything was on the table – and after Facebook's wildest year yet, that's a really big table", 18 July 2018, https://www.recode.net/2018/7/18/17575156/mark-zuckerberg-interview-facebook-recode-kara-swisher.
[13] See the official website: https://www.christchurchcall.com/call.html.
[14] Cited after Emerson T. Brooking: The Christchurch Call and the Failure of US Leadership, in: Atlantic Council of 20 May 2019, https://www.atlanticcouncil.org/blogs/new-atlanticist/the-christchurch-call-and-the-failure-of-us-leadership.
[15] See Alexander Gillespie: Christchurch Call: No clear target but let's salute a start to reform, in: RNZ (New Zealand Public Broadcast) (Opinion), https://www.rnz.co.nz/news/on-the-inside/389370/christchurch-call-no-clear-target-but-let-s-salute-a-start-to-reform.

The latest discussions in the USA on militant right-wing extremism on the Internet demonstrate dramatically how poorly self-governance of virtual platforms actually works. The neo-National Socialist group "Atomwaffen Division" (*Atomic Weapons Division*) is considered to be dangerous to the highest degree. It inspires Lone Wolves, who struck out on their own, for example in Texas, Virginia, Washington and Nevada. All are united in their homage to the Third Reich, their hatred of Jews and homosexuals. Five murders have been attributed directly to this group. Like 20-year-old Samuel Woodward murdering a homosexual Jewish student in January 2018. Woodward commended *Mein Kampf* and wrote that the National Socialist underground was "fairly cool".[16] The ideological cement is blatant. However, the group was able to continue its activities unhindered. Activists placed propaganda films on Steam and YouTube under the banner "Atomwaffen Division", in which they demanded Jews should be gassed for instance.

However, the videos can only be called up, if the user first gives their consent to receive extremist contents. Employees of both platforms must have been aware of the videos, without considering it necessary to block them. Verge, who administer Steam's site finally reacted at the end of February, and YouTube likewise.[17]

A fundamental problem remains: Steam scarcely has any registration mechanism. Only groups or users can be registered, not contents or concrete threats of violence. In the meantime, a petition page has been added, in order to make Valve aware of these problems. The appeal criticises racist accounts appearing as news feeds. A basic search for words or keywords such as "Nazi", "Jews" or "school shooting" yields thousands of results. The petition had 35,706 supporters in July 2018.[18]

One gamer complained in a German forum as early as January 2010 about the spread of numerous hate groups: "Dear Gamestar! I really have often noticed that various groups bustle about on Steam, with dubious names and

---

[16] Cf. Pro Publica (2018): "Inside Atomwaffen As It Celebrates a Member for Allegedly Killing a Gay Jewish College Student", 23 February 2018, https://www.propublica.org/article/atomwaffen-division-inside-white-hate-group.

[17] Cf. ibid. and: The Verge (2018): "Discord shuts down more neo-Nazi, alt-right servers".

[18] Care 2 Petitions (2018): "Tell This Online Platform That Allowing Hate Is Not Ok", https://www.thepetitionsite.com/takeaction/861/602/295/—This initiative was triggered by the case of "Nicolas Giampa". The teenager from Northern Virginia/USA maintains a Steam page with an SS logo and the statement: "National Socialism is here to stay." He praised Adolf Hitler and a white revolution, also described himself amongst other things using his Twitter pseudonym as a National Socialist. At the same time he was a Trump supporter and endorsed Bashar Assad's approach in Syria. When his parents confronted him in December 2017 because of his online activities and his conspicuous state of mind, he shot them. Cf. Andy Campell: "Steam, Your Kids' Favourite Video Game App, Has A Big Nazi Problem", in: Huffington Post, 8 March 2018, https://www.huffingtonpost.com/entry/steam-video-games-nazis_us_5aa006cae4b0e9381c146438.

which post questionable texts or even deliver clearly racist statements [...] I am of the opinion that Valve, based on their exclusive distribution rights in Germany and even specific sales strategies for each federal state, should at least pay attention to this on moral grounds. For it is not clear to me, that e.g. fantasy gaming demos [...] cannot be downloaded here on the basis of violence, in order that no children should get their hands on it too; however, it apparently does not interest anyone if these same children come into contact with neo-Nazi thinking." In the further course of the discussion, the gamer became more specific: "I am talking about people who have decided to use a swastika for their Steam logo, and why does Steam not react when someone writes informing them! Why then is there the opportunity to report this?"[19]

Evidently, officials in our country also let these developments slip past them. The Public Prosecutor's Office in Munich still talks today about the "World Wide Web", and in this way expresses their helplessness and the fact they are overloaded.[20] There is clearly a lack of expertise here, which is similar to other European countries. It quickly became evident during criminal proceedings against Breivik, that the two initial experts appointed by the court on the extreme right-wing online underworld, in which Breivik circulated for over a decade, really had as good as no clue.[21] And so it is long overdue here, to think outside the box and beyond national state boundaries; and to think about networking in a new way. It would easily have been possible for investigators to shadow members of the "Anti-Refugee Club" on Steam for instance, as the investigative journalist Christian Bergmann did for the TV programme ARD *Fakt*. Moreover, the community of potential mass murders on Steam existed up until September 2017. Christian Bergmann came to realisations in a very short period of time, which had previously remained hidden from 60 investigators.

The German officials' not passing information on Atchison on had fatal consequences, as the American not only sought to ensure Sonboly's posthumous fame but struck out violently in anger himself in New Mexico in December 2017. The FBI in turn searched Atchison' house in 2016, 4 months prior to the attack in Munich, because he wanted to obtain a

---

[19] Gamestar: Post in a forum "Nazi-Szene in Steam", Username: Knusper, 18 February 2010, (Rechtschreibfehler korrigiert), https://www.gamestar.de/xenforo/threads/nazi-szene-im-steam.378351/.

[20] According to Madam Speaker of the Public Prosecutor Anne Leiding in the broadcast Fakt on 15 May 2018, Report by Christian Bergmann, https://www.mdr.de/investigativ/video-197676_zc-f80c8d3a_zs-0fdb427d.html.

[21] Cf. Sindre Bangstad: „Norwegen: Ein Fall von Entpolitisierung?", in: Anna Maria Kellner (ed.): Demokratien und Terrorismus – Erfahrungen mit der Bewältigung von Terroranschlägen, Friedrich-Ebert-Stiftung, Bonn 2017, p. 46.

weapon for himself on the Net. However, the officials did not find anything whilst searching his home and came to the conclusion, Atchison was a harmless "online troll". The outcome: the American remained beneath the officials' radar from that time on. He must already have been in contact with David Sonboly at that time. German investigators learned nothing of this. There would have been grounds for getting involved here: The two were part of a virtual, international network of potential mass murderers. The absolute determination of the Bavarian officials on the subject of school bullying did not promote opportunities for police personnel to commence internal investigations regarding such a network.

Brice Current, the Sheriff there, stated when questioned by a team of reporters about the fact that German officials would possibly have been able to deliver important insights, which may possibly have been able to prevent the killing spree in Aztec: "We did not receive any information on Atchison from Germany. It is a total disappointment if they had information, but did not share it with us."[22] And thus David F. from Ludwigsburg had referred officials to Atchison, which Stuttgart State Criminal Police Office did not follow up further in spite of the concrete witness statement.[23] And so it becomes clear to us: The radicalisation process of David Sonboly via platforms from the USA such as Steam was not investigated even once, let alone discussed. International cooperation appears inevitable, if such cases really should be prevented in future.

We chanced across this David F. through the witness Florian M., who went to the police in Erfurt 2 days after the deed in Munich and handed over an USB stick there, with the information that this USB drive contained information on accessories and accomplices in the OEZ (Olympia Shopping Centre) attack. There were extracts on the USB drive from the forum on Steam. Apparently the witness, who in the meantime has disappeared from view again, was active himself on the platform, whether as a private individual or as a secret investigator. Following the murderous attack in Munich, this person, however, is supposed to have been shocked that one of the users had taken his attack plans and actually carried them out. Out of concern that the police in Erfurt would not pass this information on, Florian M. additionally reported it to police in Ludwigsburg. He also informed the police there about a potential assailant in this region. The home of David F. who was 15 years

---

[22] Quoted in the broadcast ARD Fakt on 15 May 2018, report by Christian Bergmann, https://www.mdr.de/investigativ/video-197676_zc-f80c8d3a_zs-0fdb427d.html.

[23] Cf. Ibid. David F. stated further for the record, that he knew of another person, who was planning murderous attacks worldwide. He only knew him by his nickname of "Cannibalwolf". He was from Liechtenstein.

of age at the time was searched as a result. David F. possessed the access data for one of Sonboly's Steam accounts and logged in using this 2 days after the latter's murderous assault. 5 months prior to Munich, David F. Sonboly was still writing: "Free your hate!".

The accessory prosecution lawyer Claudia Neher attempted to introduce the Steam Forum and USB stick as pieces of evidence into criminal proceedings against the arms dealer Philipp Körber. What is more, she wanted to summon the witnesses Florian M. and David F. and to allow sight of the documents on David F. for this case. The application to produce evidence was not granted in the trial, Munich Public Prosecution Service did not investigate any further, in spite of this information. After inspecting the files and prior to proceedings against the arms dealer, it had decided there was no connection between the cases "David F." and "Sonboly".[24] As Claudia Neher told the author face-to-face, in addition it was not evident either from a sociopolitical point of view or in the individual specific case in question, why Körber was not charged with aiding and abetting. The litigation would not have served the public peace.[25] In general it is unclear, whether undercover investigators were scurrying about on Steam, in any case ineffectively.

This case flags up all too clearly: investigating officials continue to think today, that users on these types of platforms mainly concern "Internet pseudonyms", which one is not able to do a lot with. It is true that users can register with Steam without needing to register any personal details: A nickname and a disposable e-mail address suffice, in order to join in discussions on the platform. Yet a simple prompt of the Internet service provider with the help of an IP address will allow us to discover who is hiding behind the nickname. As long as a user does not use any tools for IP obfuscation, it should not provide any great difficulty as a result, for criminal prosecutors to find out the identity of a user on Steam.[26]

A further problem: Terrorist activities are not barred out of commercial interests. Potential terrorists can still act on Steam to the greatest extent unprotected. They can easily hide amongst hundreds of thousands of gamers on Counterstrike alone every day. During the games, texting and voicemail

---

[24] Kira Ayyadi: „Das OEZ-Attentat undder international vernetzte virtuelle Rechtsextremismus", in: Bell Tower—Netz für digitale Zivilgesellschaft, Amadeu Antonio Stiftung, 16 July 2018, http://www.belltower.news/artikel/das-oez-attentat-und-der-international-vernetzte-virtuelle-rechtsextremismus-13977.

[25] In a discussion with the author on 10 July 2018.

[26] Cf. Daniel Mützel: „Amokläufer vernetzen sich auf weltgrößter Gaming-Seite—Polizei und Betreiber ignorieren das Problem", in: Motherboard Vice of 27 June 2018, https://motherboard.vice.com/de/article/xwmjnw/amoklaeufer-auf-steam-polizei-und-betreiber-ignorieren-problem-david-s-muenchen-attentat.

chats are possible—an ideal platform to get to know one another. Investigators have a hard time uncovering the black sheep. This is why it would appear to be more efficient, if gamers could report violations amongst one another, whenever they become aware of aggressive, hate-filled behaviour.

For example, the so-called Netzwerkdurchsetzungsgesetz (NetzDG) [*Network Enforcement Act NEA*] assumed legal effect in Germany at the start of 2018. It stipulates that online platforms such as Facebook must delete clearly culpable contents within 24 h of receiving any indication of these. In less clear cases, they have 1 week to do so. There is a threat of being fined up to 50 million Euros for violating this regulation. If the networks do not react quickly enough, users can complain to the Bundesamt für Justiz [*Federal Office of Justice*]. Computer games and video games are not, however, subject to the law, which is why there may only be limited success with them. Apparently, the gaming industry lobby succeeded in having online games removed from the initial draft of this law.[27] The emphasis on Facebook and Twitter in view of the current risk level and threats in any case appears antiquated. This is also true for Whatsapp, where relevant groups can quickly be identified and investigated. And thus, six people had their cover blown in the Austrian district of Schärding in March 2018, amongst them FPÖ [*Freedom Party of Austria*] regional councillors,[28] who sent each other images of Hitler, photos in which they posed in SS uniforms, as well as rabble-rousing images and commentaries on refugees. The police happened across this group whilst carrying out spot checks on cars and after confiscating a smartphone, then searched some members' homes immediately after this. The Bundesamt für Verfassungsschutz und Terrorismusbekämpfung (BVT) [Office for counteracting terrorism in Austria] assessed data on computers, mobile telephones and USB drives,[29] because of suspicion of re-engaging in National Socialist activities.[30]

The consideration of regarding online games as platforms for criminals, especially for terrorists has scarcely been present up until now in debates on security policy. They are an effective vehicle in such cases, as they enable communication without any protection. Investigators have not placed them

---

[27] Cf. Christina Brause: „Die wollen doch nur spielen", in: Die Welt of 6 February 2018, https://www.welt.de/print/welt_kompakt/webwelt/article173237989/Die-wollen-doch-nur-spielen.html.

[28] The FPÖ, at that time a party in the government, saw themselves forced to distance themselves from these members and immediately pressed for their exclusion from the party.

[29] Die Presse.com (2018): Razzia wegen Hitlerbildern, https://diepresse.com/home/innenpolitik/5393755/Oberoesterreich_Razzia-wegen-Hitlerbildern-bei-FPOeGemeinderaeten.

[30] In Article 9 of the treaty signed in 1955, which is a constituent part of the Federal Constitution, Austria committed to disband all National Socialist organisations and not to permit any re-engagement. This piece of legislation which is still valid today amongst other things bans under threat of punishment any engagement at all in the spirit of National Socialism.

at the focus of their attention, other than with smartphones, for instance.[31] It remains a mystery why the Bavarian Special Prosecutors entrusted with working through the murderous attack, were only aware of David Sonboly's virtual activities to a small extent. Of course, it is true the officials made a request to Valve shortly after the attack, obtaining profiles, contents of chats and IP addresses. Yet they were unable to gain really useful insights from these.[32]

Whoever considers this feeble handling of the powerful video and gaming industry will recognise, that the danger has neither been foreseen nor avoided. For a long time, a global online subculture has existed, which is highly interactive and which functions beyond national boundaries. Activists do not need to leave their own bedroom for this, do not need to go to war, or live life in the underground. A computer and an Internet connection suffice for them. We must pay attention to this in future.

Even the industry itself ignores the threat of the political risk situation. Felix Falk, Chief executive of GAME, Verband der deutschen Videospielbranche (Association of the German Video Games Industry) sees no danger of games unintentionally becoming a vehicle for radicalisation. When gamers exchange insights with one another, we are dealing with agreements and arrangements, not with political debates. Apart from this, there are only a few games in which gamers can write to one another. And in these, communication is "normally monitored by moderators and checked."[33] In response to my specific request on revelations concerning Sonboly and Atchison, Falk affirmed that no debates took place on Steam "relevant to the people's debate on public opinion".[34] Now at the very latest one unavoidably thinks of the three wise monkeys, who can see nothing, hear nothing and say nothing. Even President Donald Trump met with the company maintaining the site for Steam in March 2018, as racially motivated cases were becoming more frequent. He warned the violence in their games would have dangerous effects.[35]

---

[31] According to the Criminologist Thomas-Gabriel Rüdiger, cited after Matthias Jauch: „Immer einen Schritt zu spät", in: der Freitag vom 18. November 2011, https://www.freitag.de/autoren/matthias-jauch/immer-einen-schritt-zu-spaet.

[32] Cf. Daniel Mützel: „Amokläufer vernetzen sich auf weltgrößter Gaming-Seite – Polizei und Betreiber ignorieren das Problem", in: Motherboard Vice of 27 June 2018, https://motherboard.vice.com/de/article/xwmjnw/amoklaeufer-auf-steam-polizei-und-betreiber-ignorieren-problem-david-s-muenchen-attentat.

[33] Cited after Christina Brause: „Die wollen doch nur spielen", in: Die Welt of 6 February 2018, https://www.welt.de/print/welt_kompakt/webwelt/article173237989/Die-wollen-doch-nur-spielen.html.

[34] E-Mail on 18 July 2018 to the author from Martin Pupper, Head of Public Relations.

[35] Cf. Andy Campell: "Steam, Your Kids' Favorite Video Game App, Has A Big Nazi Problem", in: Huffington Post of 8 March 2018, https://www.huffingtonpost.com/entry/steam-video-games-nazis_us_5aa006cae4b0e9381c146438.

A definitive need for intervention exists here. Sonboly was of course reported because of his aggressive and racist statements, without anything happening. Amongst other things, David Sonboly used the name of the Winnenden spree killer Tim Kretschmer as a nickname. He wrote on Steam, "that he was the reincarnation or the ghost of Tim K. and would catch all of us." The problem: Even people who so openly wish to glorify the mass murderer Kretschmer, do not make themselves culpable by so doing. In principle, such statements are covered by freedom of expression. It does not become problematic, until specific deeds have been supported or condoned—and even then, only once the "Endorsement is suitable for disturbing the public peace."[36]

A young man of the same age had even telephoned Sonboly's father and asked him to make sure Ali sought medical help.[37] A functional early-warning system would certainly have been useful here, when people of the same age start listening intently and wish to step in. However, the gaming industry does not take this aspect seriously; there is little pressure from the political side or from officials. However, it is very clear to see from this case that lone wolves also leave traces behind which are easy to find, if one looks for them.

Groups such as the "Anti-Refugee Club" are by no means the exception on Steam. Searches on the platform for the term "Nazi" yields around 18,000 hits, for "amok" yields 1,500. Whoever inputs the name "Sonboly" will similarly detect a large number of hits. Three users had the same nickname in May 2018, as he used for his activities. Not only Sonboly and Atchison were „Brüder im Geiste" (*Brothers in Spirit*), who got to know one another through their enthusiasm for violent and killer games.[38] A Steam Group with the name "Eldigado is a god" honours Atchison's username. It had 70 members in July 2018.

We should start to penetrate this subculture more strongly—in order to protect ourselves and also to perpetuate an open society in the virtual world. The insight must be an integral part here, that globalisation can have a shadowy side and may revitalise a militant, racist-motivated hatred. Often we are concerned with young men here, born and raised in the middle of Europe themselves and who of their own free will embarked down a remote, dark

---

[36] Markus Böhm/Angela Gruber, Angela: „Amok-Kult. Wie junge Menschen Gewalttätern im Netz huldigen", in: Spiegel online, 2 August 2016, http://www.spiegel.de/netzwelt/web/amoklauf-kult-im-internet-wie-junge-menschen-amoklaeufern-huldigen-a-1105693.html.

[37] Britta Bannenberg: Expert Report on the case of David S. for the Bavarian State Criminal Police Office, Gießen, February 2018, p. 54.

[38] Cf. Martin Bernstein: Das Netzwerk der Todesschützen. Hasstiraden und Massenmord-Pläne: Über eine Internet-Plattform tauschten sich der OEZ-Attentäter mit einem Amerikaner aus, der zwei Schüler ermordete, in: Süddeutsche Zeitung of 15 May 2018, p. 30.

path away from the apparently stable paths of "polite" civil society. Often they stay at least one step ahead of investigators through their virtual networking. Sceptically, it is true that many investigators, public prosecutors and court officials hardly have any extensive knowledge of the Darknet. Usually only special investigators know how the anonymous marketplace functions, and how criminals deal in weapons for instance. Hardly any state prosecutors have ever made payments themselves using the cryptocurrency bitcoin, used as the standard currency on the Darknet and which can easily be purchased in numerous legitimate online exchanges.[39]

Yet even once the officials' opportunities for operating on Darknet have been exhausted, this does not mean they are acting correctly. It is usually only possible to penetrate criminal trading forums on the Darknet, if a suspect has first been caught and been offered a "Deal"—permitted according to § 46 b of the Criminal Code: The accused person makes his Darknet account available to investigators in exchange for a more lenient sentence, who now penetrate ever deeper into the structure of dealers as a decoy.

Even in the case of Philipp Körber, who obtained the weapon for David Sonboly and handed it over to him, it worked in this manner.[40] An investigator took over his account "Erich Hartmann", who was considered to be a reliable arms supplier in the Darknet forum „Deutschland im Deep Web" (DiDW) [*Germany in the Deep Web*], which specialised in drugs deals and the arms trade.[41] By this point the murderous attack had already taken place. At this time, investigation of the Darknet forum has already started in April 2015, and thus a good year before the murderous assault in Munich.[42]

The delivery of arms and weapons to Sonboly could, however, have been prevented. An undercover official in the German Customs Investigation Bureau was however in contact with Sonboly's pseudonym "Maurächer". Sonboly searched the Darknet for a weapon for about a year. His objective was to obtain the weapon Breivik had also used. The investigator started paying attention to Sonboly. He also had contact to the arms dealer Körber and clearly access to Sonboly's message to "Erich Hartmann": "Could you get

---

[39] Cf. Otto Hostettler: „Hilflose Ermittler. Warum Kriminelle im Darknet wenig zu befürchten haben", in: Aus Politik und Zeitgeschichte, 46–47/2017, p. 10f.

[40] Körber obtained most of the weapons he sold on the Darknet in the Czech Republic, from his contact there named "Hyena". He had clearly already obtained the Glock 17 from "Hyena", which he rebuilt himself for the left-handed Sonboly.

[41] The GTAZ, the Joint Counter-Terrorism Centre includes the BKA [*Federal Criminal Police Office*] and the Verfassungsschutz [*Intelligence Services*] as well as the Central Office of the German Customs Investigation Service, have nevertheless still not discussed this case.

[42] Cf. „Andreas Förster: Der Waffenhändler aus dem Darknet", in: Stuttgarter Zeitung of 27 August 2017, https://www.stuttgarter-zeitung.de/inhalt.muenchner-amoklauf-prozess-beginnt-der-waffenhaendler-aus-dem-darknet.d9b8dedc-8b22-4a0a-b6a0-5e51640e8769.html.

your hands on a Glock 17 with 2 magazines and 150 bullets?" This concrete enquiry should have been an alarm bell. Finally, Sonboly found a supplier in Körber—with deadly consequences.[43]

At this time, the German Customs Investigation Office in Frankfurt has a fairly precise overview of illegal trade on the Darknet. There are a large number of covert investigating officers and informants. Nevertheless, at the time of the "Sonboly" case, there were no official instructions on how to proceed with events occurring such as the sale or purchase of a weapon. We were finally able to capture Körber. Nevertheless, this was no reason to sound the all-clear: Numerous gun nuts had gathered around Körber throughout the entire Federal Republic of Germany, also in the Reichsbürger scene, and some of them had racist backgrounds. Körber stated that all his customers purchased weapons, because they were afraid of burglars and refugees. This hive of potential extreme right-wing assailants remains undiscovered up until today. The same is also true and is especially apt for the platform Steam.

5.3 Searching for a Trail in the Social Environment

The types of assailants vary widely. Nevertheless, a fixed pattern can be detected for Lone Wolf Terrorists[44]:

- They frequently combine personal and political problems
- They suffer from mental illnesses
- Their radicalisation does not occur in a social vacuum
- They communicate their openness to violence and the possibility of carrying out a massacre
- They show that they are inspired by other actors and extremist ideas
- There has been a triggering event, which triggers their specific act of violence

An important characteristic of lone wolves appears to be, that they go through a phase of self-radicalisation, which they experience sometimes in the quiet of their own room, via the Internet and social media. Nevertheless, it would be going too far merely to make the Internet responsible as the

---

[43] Cf. ARD Fakt: „Zollermittler hatte möglicherweise Hinweis auf Attentatspläne", Report: Christian Bergmann/Marcus Weller, broadcast on 12 September 2017.
[44] Cf. Mark S. Hamm/Ramón Spaaij: The Age of Lone Wolf Terrorism, New York 2017, p. 29.

stronghold of the radicalisation. Basically, lone wolves always have an affinity to an individual person, a community or a group, whether it is online or in the real world. This finding becomes even more significant, as it contradicts the assumption that lone wolf terrorists do not communicate with other people and do not follow other violent traditions.

Usually, there is an interplay between online and offline activities in the form of an overlapping of the two spheres. Are the security services primed and equipped for this? The German expert Armin Pfahl-Traughber says in this regard: "One may ask oneself for example, whether police and intelligence services defending Germany would have become aware of an Anders Behring Breivik prior to his deeds."[45] The lady in charge of the Norwegian Police's public relations, Janne Kristianen, delivered the following statement which was assessed very controversially a few days after the murderous event: "I believe, that not even the Stasi [*Secret Service of the former East Germany*] in East Germany would have been able to expose this man. He would even have slipped through the net there."[46]

Clearly, the mass murderer did not remain entirely without any traces, although he mainly just sat in his childhood bedroom. Even an Anders Breivik has good friends he has known for many years. Four men recounted the history of this man during his trial, who became increasingly more isolated, more curious and descended into a gloomy image of the world. They had known for a long time that something was not right, at the latest in 2006 when Breivik gave up his apartment and moved back in with his mother. According to their accounts, he had a downtrodden manner, hardly contacted them anymore and told them that he was working on a book on the "Islamification of Europe"—the right-wing extremist pamphlet, with which he subsequently tried to justify his murderous attacks. In rare meetings with his circle of friends, he always expressed very extreme political views. In the end his friends pressed him to meet up, as he withdrew completely. Breivik finally complied but put this back until a date after 22 July 2011.[47]

Breivik's name appeared on a list of names of people, who had ordered chemicals from a company in Poland, which can be used for making bombs. David Sonboly was also far from invisible. Whether his social phobias—as

---

[45] Armin Pfahl-Traughber: „Das "Lone Wolf"-Phänomen im deutschen Rechtsterrorismus. Eine Analyse von Fallbeispielen", in: Sybille Steinbacher (ed.): Rechte Gewalt in Deutschland. Zum Umgang mit dem Rechtsextremismus in Gesellschaft, Politik und Justiz, Göttingen 2016, p. 217.

[46] Cited after Øyvind Strømmen: Der Soloterrorist als Kulturphänomen, in: Frank Decker/Bernd Henningsen/Kjetil Jakobsen (eds.): Rechtspopulismus und Rechtsextremismus in Europa, Baden-Baden 2015, pp. 245–254.

[47] Cf. Gunnar Herrmann: „Mein Freund, der Massenmörder", in: Süddeutsche Zeitung, 29 May 2012.

the officials presented them—therefore really were definitive for his murderous deeds, remains more than questionable. Nevertheless, investigators discovered more than 140 contacts on his smartphone, in addition around 30 chats. He also had a regular partner he played football with and he delivered newspapers.

Terrorism is merely a symptom, which gives an indication of the illnesses (*and disease*) in the actor's social, political and cultural life. Precisely when looking at youths, drug dependency, alcoholism, and a general lack of drive and perspective play a special role. Terrorism may perhaps be interpreted here as a "shrill appeal", to investigate the causes for this illness.[48] Like drug addicts, lone wolves certainly do leave trails, precisely in the circle of their friends and families. Thomas Müller, one of the bestknown criminal psychologists in Europe and amongst other things once appointed profiler in the case of Franz Fuchs tells us: "If we ask people who were involved with the actor after the event, any small signal may inform them, which points towards it. An actor's environment merely lacks the attention, the sensibility to definitely take the time to interpret these signals in advance, to take steps to work against them."[49] Joe Navarro, a former FBI Agent, who has interviewed numerous terrorists and wrote the book *Hunting Terrorists: A Look at The Psychopathology of Terror* in 2005, is likewise of the opinion that all of these individuals, irrespective of their driving force and their ideology in particular, are always seeking to communicate with people from their surrounding area. We always happen upon people in the analysis after the event, who confirm discussions and feel guilty to a certain extent, as they did not interpret the signals correctly or ignored them.[50] The Norwegian Police Security Service said that they received a tip about the mosque attack from August 2019 approximately 1 year prior to the attack conducted by the white supremacist Philip Manshaus. After coordinating with the local police department, Oslo Police District, the agencies found that the tip was vague and did not indicate planning for any imminent terrorist activities. The tip was not followed up.[51]

There were such indications with David Sonboly too. Svenia G., a young woman who was his best friend at one time said, he did not make any secret

---

[48] Cf. Iring Fetscher even decades ago: „Hypothesen zur politisch motivierten Gewalttätigkeit in der Bundesrepublik", in: Hearing des Bundesjugendkuratoriums, Munich 1979, p. 11.

[49] Thomas Müller: „Jeder kann zum Amokläufer werden", in: Die Welt of 20 August 2009, https://www.welt.de/vermischtes/article4362672/Jeder-kann-zum-Amoklaeufer-werden.html.

[50] Cited after Joe Navarro: "Wounded Minds", in: Southern Poverty Law Centre: Age of the Wolf. A Study of the Rise of the Lone Wolf and Leaderless Resistance Terrorism, Montgomery/Alabama 2015, p. 36.

[51] The Guardian (2019): Norway issues right-wing terror warning for year ahead, 6 September, https://www.theguardian.com/world/2019/sep/06/norway-issues-rightwing-terror-warning-for-year-ahead.

of his murderous fantasies: "Earlier it was simply: "I had an argument with that person". Then later on he would say: "I hate this person. Some time or other I will kill him." And later on, it was always like: "I hate all these people. I hate Turks! I hate it! I simply do not want this in my life. As often as we may now have approached teachers, telling them that Ali was really extremely caught up in all of this and that he would like to carry out his ideas. We told them this, but simply got nothing back in return. They always just nodded, with 'Yes, that is just our Ali.'"

Up until today his female friend still suffers under the burden of not having done enough: "I still blame myself today, because I cannot understand, why we simply did not do something sooner. We were friends. We knew what was going on. We knew it. Ali told us about this on a daily basis and we were not able to stop it."[52] Although it would far rather have been the teachers'and the officials'place to observe this behaviour more closely.

The problems which had in the meantime arisen at school clearly also contributed to radicalising David Sonboly, and towards his forming a racist image of the world. Symbols of racism or disparaging remarks about people with a migratory background must be interpreted correctly—even if they are made by people who have a background of migration themselves and are not wearing combat jump boots. The raging addiction of young people to computers, their communication via TeamSpeak and playing violent video games in their childhood bedroom must also be discussed in an educational context. After school, Sonboly withdrew into his room and remained there for hours on end. He did not like anyone entering his room, and he spent significant portions of his time in front of his computer. He was addicted and spent practically his whole childhood in front of a computer. He set up his first account on Steam at the age of nine.[53] A deficits analysis should therefore be undertaken to the effect of whether this aspect is worthy of special consideration or not.

There are opportunities to compare conspicuous individuals such as Sonboly using a framework, to check whether they may potentially carry out a murderous act. If a few points in it are fulfilled, then we should approach the authorities. We should pay more attention to the traces and should possibly seek an external consultation[54]:

---

[52]Cited after ARD Fakt: „München-Attentat: Warum viele Hintergründe im Dunkeln bleiben", Report: Christian Bergmann/Marcus Weller, broadcast on 22 August 2017.

[53]Britta Bannenberg: Expert Report on the case of David S. for Bayerische Landeskriminalamt [*Bavarian State Criminal Police Office*], Gießen, February 2018, p. 26.

[54]On the basis of Diane M. Zierhoffer: Threat Assessment: Do Lone Terrorists Differ From Other Lone Offenders, in: Journal of Strategic Security, 7 (2014) 3, pp. 57–59.

1. Motivation (grievance, sense of mission, racism etc.)
2. Communication (with a view towards evil intentions)
3. Interest in terrorism and searching for role models (violent fantasies, running amok)
4. Behaviour in conjunction with the attacks (radicalisation process, withdrawal etc.)
5. Mental disorders (diagnoses, treatment received)
6. Organisation (planning the deed)
7. Confirmation (for instance through attempts to join onto organisations)
8. Social relationships (surroundings, emphasis on virtual rooms and space)
9. Conspicuous problems from others (especially in virtual rooms)
10. Opportunities for prevention (Racism in schools etc.)

Treating right-wing terrorism in the school environment is a challenge. As difficult as this must clearly be for teaching staff from a moral perspective too, it is demonstrated by how Norway's school dealt with the terror of the assault of 22 July 2011. Breivik's deeds, ideology and motive were neither presented nor discussed, but were systematically hushed up.[55] This should change now: The deeds are supposed to be accepted into the schools'curriculum in the foreseeable future, as was reported on the 8th anniversary on 22 July 2019.[56]

Lone wolf terrorists always pursue the goal of leaving a memorial for themselves. This chiefly occurs through extensive reporting in the media. If this is successful, these "heroes" attract copycats. With this background the question crops up, whether this subject matter of lone wolves should be recorded on film at all, or not. On the other hand, the film *Der Patriot* by Elisabeth Scharang on Franz Fuchs is a successful form of this along the lines of a documentary, based upon tape recordings of the hearings, and the individual scenes are allowed to speak for themselves. The actor's conspicuous psychological problems are just as evident as his extreme right-wing state of mind. This film broadcast in 2007 is far removed from any form of making him a hero.

As a preventive measure, in addition when teaching social studies, the virtual progression of the radicalisation process should be examined in more detail—including their own language used in chats. In order to keep up with this, teaching digital competence is indispensable—in the sphere of activities of the school itself. There are still teaching bodies, who do not have a

---

[55] Cf. Sindre Bangstad: „Norwegen: Ein Fall von Entpolitisierung?", in: Anna Maria Kellner (ed.): Demokratien und Terrorismus – Erfahrungen mit der Bewältigung von Terroranschlägen, Friedrich-Ebert-Stiftung, Bonn 2017, p. 49.
[56] Faz.net, 22 July 2019: Acht Jahre danach. Norwegische Schulen sollen Terrortat von Utøya im Unterricht behandeln, https://www.faz.net/aktuell/politik/ausland/schulen-in-norwegen-sollen-sich-mit-breivik-attentat-befassen-16296749.html.

clue about the dynamics of the virtual world. Social (however, also political) communication has changed in principle. Presentations of extremism and terrorism must also adjust to the new realities. We no longer need a party member's book or a membership card for the organisation. All-in-all, prevention demands a strategy which at first glance is a seeming paradox:

- *In the virtual life,* we must socially isolate conspicuous aggressors and shatter and destroy right-wing extremist communication bridges on virtual platforms such as Steam. Terrorists can achieve their goals that much quicker and carry out their attacks, if they exchange ideas with people with similar mindsets.[57]
- *In real life* socially isolated individuals must often regain their ties to society and must be reintegrated. Teaching and psychological services are in order here, for instance when dealing with personality disorders too. Depressive illnesses continue to be taboo for example, although in recent years there has been an awareness campaign in the media.

We can also scrutinise the role of Paediatric and Adolescent Psychiatry using the case of David Sonboly. Although he sought medical assistance, the potential for danger was not detected. The hospital could not see any reasons he would be a danger towards strangers and played down the violent and murderous fantasies with racist undertones. And so, it would have been misleading to blame society alone, when even professional staff misjudged the threat. However, this was also due to skilful manipulation by the actor himself: By his last session of treatment chronologically, the accused had evidently already acquired the ability to consciously dissemble, which means he could play down the symptoms of his illness and was able to disguise them. Even during his last appointment on 13 July 2016, 9 days prior to his murderous attack, he distanced himself from an acute risk of suicide and presenting any danger towards strangers. Therapists believed him. And therefore, in general measures must be clearly thought out, on how young people with distinct addictions to the computer and an excessive tendency towards violent video games and killer games can be treated.

---

[57] Cf. Daniel Byman: "How to Hunt a Lone Wolf. Countering Terrorists Who Act on Their Own", in: Foreign Affairs, 2/2017, p. 97.

References

1. AIVD, General Intelligence and Security Service in the Netherlands. (2012). *Jihadism on the web. A breeding ground for jihad in the modern age.* Amsterdam.
2. Bangstad, S. (2017). Norwegen: Ein Fall von Entpolitisierung? In A. M. Kellner (Ed.), *Demokratien und Terrorismus – Erfahrungen mit der Bewältigung von Terroranschlägen, Friedrich-Ebert-Stiftung* (pp. 41–51). Bonn.
3. Bazan, E. B. (2004). *Intelligence reform and terrorism prevention act of 2004: "Lone wolf" Amendment to the Foreign Intelligence Surveillance Act, Report for Congress.* Washington D.C.
4. Byman, D. (2017). How to hunt a lone wolf. Countering terrorists who act on their own. *Foreign Affairs, 2,* S. 101. https://www.brookings.edu/opinions/how-to-hunt-a-lone-wolf-countering-terrorists-who-act-on-their-own/.
5. EUROPOL. (2017). *EU terrorism and trend report 2017* (pp. 45–47). The Hague. https://www.europol.europa.eu/activities-services/main-reports/eu-terrorism-situation-and-trend-report-te-sat-2017.
6. Ebner, J. (2017). *The rage. The vicious circle of Islamist and far-right extremism.* London.
7. Fetscher, I. (1979). Hypothesen zur politisch motivierten Gewalttätigkeit in der Bundesrepublik. In *Ders. u.a.: Jugend und Terrorismus. Ein Hearing des Bundesjugendkuratoriums* (pp. 11–26). Munich.
8. Gensing, P. (2012). *Terror von Rechts. Die Nazi-Morde und das Versagen der Politik.* Berlin.
9. Hamm, M. S., & Spaaij, R. (2017). *The age of lone wolf terrorism.* New York.
10. Hostettler, O. (2017). Hilflose Ermittler. Warum Kriminelle im Darknet wenig zu befürchten haben. *Aus Politik und Zeitgeschichte,* 10–15.
11. Navarro, J. (2015). Wounded minds. In *Southern Poverty Law Centre: Age of the wolf. A study of the rise of the lone wolf and leaderless resistance terrorism.* Montgomery/Alabama.
12. Pfahl-Traughber, A. (2016). Das "Lone Wolf"-Phänomen im deutschen Rechtsterrorismus. Eine Analyse von Fallbeispielen. In S. Steinbacher (Ed.), *Rechte Gewalt in Deutschland. Zum Umgang mit dem Rechtsextremismus in Gesellschaft, Politik und Justiz* (pp. 206–221). Göttingen.
13. Strømmen, Ø. (2015). Der Soloterrorist als Kulturphänomen. In F. Decker, B. Henningsen, & K. Jakobsen (Eds.), *Rechtspopulismus und Rechtsextremismus in Europa* (pp. 245–254). Baden-Baden.
14. Zierhoffer, D. M. (2014). Threat assessment: Do lone terrorists differ from other lone offenders. *Journal of Strategic Security, 7*(3), 48–62.

6

Conclusions

Albert Einstein wrote in Betrachtungen der Persönlichkeit (*Considerations of Personality*): "If we think about our life and our ambitions, then we notice that practically all of our actions and wishes are linked to the existence of other people. We notice that according to our species, we are very similar to other sociable animals […] Only each individual person is able to think and in this way create new values for society, and indeed even set up new moral standards, according to which the life of the community is enacted. Without creative, independent thinking and adjudicating personalities, higher development of society is just as inconceivable as developing individual personalities without the fertile soil of the community."[1]

The lone wolf has perverted the positive aspects of the individual person and converted these into a terrifying form of irreparable damage—directed straight ahead towards whatever confronts them, the enemy, which is denied any individuality whatsoever. To them this means: Jews, refugees, Muslims, people of colour, etc. Internal social cohesion is replaced by antisocial explosive power.

Lone wolves are symptoms of the world in which we live, even if we are happy to suppress the causes. They are one of the mantras of our times and they will remain a significant threat in the contemporary world we live in.[2] We speak of a global phenomenon, which does not, however, affect different regions of the world to the same extent. This raises one open question

---

[1] Albert Einstein: Mein Weltbild. Wie ich die Welt sehe, Berlin 2010, p. 13f.
[2] According to the conclusions of Miroslav Mareš/Richard Stojar: Extreme right perpetrators, in: Michael Fredholm (ed.): Understanding Lone Actor Terrorism. Past experience, future outlook, and response strategies, London/New York, 2016, p. 82.

researchers in this field pointed out: "So, why are there apparently no cases of lone actor terrorism in Asia (outside of the former Soviet Union, that is), Africa or even in South America?"[3] We could easily assume here that we should look for a cause in cultural factors, for example in the individualisation of lifestyles in the West. We can add the observation to this, of: "If so, much of the Far East might already be susceptible to the risk of lone actor terrorism, in particular those areas where Western values and lifestyles have become widespread, and the same argument could be valid for South Africa and much of South America."[4]

The following is true for evaluating lone wolf terrorism: We must regard murderous deeds in a political context, and must not negate their intentions through "depoliticisation" and "pathologisation". For instance, in the court cases against Franz Fuchs, David Copeland, John Ausonius, Peter Mangs and Frank Steffen, personality disorders were to the fore, not xenophobic motives. The constitutional state disregards ideological motivations which are hard to grasp, which prevail in other regions, for example in the case of "Sonboly": Whilst the memorial dedicated to victims of the murderous deed in Munich 1 year after the event bore the misleading inscription "amok", it contained no words on terrorism. This is equally as unsatisfactory for the self-image and culture of remembrance in Munich from the perspective of the victims' relatives, as also for society as a whole.

Sonboly was not a classic spree killer running amok, who wished his revenge on former fellow pupils or teachers, but someone who looked down on certain people due to political motives. We were dealing with an act which had been planned for over a year, was targeted and executed—and not just with a spontaneous escalation of violence. It is particularly difficult for relatives and families of victims to grasp the circumstance, that the evil deeds "did not fall out of nowhere into our lap". This is precisely the reason a lot of care is required during processing and coming to terms with them, which is also being carried out in the case of Munich.

Many of the terror attacks discussed here indicate: People must pay penalties for being a part of a hated group, both as actual representatives and anonymously. Extreme right-wing online communities help, as people come into contact with one another, who otherwise in all probability would never have been able to make contact with one another. Such combining networks may on the one hand form a supporting or legitimising framework, on the

---

[3] Michael Fredholm/Hanna Runeborg: Lone actor terrorism, a lifestyle phenomenon? A research essay, in: Michael Fredholm (ed.): Understanding Lone Actor Terrorism. Past experience, future outlook, and response strategies, London/New York, 2016, p. 304.
[4] Ibid., p. 305.

other hand may be used for coordinating or organising violent actions. Officials need to modernise quickly, and at last finally take the new dimension of virtual, internationally networked right-wing extremism into consideration.

It is true not only within Islamic terrorism, but also with right-wing extremism, that: The new structure of lone wolf actors is growing at a significant pace. Whilst such actors are not included in any party or organisation, however, but acting out of political motives in spite of this, for instance based on racist views. Internationalisation and virtualisation in this case form the context: The case of Sonboly in Munich reveals examples of deficits in the policies, in particular in internal security as well as in the Justice department. The narrative of an apolitical spree killer came about all too quickly. Investigating authorities are too caught up with traditional patterns, the wish to depoliticise politically motivated terrifying acts appears to be too great. Apparently, we are measuring using two different scales, as far as our treatment of Islamic terrorism and right-wing terrorism goes.

In the case of IS single actors, it will suffice to be categorised as an Islamic terrorist if the murderous actor shouts "Allahu akbar" or an IS symbol is found in his room. This applied to the 17-year-old Riaz A. for instance, who attacked passengers with an axe and a knife on a regional train close to Würzburg in July 2016, just days before the murderous attack in Munich. The *Süddeutsche Zeitung* newspaper is correct to ask with a laconic undertone, what would a Sonboly have needed to shout, for his deed to have been allocated as being political?[5]

Civilised societies which in the past had experience of dealing with totalitarian regimes, do not wish to be subjected to the allegation of not being able to guarantee protection for stigmatised groups in the population. On the contrary they commit themselves to preventing violence directed against people. As the phenomenon of the lone wolves shows, however, this only succeeds in delivering results to an unsatisfactory extent. The consequence is an uncomfortable debate, and also because the struggle of the animosity of "an entire state" against "an individual" appears unfair. As a reaction, the response is to form new institutions and commissions, with the additional burdens of administration. However, the problem remains, leaving some facades appearing fragile and crumbling.

What can we derive from this, if we express our lack of an ability to defend democracy from its enemies according to cyclical patterns? Anyway, there are few organisations operating which proceed against extreme right-wing virtual terror networks, which animate lone wolves to perpetrate their deeds.

---

[5] Cf. Lena Kampf/Kassian Stroh: „Die Tat eines „echten Deutschen"", in: Süddeutsche Zeitung, 4 October 2017, p. 35.

These conceal themselves for example behind the veil of gaming platforms, and the commercially driven companies operating these sites can only be forced to intervene with difficulty. In the case of Atchison, even the FBI was not able to recognise the rapid pace, although the right-wing extremist actor left numerous signs in his wake. David Sonboly was even named in person. It would have been easy to proceed against the "Anti-Refugee Club", where racist thoughts were still being exchanged long after the murderous attack in Munich, up until September 2017. Whoever had speculated Sonboly was active in such a virtual and international network, would certainly have been reprimanded as being an advocate of conspiracy theories, without the revelations of December 2017.

The reference to the individual case and the focus on motives such as troubles of the heart or bullying at school counteracts a necessary as well as uncomfortable debate, as it frees society from any share of responsibility. Said differently: As with the case of Sonboly, the officials were hoodwinked by the single actor, who is distinguished by a high susceptibility to being aggrieved. Everyday occurrences became humiliations and impertinences to him. From this perspective we can explain the political direction of impact, for instance, if ethnic minorities are made our target in the polarising debate on refugees.

Native, indigenous people in the corresponding countries likewise feel they are concerned, whenever someone in their ranks mutates into a terrorist. Many Norwegians felt injured and sad following the attacks of 22 July 2011. The same is true for the inhabitants of New Zealand, who likewise had no experience of having experienced terrorism. Solidarity has its limits, however, Reinvigorated right-wing populist parties and movements instrumentalise the deeds in real time. This was the case immediately on the evening of 22 July 2016, for instance when the populist right party „Alternative für Deutschland" (AfD) [*Alternative for Germany*] conjured up the terrifying Islamification and „Willkommenskultur" [*Welcome Culture*]—without waiting for any insights whatsoever. There is a need for serious and dependable reporting precisely in times, when the established media had suffered cutbacks and parallel worlds exist. The virtual rumour mill clearly makes this difficult—with a public which quickly thinks of Islamic terrorist attacks.

The subject of "immigration" is central to right-wing terrorism. All actors come from societies in which there are fierce and controversial struggles around the question of immigration. The sustained, heated debate on refugees may continue to sow seeds for further violence. Individuals, who at any rate have mental problems, find their scapegoats here and with them a plan to project their own plight and misery onto. The attempt to explain terrorism exclusively using psychological theories and in this way to reduce its significance clearly does not go far enough and merely has the effect of a sedative to calm the population according to political measures. The murderous deeds do not arise through emotions or false illusions but are based on planning in minute detail. For instance, Breivik prevented himself from being perceived as being ill and mentally incompetent. That would have been a "fate worse than death". He was concerned merely with the political dimension of his terrible deed.[6]

Terrorist actors in all likelihood will express themselves to third parties very conspicuously long before their murderous deeds—using real as well as virtual communication channels. For instance, Sonboly was blocked time and again by online gamers the same age as him, as he made no bones of his violent fantasies. This is typical for such actors: They spend their time with indexed computer games which glorify violence, in order to experience violence as an approach to a solution. Society itself must learn to identify behaviours which serve as a warning and to report these as soon as possible. This becomes clear, whenever a person states they are a "military detachment" in a combative mentality, openly expresses sympathy for using weapons, identifies himself with former actors of murderous deeds and murderous violent deeds as well as appears to be inspired by a missionary-like compulsion.

Lone wolf terrorists with right-wing motives are not only mentally conspicuous but are also part of a larger ideological pack. They demonstrate that they are pleased by displays of aggression—for instance with discussions on terrorism in the media and virtually—and see an effective means here to articulate their problems and desires. They mix grandiose political grievances with murdering people who have done nothing to them and whom they have no personal connection to. Their racist image of the world divides the world into friends and enemies; their hatred is directed towards minorities. Many such ideological convictions sound abstruse and laughable. We know this from examples throughout history, for instance, the burning of witches, who were supposed to have sunk ships and changed people into cats, the plan to exterminate all Jews in Europe, because their blood was supposedly poisoning the Aryan race, or the execution of all Cambodians who wore spectacles, because this was allegedly proof they were intellectuals, and in this way were enemies of the Communist regime.[7] Eric Hoffer had already stated in 1951: "All the true believers of our time – whether Communist, Nazi, Fascist, Japanese or

---

[6] Cf. Tore Wehling, Tore/Stefan Hansen: „Breivik, Terrorist oder Amokläufer?", in: Joachim Krause/Stefan Hansen (eds.): Jahrbuch Terrorismus 2011/2012, Opladen 2012, p. 121.
[7] Cf. Steven Pinker: Gewalt. Eine neue Geschichte der Menschheit, Frankfurt on Main 2011, p. 825.

Catholic – declaimed volubly (...) on the decadence of the Western democracies."[8]

A Breivik, who stylised himself as a Knight Crusader and wished to save Europe from Islamification, can join on to this chain of thought almost seamlessly. And likewise, for actors who appear from an anonymous background and then wish to trigger a race war or like a Sonboly wish to exterminate all Turks. Radicalisation should be considered to be a social process. It would be fatal, merely to explain the new terrorism of right-wing actors through readily available opportunities to access the Internet. Undesired side effects in the form of single actor terrorism become possible in particular, whenever a society is split down the middle on immigration questions for instance, whenever verbal radicalism become the norm. Arguments between right-wing populist and radical forces should not lead to the centre running along behind as a duplicate or copy of the original and adopting the same views and formulations. Such developments lead to legitimising politically isolating, extracted demands and requirements, for instance on the subject of refugees.

At the latest at this point, the question arises of the self-concept of modern societies, which are prompted to develop finer sensors for a narcissistic pattern and extreme right-wing messages. More monitoring must be devoted to far right cultures. We are quite simply concerned with developing competency: In the end, new, virtually networked types of actors have developed, who continue to only be sporadically perceived as a danger both in society, in public and in the media, with general ambivalence being at fault. The authorities avoid holding the necessary debate we need in order to follow new routes, so as to be able to detect right-wing violence—if you like. Homage is given to terrorists on the public platform "Encyclopaedia Dramatica" and these are given a numeric score. In spite of my information, these entries continue to exist and are constantly being updated (in 2019 by Christchurch and El Paso).[9] Along with the virtual portrait gallery on Steam, there are numerous groups with the name "Breivik", for instance. The constant attitude of a lack of responsibility from the gaming industry, which denies racism is present and says it does not detect any debates relevant to society in their forums, is one last thing. Ignoring dangerous networking on apparently harmless gaming platforms is just as dangerous as an apparently intentional depoliticisation of attacks by lone wolves according to the motto: "What may not be, cannot be." The necessity will grow here, to hold a debate on right-wing domestic (*homeland*) terrorism and its causes.

---

[8] Eric Hoffer: The True Believer, New York 1951, p. 163.
[9] https://encyclopediadramatica.rs.

References

1. Einstein, A. (2010). *Mein Weltbild. Wie ich die Welt sehe.* Berlin.
2. Fredholm, M., & Runeborg, H. (2016). Lone actor terrorism, a lifestyle phenomenon? A research essay. In M. Fredholm (Ed.), *Understanding lone actor terrorism. Past experience, future outlook, and response strategies* (pp. 303–306). London/New York.
3. Hoffer, E. (1951). *The true believer.* New York.
4. Mareš, M., & Stojar, R. (2016). Extreme right perpetrators. In M. Fredholm (Ed.), *Understanding lone actor terrorism. Past experience, future outlook, and response strategies* (pp. 66–86). London/New York.
5. Pinker, S. (2011). *Gewalt. Eine neue Geschichte der Menschheit.* Frankfurt/Main.
6. Wehling, T., & Hansen, S. (2012). Breivik, Terrorist oder Amokläufer? In J. Krause & S. Hansen (Eds.), *Jahrbuch Terrorismus 2011/2012* (pp. 121–148). Opladen.

Index

A

Aaronson, Trevor 1
AIVD, General Intelligence and Security Service in the Netherlands 153
Albrecht, Richard 50
Albrecht, Stephen 131
Al-Qaeda 1, 7, 13, 52, 53, 83, 145
Alternative for Deutschland (AfD) 99, 103, 105, 138
Amir, Yigal 37
Amok 6, 16, 19, 21, 23, 31, 49–51, 63, 95, 99, 100, 102, 104, 108, 110, 115, 135, 146, 154, 155, 160, 162–164, 167, 169, 174, 177
Amri, Anis 54, 55, 58
Arco-Valley, Count 35
ARD Fakt 50
Arendt, Hannah 111
Atchison, W. 19, 20, 100, 101, 158, 159, 162, 163, 176
Atomwaffen 157
Ausonius, John 73, 77–79, 91, 93, 113, 118, 119, 174

Aztec, New Mexico 19, 23, 159

B

Bachmann, Lutz 144
Backes, Uwe 4, 57, 111, 124, 126
Bahners, Patrick 17
Bakunin, Michail Alexandrowitsch 34
Bangstad, Sindre 158, 169
Bannenberg, Britta 17, 21, 49, 95, 101, 105, 108, 115, 163, 168
Barr, Nathaniel 55
Bartlett, Jamie 127
Bartsch, Matthias 40
Baumgärtner, Maik 95, 103
Bayerischer Rundfunk 16, 103
Bayerisches Innenministerium 96
Bayerisches Landeskriminalamt (BLKA) 19–21, 101, 168
Bayuwarische Befreiungsarmee (BBA) 73
Bazan, Elizabeth B. 152
Beam, Louis (Leaderless Resistance) 42, 43

Beck, Ulrich 9
Berger, J.M. 41
Bergmann, Christian 18–20, 50, 101, 158, 159, 165, 168
Berlekamp, Hinnerk 140
Bernhard, Petra 11
Bernstein, Martin 17, 18, 20, 102, 163
Berntzen, Lars Erik 146
Betts, Connor 37
Bewarder, Manuel 53
Bierhoff, Hans-Werner 112
Binder, Sepp 9
BKA Bundeskriminalamt 20, 21, 23, 164
Blaues Erwachen (Blue Awakening) 144
Blood & Honor 12, 43
Blücher, Erik 12
Böckler, Nils 48, 109
Bohn, Caroline 124
Böhnhardt, U. 10, 12, 44
Breivik, Anders Behring 1–3, 8, 15, 17, 30, 42, 56, 69, 73, 80–86, 90, 91, 96–98, 106, 110, 111, 113–120, 127, 133, 134, 141, 142, 145, 146, 151, 154, 158, 164, 166, 169, 177, 178
Bundesamt für Verfassungsschutz und Terrorismusbekämpfung/domestic intelligence services and the office for counteracting terrorism in Austria (BVT) 143
Bundesministerium für Inneres (Austrian Federal Ministry of the Interior) 144
Burgis, Tom 69
Burke, Jason 41, 118
Butter, Michael 136
Byman, Daniel 55, 170

C

C18 12
Caliphate 53
Campell, Andy 135, 157, 162
Camus, Renaud 88, 141, 143
Christchurch 2, 3, 85, 86, 89, 90, 118, 120, 132, 133, 141, 143, 144, 156, 178
Christchurch call 156
Christ, Michaela 49
CNN 16, 37
Cobain, Ian 69
Communist Party of Finland 109
Communist Party of Germany (KPD) 38
Connor, Jeffrey 147
Cox, Jo 25, 69, 152
Crusius, Patrick 3, 130, 131

D

Darknet 13, 98, 102, 134, 136, 164, 165
Davey, Jacob 142
Diehl, Joerg 3
Donovan, Joan 132
Doumer, Paul 36
Dubiel, Helmut 128
Dümer, Viktoria 14

E

Easson, Joseph J. 29
Ebner, Julia 52, 128, 129, 142, 152
Eckhard, Jesse 4, 43, 111, 124, 126
Einstein, Albert 173
Eisner, Kurt 35–37
11 September 2001 ['9/11'] 1, 2, 9, 52, 126, 136, 137, 152
Elser, Georg 37, 38
English Defence League (EDL) 81, 126, 127
Ernst, Stephan 39–41
EUROPOL 154

Euskadi Ta Askatasuna (ETA) 10
Evans, Robert 133

F

Facebook 8
FBI 1, 23, 31, 32, 43, 64, 158, 167, 176
Fekete, Liz 142
Fetscher, Iring 167
Fiedler, Peter 112
Flade, Florian 53
Flynn, Carol Rollie 147
Fortuyn, Pim 39
Fredholm, Michael 36, 57, 65, 173, 174
Freedom Party of Austria (FPÖ) 77, 116, 138, 161
French Revolution 34
Friedrich, Hans-Peter 11
Friedrichsen, Gisela 75
Fuchs, Franz 4

G

Garaude, Pauline 30
Gardell, Mattias 82, 93, 117
Gartenstein-Ross, Daveed 55
Gärtner, Benjamin 41
Gensing, Patrick 154
German domestic intelligence services (Verfassungsschutz) 41, 44
German Federal Ministry of the Interior (Bundesministerium des Inneren) 11
German homeland secret services 12
Gigerenzer, Gerd 9
Gill, Paul 111
Gorguloff, Paul 36
Gräfe, Sebastian 13, 43
Gudehus, Christian 49
Gujer, Eric 50

H

Hammer, Max 12
Hamm, Mark S./ Spaaij, Ramon 8, 13, 30, 31, 45, 107, 113–115, 165
Hansen, Stefan 81, 177
Hartleb, Florian 19, 81, 84, 130
Hegemann, Hendrik 29
Heitmeyer, Wilhelm 109
Herrmann, Joachim 18, 155
Hitler, Adolf 5, 24, 37, 38, 43, 44, 52, 65, 68, 71, 83, 95, 96, 109, 151, 157, 161
Hodgkinson, James T. 36, 37
Hoffer, Eric 32, 177, 178
Hoffmann, Jens 48
Hoffmann Paramilitary Group 46
Horgan, John 104
Horn, Alexander 18
Hostettler, Otto 164
Hudson, Rex 66

I

Identitarian Movement Germany (IBD) 88, 139, 141–144
Irish Republican Army (IRA) 10
IS (ISIS) 7, 30, 53, 55, 88, 115, 145, 175
Islam, (Islamic, Islamification,..) 1–3, 6–9, 13, 16, 19, 24, 25, 33, 36, 39, 46, 47, 52–54, 56, 58, 81, 84, 88, 92, 98, 99, 113, 119, 125–128, 130, 136, 142, 144, 146, 155, 166, 175, 176, 178

J

Jackson, Paul 45
Jarren, Otfried 131
Jaschke, Hans-Gerd 124
Job, Nina 23
Jokela, Pekka 109

K

Kaalep, Ruuben 144, 145
Kaczynski, Theodore ("Ted") John 31, 83, 112
Kahlenberg, Battle of 83
Kahl, Martin 29
Kahr, Robert 16
Kain, Alexander 21
Kallis, Aristotle 45
Kaplan, Jeffrey 32, 35, 82, 109
Karadžić, Radovan 2
Kellerhoff, Sven Felix 36, 38
Kennedy, John F. 38, 69
Kennedy, Robert F. 38
Khosrokhavar, Farhad 146
Knobbe, Martin 95, 103
Koehler, Daniel 5, 128
Köhler, Gundolf 46
Kommunistische Partei Deutschland 38
König, Michael 6
Korea, North 33, 87, 109
Krause, Joachim 81
Kraushaar, Wolfgang 48, 52
Kron, Thomas 29
Kühnen, Michael 56, 123, 124
Ku Klux Klan 41, 42, 69

L

Lang, Hermann 116
Laphshyn, Pavlo 94, 153
Law Randall P. 4
Leaderless resistance 42, 43, 167
Lenin 35
Leonhard, Cecilia 85
Leuschner, Vincenz 110, 117
Library of Congress 30
LKA Bayern 19, 20, 101
Logvinov, Michail 23
Lööw, Heléne 32, 35, 82, 109
Lübcke, Walter 39–41

M

Mair, Thomas 66, 69, 70, 72, 111, 113, 116, 118
Malkki, Leena 32, 35, 82, 109
Mangs, Peter 92, 93, 106, 111, 117–119, 154, 174
Mareš, Miroslav 36, 65
Martin, Gus 65
Maryland, University of 9, 10
Masala, Carlo 53
Masaryk, Tomas Garrague 36
McVeigh, Timothy James 41, 46, 64, 94
Mecca 13
Meier, Mischa 37
Metzger, Tom 41
Miller-Idriss, Cynthia 123
Mishra, Pankaj 8
Mundlos, U. 10, 12, 44
Musharbash, Yassin 5

N

Nash, Jay Robert 31
National Socialism 5, 8, 10, 12, 41–43, 46, 55, 56, 68, 69, 71, 83, 94–96, 101, 107–109, 115, 135, 137, 145, 157, 161, 163
National Socialist Underground (NSU) 8, 10–12, 17, 23, 40, 41, 43, 45, 117, 153, 154
Navarro, Joe 167
Nedopil, Norbert 114
Neumann, Peter A. 30, 39, 47, 53, 57, 58
Nurmi, Johanna 109

O

Obama, Barack 2
Oksanen, Atte 109
Ordine Nuovo 10
Osterhammel, Jürgen 34

Oswald, Lee Harvey 38
Öztürk, Bilgehan 45

P

Palestinian Liberation Organisation (PLO) 4, 37, 38
Pantucci, Raffaello 45
Parveen, Nazia 69
Pfahl-Traughber, Armin 68, 78, 166
Pierce, William L. 41, 42, 69
Pinker, Steven 46, 64, 177
Pink Panther cartoon 11
Preuß, Thorsten 50
Price, Matthew 133
Priester, Karin 24
Prism 128
Progress Party (in Norway) 82, 84
Propaganda of the deed 34, 35, 39
Pucket, Kathleen M. (FBI) 32

R

Rabert, Bernhard 56
Rabin, Yitzhak 37
Rapoport, David C. 13
Räsänen, Pekka 109
Red Army Faction (RAF) 10, 34, 47, 48, 64
Red Brigades 10
Reichsbürger (Reich Citizens) 138–141, 146, 165
Reker, Henrietta 67
Remschmidt, Helmut 112
Richardson, Louise 33–35, 39
Roten Frontkämpferbund (RFB, Red Front Fighting Alliance) 38
Royal United Services Institute (RUSI) 8
Roy A. / McGowan M. 3
Rudolph, Eric 64
Rumiyah 54
Runeborg, Hanna 57, 174

S

Saimeh, Nahlah 56
Salafist 54, 58, 103
Sanders, Bernie 36, 37
Schild, Georg 37
Schindling, Anton 37
Schliefsteiner, Paul 4, 73
Schmid, Alex P. 29
Schmidt, Colette M. 144
Schmidt, Martin 112
Schmidt, Ulrich 12
Schneider, Hans Joachim 30
Schulte von Drach, Markus C. 49
Seeger, Thorsten 109
Segashi, Arbnor 50
Seierstad, Åsne 56, 81, 85, 91
Sellner, Martin 88, 89, 143–145
Shakespeare, W. [Hamlet] 9
Shekhovtsov, Anton 94
Simon, Jeffrey D. 4, 13, 30, 31, 37, 46, 65, 145
Sirhan Bishara Sirhan 38
Sitzer, Peter 109
Slyomovics, Nettanel 38
Sonboly, David Ali (Hamenadi) 8, 15, 17–20, 23, 24, 50, 92, 95–106, 110, 113–116, 118, 150, 151, 154, 155, 158–160, 162–168, 170, 174–177
Soros, George 136, 142
Speit, Andreas 139, 140, 143
Spengler, Oswald 130
Spitzer, Manfred 114, 125
Stalinism 56
Steam (gaming platform) 14, 20, 23, 99–101, 118, 134–136, 154, 157–160, 178
Steffen, Frank 66–69, 72, 111, 113, 114, 119, 151, 174
Steinbach, Peter 38
Steinbach, Sybille 166
Stojar, Richard 36, 65, 173
Strømmen, Øyvind 78, 166
Sturm, Roland 42, 43

Sundermeyer, Olaf 11
Sunstein, Cass R. 131, 132
Sun Tzu 1
Sweinung, Sandberg 146

T

Taleb, Nassim Nicholas 6
Tarabay, Jamie 134
Tarrant, Brenton 2, 3, 73, 85–91, 111, 113, 118, 133, 134, 143–146
Taylor, Matthew 69
Temme, Andreas 41
Theweleit, Klaus 115
Thier, Judith 49
Thule Society 36
Traini, Luca 25, 66, 70, 72, 118, 134
Trump, Donald 32, 36, 37, 102, 120, 128, 130, 131, 156, 157, 162
Tuchel, Johannes 38
Turchie, Therry D. 32
Twitter (tweets) 1, 8, 16, 37, 130, 145, 155, 161

U

Unabomber 31, 83, 112
Utopian Socialists 35

V

Van der Graaf, Volkert 39
Vogeley, Kai 103
Vuori, Miika 109

W

Waldmann, Peter 7, 29, 115
Wehling, Tore 81, 177
Wehrsportgruppe Hoffmann 46
Weimann, Gabriel 31, 32, 52
Welcome Culture (Germany, Angela Merkel) 40, 68
Weller, Marcus 18, 50, 165, 168
Welzer, Harald 113
Wilkinson, Paul 1
Wolf, Tobias 144
World Risk Society 9

Y

Yozgat, Halit 40, 41

Z

Zaugg, Wolfgang Alexander John 11, 78
Zehnpfennig, Barbara 24, 111
Zeiger, Sara 45
Zierhoffer, Diane M. 168
Zschäpe, Beate 10, 44

Lightning Source UK Ltd.
Milton Keynes UK
UKHW021826250521
384375UK00002B/2